By the same authors

MICHAEL O'NEILL

Literary Criticism

*The Human Mind's Imaginings: Conflict and Achievement in
Shelley's Poetry*

Percy Bysshe Shelley: A Literary Life

Poetry

The Stripped Bed

GARETH REEVES

Literary Criticism

T. S. Eliot: A Virgilian Poet

Selected Poems of George Herbert (ed.)

Poetry

Real Stories

AUDEN, MACNEICE, SPENDER: THE THIRTIES POETRY

Michael O'Neill and Gareth Reeves

MACMILLAN

First edition 1992

Published by
MACMILLAN EDUCATION LTD
Houndmills, Basingstoke, Hampshire RG21 2XS
and London
Companies and representatives
throughout the world

Typeset by Footnote Graphics, Warminster, Wiltshire

Printed in Hong Kong

ISBN 0–333–45117–1 (hardcover)
ISBN 0–333–45118–X (paperback)

A catalogue record for this book
is available from the British Library

Contents

Acknowledgements

We are grateful to the University of Durham for granting us terms of Research Leave during which we have been able to work on and finish this book, and to the staff of the University Library for all their help. We owe a special debt to students who took our Special Topic course on Poetry of the 1930s; the book has its origins in the teaching of that course.

Excerpt from *The English Auden: Poems, Essays and Dramatic Writings 1927–1939* edited by Edward Mendelson, and *The Orators* by W. H. Auden, are reprinted by permission of Faber and Faber, Ltd. Excerpts from *W. H. Auden: Collected Poems* by W. H. Auden, copyright © 1934, 1937, 1940, 1945 by W. H. Auden and renewed 1962, 1965, 1968 by W. H. Auden, are reprinted by permission of Random House, Inc. Excerpts from *Poems* (1933; 2nd edn 1934), *The Still Centre*, *Collected Poems 1928–1953*, and *Collected Poems 1928–1985* by Stephen Spender, copyright © 1934, 1942 by Stephen Spender, renewed 1962 by Stephen Spender, are reprinted by permission of Random House, Inc., and Faber and Faber, Ltd. Excerpts from *The Collected Poems of Louis MacNeice* edited by E. R. Dodds are reprinted by permission of Faber and Faber, Ltd. The excerpts from 'Preludes' in *Collected Poems 1909–1962* by T. S. Eliot, copyright 1936 by Harcourt Brace Jovanovich, Inc., copyright © 1964, 1963 by T. S. Eliot, is reprinted by permission of Harcourt Brace Jovanovich, Inc., and Faber and Faber, Ltd. The excerpt from 'From the Canton of Expectation' in *The Haw Lantern* by Seamus Heaney, copyright © 1987 by Seamus Heaney, is reprinted by permission of Farrar, Straus and Giroux, Inc., and Faber and Faber, Ltd. Excerpts from *The Poems of Laura*

Riding: A New Edition of the 1938 Collection are reprinted by kind permission of Laura (Riding) Jackson and Carcanet Press, Ltd.

The book is very much a joint venture. However, Michael O'Neill is primarily responsible for Chapters 2, 5, 6 (except the final section) and 8; Gareth Reeves is primarily responsible for Chapters 1, 3, 4, 7 and the final section of 6 (on *In Time of War*).

Note on Texts and Abbreviations

Except where indicated otherwise, all quotations from Auden's poetry are taken from *The English Auden: Poems, Essays and Dramatic Writings 1927–1939*, ed. Edward Mendelson (London, 1977). This work is hereafter referred to as *EA*. Auden's poems are referred to by first line or title, as in *EA*.

Except where indicated otherwise, all quotations from MacNeice's poetry are taken from *The Collected Poems of Louis MacNeice*, ed. E. R. Dodds (1966; rpt London and Boston, 1979). This work is hereafter referred to as *CPM*.

Except where indicated otherwise, all quotations from Spender's poetry are taken from the collections he published in the 1930s. See the opening section of Chapter 2 for fuller details.

Other abbreviations used in the book:

Casebook   *Thirties Poets: 'The Auden Group'*, A Casebook, ed. Ronald Carter (London and Basingstoke, 1984).

CPS(1)   Stephen Spender, *Collected Poems 1928–1953* (London, 1955).

CPS(2)   Stephen Spender, *Collected Poems 1928–1985* (London and Boston, 1985).

CSPA   W. H. Auden, *Collected Shorter Poems 1927–1957* (1966; rpt London, 1969).

Cunningham	Valentine Cunningham, *British Writers of the Thirties* (Oxford and New York, 1988).
DE	Stephen Spender, *The Destructive Element: A Study of Modern Writers and Beliefs* (London, 1935).
Everett	Barbara Everett, *Auden* (Edinburgh and London, 1964).
Fantasia	D. H. Lawrence, *Fantasia of the Unconscious* (1923; rpt London, 1933).
Fuller	John Fuller, *A Reader's Guide to W. H. Auden* (London, 1970).
Hynes	Samuel Hynes, *The Auden Generation: Literature and Politics in England in the 1930s* (London and Boston, 1976).
Longley	Edna Longley, *Poetry in the Wars* (Newcastle upon Tyne, 1986).
Mac	Edna Longley, *Louis MacNeice: A Study* (London and Boston, 1988).
Mendelson	Edward Mendelson, *Early Auden* (London and Boston, 1981).
PBSCWV	*The Penguin Book of Spanish Civil War Verse*, ed. Valentine Cunningham (1980; rpt Harmondsworth, 1983).
PFS	*Poems for Spain*, eds Stephen Spender and John Lehmann (London, 1939).
SAF	Louis MacNeice, *The Strings Are False: An Unfinished Autobiography* (1965; rpt London and Boston, 1982).
SC	Stephen Spender, *The Still Centre* (London, 1939).
SCM	*Selected Literary Criticism of Louis MacNeice*, ed. Alan Heuser (Oxford, 1987).
Smith	Stan Smith, *W. H. Auden* (Oxford and New York, 1985).
SPS	Stephen Spender, *Selected Poems* (London and Boston, 1965).
SP33	Stephen Spender, *Poems* (London, 1933).
SP34	Stephen Spender, *Poems* 2nd edn (London, 1934).
T	Stephen Spender, *The Temple* 2nd edn (London and Boston, 1989).

*The Thirties
and After*   Stephen Spender, *The Thirties and After: Poetry,
                 Politics, People 1933–75* (Glasgow, 1978).
WHACP   W. H. Auden, *Collected Poems*, ed. Edward Men-
                 delson (London, 1976).
WWW   Stephen Spender, *World Within World* (1951; rpt
                 London, 1977).

Introduction

Poetry written during the 1930s has received thoughtful consideration in recent years, most notably in Samuel Hynes's judicious *The Auden Generation* and Valentine Cunningham's pyrotechnical *British Writers of the Thirties*. Both books seek to read literary texts in the light of cultural and historical contexts: Hynes offering an analysis of 'the growth of literary forms' (Hynes, p. 9) in the decade, Cunningham announcing provocatively that 'all texts and contexts will be thought of here as tending to lose their separate identities, collapsing purposefully into each other and existing rather as what we might call (con)texts' (Cunningham, p. 1). The present study is more interested in the detailed examination of particular poems than either of these books. We agree with Hynes that 'a close relation exists between literature and history' (Hynes, p. 9), and we can see with Cunningham the advantages of viewing 'A period of history and its literature' as 'a sign-system, or set of sign-systems, of signifying practices, composing a structural and structured whole' (Cunningham, p. 1). Yet, more strongly still, we believe that literary texts arouse what Helen Vendler calls 'the phenomenon of aesthetic response' and that, in the same critic's words, 'Aesthetic criticism begins with the effort to understand the individual work'.[1]

That said, the idea of literature's intrinsic value, or unique status, was far from being taken for granted by the three poets of the thirties – W. H. Auden, Louis MacNeice and Stephen Spender – whom we regard as major and on whom we concentrate in this book. All three were suspicious both of art as propaganda and of art for art's sake. Their ambivalent feelings

1

about Yeats's poetry serve to focus this point. Spender, for instance, remarks that 'Yeats has found, as yet, no subject of moral significance in the social life of his time' (*DE*, p. 131); yet in the same work he is obviously drawn to, while often critical of, 'individualist writers' (*DE*, p. 19) such as Henry James, W. B. Yeats, T. S. Eliot and D. H. Lawrence. Spender's own poetry is indebted to the example of these 'individualist writers', whose awareness of 'a world without belief' (*DE*, p. 14) clears the ground for the contemporary artist's anti-modernist need to 'somehow connect his life again with . . . political life and influence it' (*DE*, p. 19). His poems are remarkable both for their individualism and for their obsession with 'political life'. Accordingly, Chapter 2 analyses and evaluates the presentation of subjectivity in some of the more obviously personal (though by no means apolitical) poems from *Poems*, 1933 (and 1934), while Chapter 5 begins by discussing the more obviously political poems in the same volume before moving on to an account of his subsequent poetry in the decade.

For his part MacNeice's sense of what poetry was or should be shows a tenacious intelligence that emerges in his reflections on Yeats's significance. In *The Poetry of W. B. Yeats* (published in 1941), he formulates this flexible account of art's duty to itself and to life: 'art is autotelic in so far as its value . . . is non-utilitarian; it is not autotelic if that is taken to mean that it neither comes from life nor affects it, and that therefore it can be understood without reference to life'.[2] Interestingly, in the Preface to his study of Yeats, MacNeice comments that in his critical work *Modern Poetry* (1938) he 'overstressed the half-truth that poetry is *about* something, is communication. So it is, but it is also a separate self'.[3] That understanding of poetry as moving between 'communication' and 'a separate self' is embodied in MacNeice's work, and informs this book. Though all three poets experienced the temptation to see poetry as sealed off from history, they continually sought to negotiate between word and world. Auden veers between the view that 'poetry makes nothing happen' ('In Memory of W. B. Yeats') and the view that poetry's purpose is to 'Make action urgent and its nature clear' ('August for the people and their favourite islands'). Spender describes himself as being 'hounded by external events' (*WWW*, p. 137), where 'hounded' captures the poet's mixed feelings about 'external events', regarded as at once unavoidable and intrusive. And MacNeice's finest achievement of the decade, *Autumn Journal*, points up, and thrives on, clashes between pattern and flux, 'a single purpose' and 'A jumble of opposites' (*Autumn Journal*, XVI), poetic form and historical crisis.

Yet the place where these veerings, ambivalences and clashes can be observed, and their workings most fruitfully investigated, is the poetry itself. 'All I have is a voice', Auden writes in 'September 1, 1939', and the concern of the three poets with 'voice', with mediating between possible styles of utterance and with discovering modes of address that sell neither writing nor living short, means that issues of tone and mood are unusually important in a consideration of their work – and are often foregrounded by the poets themselves. Certainly our book seeks to give a challenging, at times distinguished body of poetry the close attention it deserves. Such an aim explains, indeed demands, the book's critical method, that of detailed readings of individual poems. This method is unfashionable in some quarters because of its associations with New Criticism. But our readings do not necessarily subscribe to the assumptions underpinning the critical practice of this school. We have much sympathy with, say, Cleanth Brooks's objection to what he stigmatizes as 'the heresy of paraphrase';[4] Auden especially has suffered from the belief that his poems are coded allegories or intellectualized parables, and in our readings of his poetry throughout the decade (not merely the overtly enigmatic earlier work) we lay emphasis on the poems as linguistic events that often derail paraphrase. We, too, like Brooks, see the critical act as committing the critic to 'judgments about a poem *as a poem*',[5] even as we share his awareness of the risks and difficulties involved in making such judgements.[6] But we depart from the practice of many New Critics by paying more than lip service to the idea that poems are experiences just as much as structures, processes that unfold in time just as much as completed designs.[7]

Our criteria of poetic achievement differ accordingly. Intent on what F. R. Leavis calls 'a kind of re-creative possession'[8] of the poetry, we do not view the achieved poem as inevitably forming a system of balanced tensions, or 'pattern of resolved stresses'.[9] We are sympathetic to poems (such as Spender's 'Moving through the silent crowd') that concede the limits of poetry in the face of tricky or complex subjects. Though such concessions involve artful effects of language, evaluating them

demands 'moral' as well as 'technical' judgements, to borrow
terms from Auden, who says that there are two questions to be
put to a poem: 'The first is technical: "Here is a verbal
contraption. How does it work?" The second is, in the broadest
sense, moral: "What kind of guy inhabits this poem?"'[10] Stan
Smith quotes this in his deconstructionist study of Auden,
stressing Auden's sense of the 'verbal contraption' as primary
(Smith, p. 3). For us, too, the 'verbal contraption' is primary,
but our understanding of the relationship between 'verbal contraption' and 'guy' inhabiting it is not the same as Smith's. For
Smith, the 'guy' is the product of the 'contraption' (see Smith,
p. 3); for us, the 'guy', as poet, is a presence in, while shaping the
development of, the 'contraption'. This is not to deny that all
three poets know that the self written about, and even the self
writing, can seem far from unitary; many of their finest effects
derive from this awareness. We are, therefore, alert to the
creative potentialities of contradiction, even muddle, the more so
when, in our view, it can be shown to be contradiction or muddle
of which the poem is, however subliminally, aware. Our reading
of Auden's 'Spain', for instance, traces, and finds value in,
irresolutions and tonal swervings. Again, we argue that Auden's
In Time of War, often treated as conceptually coherent, conveys
an awareness of its attempts to reconcile divergent impulses, and
is no less compelling for being shown to do so. In a comparable
way, our account of Spender's 'The Pylons' brings out the
abrupt yet fluid interplay of attitudes in a poem often thought of
as simply propagandist. And we argue that division and doubleness lie close to the heart of MacNeice's 'Snow' as in much of the
poetry he wrote in the thirties.

  If, then, the poetry written by Auden, MacNeice and Spender
in the thirties has intrinsic value, it has it by virtue of its
dealings with the extrinsic. Bearing this in mind, our book has
something of a double rhythm. Chapters move between discussion of a range of poems by a particular poet (Chapter 3
examines poems by MacNeice from all periods of the decade,
and Chapter 6 is on the Auden of the mid-to-late thirties) and
consideration of single long works (*The Orators* and *Autumn
Journal*) or, in the case of the final chapter, poems written about
a specific historical event, the Spanish Civil War (1936–9).
Fascination with the intricate relationship between external
pressures and poetic achievement in the period underlies our

study. To discuss, as Chapter 8 does, Auden's 'Spain' alongside sections VI and XXIII of MacNeice's *Autumn Journal*, as well as Spender's 'Port Bou' or 'Two Armies', is to sharpen one's sense both of the individuality of the poems and of the common challenges and problems the poets faced.

Coverage of all the writings of the three poets in the period is not attempted, though many are given substantial attention. Our watchword here is achievement. Spender's long poem, *Vienna*, and his play, *Trial of a Judge*, are considered because they bear centrally on the nature of his poetic distinction. Indeed, we undertake a critical re-assessment of Spender's poetry in the belief that his quality as a poet has been ignored or underplayed. And Auden's *The Orators*, that intriguing, problematic, pivotal work, is, as mentioned above, the subject of a full-length chapter (the fourth). In it, we argue that the work looks, often playfully, at Auden's early manner, its fusion of riddle and mystery, and forwards to seemingly more accessible and composed poems such as 'Out on the lawn I lie in bed', a forward look that prepares the ground for our view that Auden's poetry in the later thirties is less hospitable to purely conceptual analysis than is sometimes acknowledged. However, plays such as *The Dog Beneath the Skin*, *The Ascent of F6* and *On the Frontier*, written by Auden in collaboration with Christopher Isherwood, are, we think, less bound up with what makes Auden a major poet and are therefore excluded from the book (this is not to deny the intermittent fineness of passages from these plays, the opening chorus of *The Dog Beneath the Skin*, say).

Where comparisons with poems by, among others, John Cornford, C. Day Lewis, Bernard Spencer and Rex Warner clarify the achievement of our three poets, they are offered. Again, Auden's and Spender's dealings with the issue of leadership in their poetry are defined by being put beside T. S. Eliot's in *Coriolan*. And we examine the style of Auden's earliest poems in the light of the important but little investigated influence of Laura (Riding) Jackson. Ours is, then, an author-centred study, and makes no apology for being so. Though it may be possible to abstract from the literature of a decade common 'signifying practices', the quality and independence of the poetry composed by Auden, MacNeice and Spender in the thirties prompt us to inspect and respect the particularity each writer attained in his work.

1
Auden (1)
'An altering speech'

1

Few would dispute that Auden's early poetry is arresting, but there is less agreement as to why.[1] Does it arrest in spite or because of the ellipses, rhetorical effects, posings, disruptions, syntactical swervings, dislocations, obscurities? Is it better or worse for the fact that, in Justin Replogle's words, its author seems to have 'often cared more about the liveliness of the total verbal performance than about philosophy, ideas, social themes, or his role of cultural critic'? (Casebook, p. 118). And is any lack of coherence of this sort accompanied by a lack of emotional depth? Spender is an interesting witness: he may complain that Auden's early poetry is 'intellectually over- and emotionally underdeveloped',[2] but in his poem 'Auden's Funeral' a moving section in brackets ends with lines Spender set up on his press for the privately printed *Poems* (1928), as if to pay tribute to the capacity of Auden's early poetry to penetrate deeply with a phrase or an image. Stan Smith's deconstructionist approach makes the very disruptions and dislocations of this poetry its *raison d'être*, arguing that it represents 'the crisis of the subject . . ., which constantly dissolves the problematic self back into the nexus of language' (Smith, p. 34). From a different perspective Seamus Heaney has likewise argued that the early poetry owes its fascination to its 'oddly unparaphraseable rifts' and 'defamiliarizing abruptness', to the fact that what is most alluring is its stand-offishness, its propensity to baffle and be baffled.[3]

Central to this bafflement is the elusiveness of the poems'

6

speakers: Auden, claims Heaney, 'carried the English lyric well beyond the domestic securities of the first person singular'.[4] This claim is borne out by the first poem Auden came to consider publishable: 'Who stands, the crux left of the watershed' (later titled 'The Watershed').[5] The opening mingles abruptness with mystery: it may talk about standing, but it catches the reader off-balance as we wonder who this 'who' is, whether it is to be identified in some way with the poem's speaker, or with an addressee who may or may not include the reader. It possibly intimates a direct question, but by the third line it turns out to be the start of a pseudo-latinate dependent clause ('Whoever stands . . . sees . . .'). Disorientation is compounded by questions about location, about what is literal and what is metaphor: we suspect this is a psychological as well as social narrative, that the 'watershed' is possibly an inner point of change and challenge, that 'chafing' intimates a state of mind, that 'Snatches of tramline running to the wood' leads into a *selva oscura* of individual and racial memory, that 'industry' is in a state of psychological 'coma', that the 'flooded workings' are perhaps the untapped workings of memory. 'Crux' intimates crossroads both literal and figurative: there is something crucial, a point of no return, a choice to be made, a conundrum.

When in the second verse-paragraph speaker and location appear to become more defined, it is only to define their unfamiliarity, their state of being 'cut off'. The 'who' of the start becomes a 'stranger', who in turn becomes a 'you' directly addressed; and if we have been inclined to identify that 'who' with the poem's speaker, then the 'you' turns into the other half of a divided self; or it may teeter on the edge of being all our selves, a sort of Everyman. Self-definition comes about with the sense of exclusion: 'Stranger, turn back again, frustrate and vexed: / This land, cut off, will not communicate'. Failure to communicate is what is most urgently communicated. Even when, with that bewitching image of alienation, 'Beams from your car may cross a bedroom wall', there is a sense of closing in, what is closed in on is ambiguously negated: 'They wake no sleeper' means either that there is no-one to arouse, or that whoever (or whatever – the past, comatose memories?) is sleeping will not be aroused. This is gestural poetry: 'It lay in flooded workings until *this* . . .'; 'But seldom *this*' (emphases added). Phrasing mimics precision, as in the curiously passive 'some acts are chosen'. Who or what is doing the choosing: the speaker as he defines his poetic terrain, or history, the arbitrary arbiter (i.e. some acts are by chance recorded)? Chafing unease is conveyed by the circumlocutory 'wooden shape', and by the syntactical slippage at the end of the first verse-paragraph, where the main verb shifts uncomfortably between 'died' (in 'one died / During a storm') and 'nosed' (in 'nosed his way'). The trappings of industrial decline are precisely conjured up, but only in keyhole detail, leaving the larger narrative elusively in 'snatches'. Does 'went to ground' gesture at a (haunting) return?

The authoritative air, typical of the early poetry, comes not only from the speaker's superior viewpoint ('Below him sees'), but also from the commanding voice. But it *is* only an air, of one not in command but who would command. The urgent tone mingles anticipation and fear. For instance the fricatives in the phrase 'frustrate and vexed' make it sound excited in its dumbfoundedness. The iambic drive carries the reader past the syntactic uneasinesses already noted, and gives some sort of shape, for instance, to 'Be no accessory content to one', allowing 'content' to hover between 'cóntent' and 'contént', between 'meaning' and 'contentment'. The sound of 'Aimless for faces rather there than here' gives direction to the line's fearful directionlessness. The conclusion is baffled and baffling, but impressively risks a weighty rhetoric:

> . . . you may hear the wind
> Arriving driven from the ignorant sea
> To hurt itself on pane, on bark of elm
> Where sap unbaffled rises, being Spring;
> But seldom this. Near you, taller than grass,
> Ears poise before decision, scenting danger.

The riskily grand note of the first four lines here recedes before the urgently haunting uncertainty of the last one-and-a-half. In between, the phrase 'But seldom this' is abrupt, tense but reticent: does 'this' point forward to the last sentence, or backward to the 'situation' of the whole poem?

A striking uncertainty of this poem, and of many of the early poems, is the extent to which landscape becomes metaphor for psychological state. Later poems such as the 'Prologue' to *The*

Orators and 'In Praise of Limestone' openly follow this practice. But in 'The Watershed' an outer world seems to mirror an inner by happenstance. In the concluding lines the speaker comes up against himself as if by chance, surprising himself. There seems to be an implicit contrast: outside the self in the springtime world the 'sap' is 'unbaffled', but within is bafflement. The last lines enact a closing in: 'Near you, taller than grass . . .'. The synecdoche, 'Ears poise', unnervingly permits the listener, the one who scents danger, to be other than a hunted hare (say) out there. We then come abruptly up against the abstract word 'decision', which portentously introduces the mental world of human choice. But with the final phrase we are immediately thrown back onto the impending outer world: 'scenting danger'. If the poem at times pits the 'uncommunicative' world of social reality against a psychological world, it ends by discovering that inner reality is equally baffling. The dismantlements, the disappearing snatches of tramline, are as much in here as out there. The result is total impasse. Escape turns into exclusion. The speaker is 'cut off' from himself. Like many of Auden's early poems, this is a masterfully articulate performance enacting a sense of inarticulacy: divided against itself, it nevertheless projects a highly distinctive voice.

The metaphorical status of 'The Watershed' may be uncertain, but there can be less doubt that 'Control of the passes' asks to be read as a metaphor for psychological division. Even so, with its combination of the seemingly specific and the mysteriously unspecific, it resists definition. The features of the frontier landscape are abruptly presented as if we knew our way around. The cosy-sounding 'Greenhearth' has a spuriously familiar ring. 'They' are made to sound like our habitual enemy. Frequent use of the definite article, a common trick in the early poems, contributes to the impression of familiarity even as it renders the impression suspect. As Bernard Bergonzi writes, 'The definite article points to the recognisable if not to the already known. It recalls an actually or possibly shared experience' (Casebook, p. 192). The poem's sonnet form also has a familiar air without being quite what it seems, for, along with the assonance and consonance, it gives the mistaken impression that the poem rhymes.

As in much of the early poetry lack of context gives the poem its generalizing power. The effect is paradoxical: starkly presented detail makes for suggestiveness. Darkness is screened by surface clarity of local phrase and image – 'Woken by water / Running away in the dark'. What compels is the powerful but complex emotional undercurrent released from a specific context. 'He often had / Reproached the night for a companion / Dreamed of already': is the night, here fleetingly but hauntingly personified, reproached for not providing the companion dreamed of (i.e. the reproach is a demand for such a companion), or is it reproached for providing a companion who does not come up to the dream of one? The syntactical haziness – for it comes over as that, not as poised ambiguity – captures the combination, felt in much of Auden's early poetry, of desire and resistance, anticipation and fear. The conclusion, 'They would shoot, of course, / Parting easily who were never joined', retreats into a further complex of emotions. 'Of course' signifies stoical compliance in the inevitable and familiar, a resistance to disappointment. The last line's quiet ripple of syllables intimates the guilt of acquiescing in the easy parting, as well as resignation, regret and incomprehension.

2

The protagonists of Auden's early poetry cannot escape their past: they are determined by it whether they resist or acquiesce. This is the conundrum acted out in *Paid on Both Sides*. The possibility of escape from the ancestral feud is presented in Dick's decision to 'get away from here' and start a new life in the Colonies. John Nower's determination to stick it out (he refuses to take Anne Shaw's advice and join Dick) changes nothing, and the 'charade' is largely a choric elaboration, through individual voices and set pieces for 'Chorus', of this state of impasse. Every move forward can be interpreted as a move back: 'Restore the dead; but comes thence to a wall'. Compliance with the feud ethos (in the Anglo-Saxon pastiche of 'I wished to revenge Quit fully / Who my father At Colefangs valley / Lying in ambush Cruelly shot / With life for life') resolves nothing, for Nower is left to face himself. The two warring factions can be taken to represent the divided self, and the shooting of the Spy (who is from the enemy household, a Shaw) to be Nower's guilty recognition of his inheritance: in the Spy's words, they are

'Sharers of the same house'. Nower, that is, shoots himself, and is then reconciled to himself in a psychological resurrection ('The Spy gets up') heralding his awakening to his buried self. This recognition comes in the central 'trial' scene, which, Mendelson argues, takes place as a dream fantasy by Nower in which subconscious impulses surface. (See Mendelson, pp. 50–2.)

Just before Nower subsides into this dream, and directly after the actual, as opposed to fantasy, shooting ('A shot outside followed by cheers'), he comes to a sudden recognition that his participation in the ancestral antagonisms has led nowhere: after much knockabout and tonal byplay in the charade, the air is abruptly cleared by his soliloquy beginning 'Always the following wind of history / Of others' wisdom makes a buoyant air'. 'Others' wisdom' is what Auden's early poetry is at pains to shake off, but in the process it learns that inheritance defines identity. In this soliloquy fear mingles with anticipation at the prospect of 'pockets where / Is nothing loud but us', a phrase which, because of its elliptical expression, sounds apprehensively but excitedly narcissistic. 'Abrupt, untrained, competing' could be describing the early Audenesque style. Nower's dismissal of the elders' lessons of war, sex, heroism and 'emigrating from weakness' (presumably what Dick does), sounds emotionally forthright. But less easy to pin down is his ensuing desire to escape the historical process entirely and revert to an unchanging condition which is also unnatural, without issue. The immaturity of this vision verges on comedy. 'Younger than worms, worms have too much to bear' is in high-flown adolescent mode. The rhetoric of this puerile Hamlet verges on the facile: 'Yes, mineral were best: could I but see / These woods, these fields of green, this lively world / Sterile as moon'.

The Chorus's subsequent speech, beginning 'The Spring unsettles sleeping partnerships', offers no way out. Fuller remarks of this speech that in contrast to Nower's sterile vision, 'by a hideous inversion of values, only capitalism appears to be fruitful' (Fuller, p. 20). But is it appropriate to infer such a scheme from the speech, with its abrupt transitions; and is its effect 'hideous'? The impression it gives of delighting in verbal conjuring tricks runs counter to any sense there may be of social analysis. The pararhyme is not so much ominous (an effect this technique can create elsewhere) as excited. 'Sleeping partnerships' almost preens itself on the way it punningly makes industry collude with love, so that either the dubious innuendo from the business world infects the world of love, or the fecundity of love infects the business world. 'Casting process' similarly implies a cross-fertilization between industrial manufacture and human conception. Barbara Everett provides a helpful perspective when she writes that 'If *Paid on Both Sides* can be held to be, in intention, an analysis of the murderous death-pangs of capitalist society, then the intention dissolves into a fascinated, almost genial contemplation of the heroics – and the heroism – of a struggle to the death.' (Everett, p. 16). In this speech by the Chorus the racing boys, the declaration of war, the treaty, the scrum, the troops are 'Audenesque'. The scrum-bomb simile ('Here a scrum breaks up like a bomb') plays with violence even as it conjures it up: is this an image for the terror that underlies all we do, or schoolboy heroics? Is it startling for visual 'accuracy', or does it rely more for its effect on its alliterated staccato? 'Troops / Deploy like birds': does this do anything more than pretend to a surprising accuracy? The poetry gestures at social disintegration with gleeful verbal energy. The result is a curiously excited emotional deadlock.

Unable to see a way forward, *Paid on Both Sides* is stymied, as the Chorus is aware: 'O how shall man live / Whose thought is born, child of one farcical night, / To find him old?' Behind this elliptical utterance hovers the notion that the faculty of thought which distinguishes mankind condemns him to living in the past. This is confirmed near the start of *Paid* by the speech which John's mother Joan makes in the symbolic setting of 'child and corpse', new-born son and newly murdered husband, in which she talks of the new-born as being in thrall to his past, a ghost even as he comes into the world: 'new ghost learns from many / Learns from old termers what death is, where'. 'New ghost' deliberately confuses newly-dead husband and new-born son; and old timers have become 'old termers', that is, life has become a life-term of imprisonment in the shadow of death. The Chorus implies that retreat to an innocent time is impossible. The familiar trap beckons: man 'dreams of folk in dancing bunches' but 'learns, one drawn apart, a secret will / Restore the dead'. The writing is loadedly ambiguous: bring the dead back to life; revenge the dead. The dead can only be recalled by further death. Hence emerges a complex of feelings, of guilt and betrayal:

Outside on frozen soil lie armies killed
Who seem familiar but they are cold.
Now the most solid wish he tries to keep
His hands show through; he never will look up,
Say 'I am good'. On his misfortune falls
More than enough. Better where no one feels,
The out-of-sight, buried too deep for shafts.

These lines capture the 'double-mindedness' which Everett describes: 'The hero has in him the inherited blood of the Truly Strong Man, the heroic saga-hero . . . . On the other hand, he has the conscience and sensibility of the Truly Weak Man, the war-hating poet who longs for peaceful love.' (Everett, p. 18). 'His hands show through': whatever he does, whether or not he participates in the ancestral feud, is an act of betrayal. The use of pararhyme, a technique most famously employed by Wilfred Owen in his First World War poems, is highly appropriate here. The quizzical gravity it lends a poem such as Owen's 'Strange Meeting' (a line of which, 'Even with truths that lie too deep for taint', Auden appears to be echoing) carries over into *Paid*. In Owen's poem pararhyme resists full-throated heroics; it chokes back; it gives voice to the seared conscience. Owen's 'strange friend' declares 'Courage was mine'; he had 'mystery' and 'mastery' when he was alive; he was the war-hating hero. Nower becomes, intermittently, his descendant.

At the start of the 'trial' scene Nower, the guilty 'accuser', speaks in the voice of patriotic honour, like Owen's scorned mouther of 'the old Lie: Dulce et decorum est / Pro patria mori': 'I know we have and are making terrific sacrifices, but we cannot give in. We cannot betray the dead. As we pass their graves can we be deaf to the simple eloquence of their inscriptions, those who in the glory of their early manhood gave up their lives for us? No, we must fight to the finish'. This is the public school version of the heroic mentality, and is overlaid with an irony pointed up by the farcical setting (the 'gigantic feeding bottle', 'Xmas as president', the jury 'wearing school caps', etc.). Nevertheless, not to 'betray the dead' remains at the centre of the charade: burying the dead is no answer if it means forgetting the past, which is why the witness Bo's ensuing speech comes over as inadequate, for all its grave air – an air evidently borrowed from T. S. Eliot's 'The Burial of the Dead', which, like

Bo's speech, is about the burial places of memory. It is typical of *Paid*'s disorientating registers that neither Nower's ironical prose nor Bo's resonant poetry can be taken at face value. Is Bo a witness for the defence or the prosecution? His last line, at any rate, knows what it is saying:

> In these days during the migrations, days
> Freshening with rain reported from the mountains,
> By loss of memory we are reborn,
> For memory is death; by taking leave,
> Parting in anger and glad to go
> Where we are still unwelcome, and if we count
> What dead the tides wash in, only to make
> Notches for enemies. On northern ridges
> Where flags fly, seen and lost, denying rumour
> We baffle proof, speakers of a strange tongue.

The ellipses enhance the resonance. Fuller indicates one way to take this speech: it implies 'that some break is possible', and 'continuing the military imagery, [it] elaborates the possibility of a change of heart. Decision, action and conviction are, it seems to say, still possible.' (Fuller, p. 23). If there is to be any legacy from the feud, if we count the dead, it must not be out of a spirit of revenge, but only so as to put the dead to rest by burying them, by making 'notches for enemies'. However, burying the dead may not be putting the past to rest but, on the contrary, suppressing it. It could be that 'By loss of memory we are reborn', but burial is not loss. Furthermore, the lines question the nature of such a rebirth, for it sounds more like escape, a 'migration'. A characteristically ambiguous frontier, a watershed for some sort of 'significant action', in Heaney's phrase,[6] is imaged in those 'northern ridges', which, with their 'seen and lost' flags, seem to denote confusion and isolation as much as new life. 'Memory is death' if it imprisons present action in ancestral patterns of behaviour; it may be retrogressive. But memory may be liberating if it can reveal where we stand in relation to the past; it can lead to a new identity. 'Speakers of a strange tongue' captures this doubleness.

A similar doubleness emerges from the interplay between Nower's 'soliloquy', 'There is the city', and the ensuing chorus 'To throw away the key and walk away'. In his soliloquy,

Nower's Utopian dream precedes his departure by horse to join Anne Shaw. The psychological landscape contrasts an urban setting, which symbolizes Nower's present life, with a pastoral vision in the last verse-paragraph. In the middle verse-paragraph, 'love', in the form of a locomotive, brings about the transition from urban to pastoral. The city used to exist in a prelapsarian state, as it were ('There is the city, / Lighted and clean once'), but is now a projection of Nower's acute sense of guilt: 'And I / Letting to cheaper tenants, have made a slum'. The slum is associated with inherited evil, the ancestral curse which Nower carries with him: 'Houses at which the passer shakes his fist / Remembering evil'. The metaphor of Nower's murky psyche as a slum landlord becomes explicit: 'Pride and indifference have shared with me, and I / Have kissed them in the dark, for mind has dark'. Riven by class guilt, he fears he will become an agent for passing on evil, a cursed ancestor in his turn: 'midnight accidents / In streets where heirs may dine'.

Whether the new society of love envisioned by Nower represents wish fulfilment or a profounder Utopianism is decidedly uncertain. In his soliloquy's second verse-paragraph the love-locomotive performs that 'abrupt exile' which is shortly to be scorned by the Chorus (Nower's imminent marriage to Anne being a form of such exile, as is Dick's emigration). In the last verse-paragraph the vision of a new dawn is tempered and qualified by a bracing air ('Wind from the snows'), and is there not something head-in-the-clouds about the headiness of this highly Audenesque aerial perspective? The panoptic gazer who 'sees all', who godlike surveys the prospect and yet homes in on detail, may be 'refreshed' at the new life spread out below, but it sounds like a bucolic never-never land: 'The tugged-at teat / The hopper's steady feed, the frothing leat'. Programmes for the future too easily slip into escapist idylls out of the past. Another way of putting it might be that the past cannot, by definition, provide terms for what will be: the old urban-pastoral opposition is inadequate to the task.

The ensuing chorus in *Paid* ('To throw away the key and walk away') reinforces such questionings by weighing easy escape, 'abrupt exile', against some lasting and genuine change, be it psychological or historical, individual or collective. The gradual ascent, 'An altered gradient at another rate', contrasts with Nower's explosively Utopian, 'bursting' ascent of love, and raises doubts about Auden's own panoptic propensities. The distant view that 'sees all' is associated with speculative under-standing, the emotional terrain mapped out by previous genera-tions, as opposed to direct experience: 'Learns more than maps upon the whitewashed wall / The hand put up to ask'. Inherited experience provides only theoretical knowledge and is therefore all one to the present: 'All pasts / Are single old past now'. Yet this vision of the gradual as opposed to abrupt ascent sounds as though it may be qualifying itself, perhaps inadvertently, even as it unfolds. Is the fact that it 'makes us well / Without confession of the ill' to be unequivocally applauded? Even more mystifying is the unexpected plunge downward as an image for 'the future': 'Not swooping at the surface still like gulls / But with prolonged drowning shall develop gills'. 'Prolonged drowning' seems to denote rebirth not by 'loss of memory' (as in Bo's speech), but by immersion below the floor of memory; but this is 'a purification and re-birth for which there is no language' (Everett, p. 17). It is a quickening gesture towards a way out of the impasse into which *Paid* has driven itself, but it remains a gesture. At the level of plot it provides no solution: the feud continues as before.

3

Typically the lovers of Auden's early poetry are stymied like Nower. Though playing familiar parts, they are as lost as ever: 'Another I, another You / Each knowing what to do / But of no use' ('Again in conversations'). Their living according to inherited patterns of behaviour estranges them from feeling and experiencing: 'Before this loved one / Was that one and that one / A family / And history / And ghost's adversity' ('Before this loved one'). No one encounters another as a pure self – even were that possible. 'The loving individual, still pursued by a past but pursuing a present, becomes an uneasy ghost' (Everett, pp. 24–5), a 'new ghost' like Nower's at the start of *Paid*, re-enacting the past, reliving the dead: 'the heart's changes / Where ghost has haunted / Lost and wanted' ('This lunar beauty'). Auden wrote, quoting Freud, 'The driving force in all forms of life is instinctive; a libido which of itself is undifferentiated and unmoral, the "seed of every virtue and of every act which deserves punishment" ('Psychology and Art To-day', *EA*,

p. 339). Instinct becomes suspect when, unknown to the posses-
sor, it conveys ancestral behaviour: ' "Good day, good luck" / Is
no real meeting / But instinctive look / A backward love'
('Before this loved one').

The past presses upon the lovers of the poem 'The strings'
excitement, the applauding drum' to produce a nervous energy.
This is largely the result of the edgily off-rhymed *terza rima*:
'praise-grass', 'advice-eyes', 'come-form', and especially the
uneasy discordance on which the poem ends, 'cries-Ice'. Lovers
do not act their own desires, but perform *déjà vu* scenarios,
ancestral parts:

> It is your face I see, and morning's praise
> Of you is ghost's approval of the choice,
> Filtered through roots of the effacing grass.

The lover's aubade is only a ghostly repetition. 'Roots' and
'grass' conjure up the dead. 'Effacing' has a seductive oblivion
about it, all the more so for punningly calling up 'the ancestral
face' and punningly 'effacing' in ghostly fashion the 'face I see'.
Behind these lines hovers the notion that the lovers' relationship
is spectral and deathly because the terms in which love is
expressed are weighed down by the past; the ancestral ceremony
of love frustrates their emotions. The first line of the poem,
therefore, is a metaphor both for their emotional state and for the
way it is expressed; the two cannot be separated. 'And all
emotions to expression come', the poem declares, mingling
triumph with regret: our emotions come down to this, the
expression of them; emotions reveal themselves in their expression (in this poem I am writing); all there is left of the relationship
is, guiltily, the expression of it; it is over even as it happens,
made ghostly by being contemplated, put into words. This poem
acknowledges what lies close to the heart of much of Auden's
poetry: its awareness of itself as an act of utterance.

'Expression' is an expressive pun, central to the poem: 'It is
your face I see', and the loved one's facial 'expression' betrays
the ancient ways of love, its wiles and stratagems, 'Recovering
the archaic imagery'. Again opposed emotions mingle: is this
recovery undertaken in a spirit of resignation or triumph? Does
'archaic' imply the outmoded or the revered, or both? The poem
itself has been 'expressing' the lovers' relations in terms of

'archaic imagery', of love as a battleground. Auden even makes use of the traditional courtly love notion that love enters through the eyes:

> Fear, taking me aside, would give advice
> 'To conquer her, the visible enemy,
> It is enough to turn away the eyes.'
>
> Yet there's no peace in this assaulted city
> But speeches at the corners, hope for news,
> Outside the watchfires of a stronger army.

But the poem makes the archaic imagery sound contemporary, converting the old battleground into a psychological arena. A similar conjunction of warfare, facial expression and verbal expression, in what turns out to be a lovers' relationship, occurs in the poem beginning 'Sentries against inner and outer, / At *stated* interval is feature; / And how shall enemy on these / Make sudden raid or lasting peace?' (emphasis added). It goes on to focus on 'the mouth / . . . that you may parley with', which in the end performs the familiar betrayal in 'archaic' patterns of behaviour: the 'close kiss / . . . / Given long since, had it but known'.

As a poem 'The strings' excitement' steps even further back from itself with the lines, 'This longing for assurance takes the form / / Of a hawk's vertical stooping from the sky'. The stand-offish expression 'takes the form' acknowledges the poet's-eye view of the relationship, that he is casting a cold eye on it even as it unfolds. As in many of the 'love' poems, there is a guilty but honest air of non-committal 'taciturnity'. Yet paradoxically this vantage-point gives the experience significance. The loved one's tears grandly turn into the meaningless, unfathomable tears of all the world, both scorned and given tragic significance by the epithet 'lunatic': 'The lunatic agitation of the sea'. Similarly, 'agitation' is dismissive (in relation to human emotion) as well as portentous (in relation to the sea). With its appeal for glacial oblivion, for an 'Age of Ice', the last stanza gives scorn an air of tragic immensity, the phrase 'Massive and taciturn years' conveying seductively powerful obliteration. It is a taciturnity that would silence all utterance, including love poems and the need for their 'expression'. But the poem ensures that emotions do indeed come to expression, the refusal to weep eliciting the line 'While this despair with hardened eyeballs cries', whose open vowels cry out against the tearlessness of the glacial eyes. The question self-indictingly left open by the poem is: does such rhetoric 'express' or repress? Is not what is guiltily being expressed repression, the inability to feel? Is it true that 'all emotions to expression come'? If so, then the poem is saying that those that do not come to expression do not exist. The poem goes round in guilty circles.

The poem 'Taller to-day, we remember similar evenings' represents an insecure and 'passing' moment of lovers' happiness. The beguiling distractions from which it would escape have to do with the past, memory, the historical sense (the 'windless orchard' as opposed to 'the following wind of history / Of others' wisdom'), in the poem all involved with expression: the urge to define inevitably draws in the world of time. The poem begins by beguiling the reader. 'We', always a tricky word in early Auden, unsettlingly co-opts the reader, a tendency reinforced by the fact that for several stanzas the poem's occasion is uncertain. To begin with, the poem reads as some sort of metaphor for the Audenesque watershed experience, suspended between intimations of a mysterious past and of a threatening future. One hesitates even to call this a 'love' poem until fended off in line fifteen by 'though no nearer each other'. 'We remember *similar* evenings' (emphasis added), but this one, as the poem later intimates, is unique: intimating, too, that always to be looking away from the present, to be making comparisons, to be looking backwards or forwards, is a feature of consciousness. In the first stanza the syntax beguilingly blurs past and present so that what is being remembered is, in ghostly fashion, indistinguishable from what is happening: are we 'walking' now, as we 'remember', or are we recalling a time when we walked together one evening? From one perspective the distinction is immaterial, because what we recollect is similar to our present situation. But from another, the blurring is essential to the poem's concern with the difficulty of isolating a moment, of capturing its uniqueness, of finding it 'sufficient now'.

The second and third stanzas (unfortunately omitted in the revised version) exclude even as they recall extraneous experience. The second recollects what sounds like childhood fantasy with familiar Audenesque spoof mystery. 'The sofa

hiding the grate' intimates the childish perspective ('to-day' we
are 'taller') and world, as do the teasingly conspiratorial lines
about the figure turned to the window and the knowingly
mysterious Captain Ferguson. But the mood is valedictory,
'hearing our last'; and the next stanza presents figures isolated
from their context, the dramas in which they participated lost to
time. The passive construction, 'it is seen', makes the examples
of failure (the one who 'went blind in a tower' and the one who
'broke through, and faltered') seem inconsequential, outside the
watchers' islanded hour. It contrasts with the active 'we see' two
stanzas later, at this moment of precarious happiness: 'But
happy now, though no nearer each other, / We see the farms
lighted all along the valley'. This landscape reflects the watchers'
active contentment, which is not dependent on some future
'dawn':

> Noises at dawn will bring
> Freedom for some, but not this peace
> No bird can contradict: passing, but is sufficient now
> For something fulfilled this hour, loved or endured.

Here, in the last stanza, 'freedom' and 'peace' quietly enter from
the world of feud and warfare hinted at earlier in the poem and
sustain this shared momentary oasis, the transitoriness of which
is reinforced by the isolation and suspension of the word
'passing' (an effect lost in the revised version: 'passing but here,
sufficient now . . .'). Behind the word hovers the elegiac 'passing
away'.

The encroachments on 'this hour' are mirrored in the poem's
veering diction. The second stanza seems not to take itself
seriously; likewise the ominous fourth stanza undermines itself.
'Nights come bringing the snow, and the dead howl / Under the
headlands in their windy dwelling' moves from the theatrical-
sounding to the possibly spoof: 'windy' may contrast with
'windless' in the first stanza, 'the following wind of history'
blowing strongly in the fourth; but 'windy' – as opposed to
'windswept', say – has a touch of mockery. Theatrical, too, is the
intimation of a conflict which one hesitates to read as the journey
of Everyman: 'Because the Adversary put too easy questions /
On lonely roads'. Against this showily uncommunicative idiom
is weighed the reflective reserve of the last stanza, where the

two negatives in 'not this peace / No bird can contradict' convey unshowy affirmation. This poem, like 'From the very first coming down', is 'afraid to say more than it means': it implicitly searches for a style that is 'sufficient', that does not distort the truth of 'no nearer each other', that maintains, again in the language of 'From the very first', a 'decent' reserve. The effort not to say more than is meant can be felt in the precisely vague last line: the uncertainty, even evasiveness, of 'something' and of 'loved or endured' sounds like truth-seeking, not uncommunicative secretiveness. This secret 'something' is different from the secretive references to 'Captain Ferguson', 'the Adversary' and the rest. Something has been rescued from the impasse, not least a style and a voice.

In 'From the very first coming down' evasiveness is exacting. The poem's tone shields insecurity; being in the know conveys, even as it masks, bewilderment. Fear of feeling combines with fear of an incapacity to feel: 'Always afraid to say more than it meant'. Apprehension can be glimpsed behind the chiselled authority of the phrasing, behind 'the stone smile'. The poem tries to be in command of experience in the act of submitting to it. The delay until the end of the first verse-paragraph of the poem's motivating event, the arrival of a non-committal letter from a lover, throws the opening into mysterious relief. Parts of speech are not always clear, and tenses shift unnervingly. 'Coming' at the start could on first reading sound like a present participle, but seems to resolve itself into a gerund, the action of descending performed by both the 'you' and the 'I'. There is an allegorical air: mankind's descent, Adam and Eve coming down from Milton's 'happy seat' of Paradise, so to say. The noun phrases 'with a frown' and 'a lost way', where one would normally expect participial ones ('frowning', 'having lost the way'), reinforce the effect of a mysteriously symbolic journey. The present tense, 'remain', quickly gives way to the past 'heard' and 'found'; but with the sense of an ending a new beginning comes into play, 'completed *round*' (emphasis added) encompassing notions of both finishing and starting again, satisfaction and frustration. The new beginning sounds played out with familiarity even as it is intimated, the outcome implicit in the setting out: 'love's worn circuit re-begun' is not a beginning again in the active voice, but a passive construction with a past sound, disillusion undermining the latent thrill in the fleeting electricity metaphor and in the 'very first' of the poem's opening. 'Completed round' and 'worn circuit' simultaneously reinforce and contradict each other.

Beginnings and endings merge in the continuum of repetition: 'Endless with no dissenting turn'. Even when the future tense does arrive it immediately collapses into the past, ushering in the disappointment of familiarity; it is known beforehand that anything about to happen will recall what has already happened:

> Shall see, shall pass, as we have seen
> The swallow on the tile, Spring's green
> Preliminary shiver, passed
> A solitary truck, the last
> Of shunting in the Autumn.

A sense of things passing is continually and elusively present here: 'shall pass' slides into 'passed', which could be the active past tense or past participle. Beginnings involve premonitions: the shivering word 'preliminary' quickly gives way to 'last'. The poem looks with apparent indifference at the past and future between which it is suspended, a new relationship already intimated before it is clear to the reader that the old one has ended. As in the poem 'Love by ambition', love is 'Aware already / Of who stands next / And is not vexed / And is not giddy', and with a sense of *déjà vu* 'Foretells his own death and is faithless' – words which are also appropriate to the ungiddy stylistic poise of 'From the very first coming down'.

The effect of this collapsing of times, of past into present into future, is to place the reader in an atemporal arena where what will happen already has; and the speaker, at the outset anticipating the outcome, can present a knowing and disillusioned outlook on experience before the reader is quite aware of the immediate occasion. (For this reason the poem is more arresting in its original, untitled form; later it was titled 'The Letter', and then 'The Love Letter'.) The apprehension of circularity, in the seasons and in love, that there is nothing new under 'the sun', comes even as this particular story of fracturing love unfolds. The effect is a highly self-conscious knowledge of the ways of love even as they reveal themselves, a knowledge that traps the speaker in its own knowingness, for the knowledge becomes part

of the experience, disabling even as it clarifies. As in 'Taller to-
day', therefore, self-consciousness stymies; at the same time it is
responsible for the inclination to allegorize, to turn experience
into the typical. After the quasi-symbolic landscape of 'valley',
'sun', 'sudden bird', it is a small step to the 'year's arc' and
thence to 'love's worn circuit'. The landscape takes on an inward
feel: the 'new valley' has the ring of emotional dispensation, the
'lost way' of psychological cul-de-sac, and one answer to the
question as to where it is that 'you certainly remain' is in the
memory. 'Certainly' has the air of an internal debate going on,
emotional stirrings beneath the unruffled surface.

The poem's diction betrays emotion held in check. Colloquialism parries with something more formal. For instance the
colloquial 'Thought warmed to evening *through and through*'
(emphasis added) plays off against the stilted line preceding, 'To
interrupt the homely brow', and the laconic 'Speaking of much
but not to come' two lines later, where the elliptical syntax
barely acknowledges regret. The second verse-paragraph in
particular is remarkable for elusively complex but deep emotion.
In its first three lines, the multiple negatives and roundabout
syntax want to hold wounded feelings at bay. 'Decent', in 'I,
decent with the seasons, move', is two-edged: the speaker
defends himself by claiming that he is only moving according to
the customary 'circuits', answering faithlessness with faithlessness in the time-honoured fashion. But he is also being politely
civil, refusing to be aroused where arousal would do no good.
The final sentence, artfully articulated over six lines, the repeated 'different' shadow-boxing with indifference, 'always'
balancing 'never', the repeated 'more' playing off against a sense
of less, presents a poised, stonily smiling exterior to fend off guilt
and fear. The poem may be afraid to say more than it means, but
it means much more than it lets on. The last lines may want to
sound cool and stand-offish, but the very insistence of their
denial gainsays the indifference they lay claim to: the phrases
'never was more' and 'always afraid to say more' are not
'reticent' in the emotional holding-back which they enact. Such
writing sees through the mask of 'English' reserve with its stiff
upper lip, and gives the lie to those who, in that phrase by
Spender, find Auden's early poetry 'intellectually over- and
emotionally underdeveloped'. That is to take the poetry too
much at its own word. The manner in which it lays claim to

emotional detachment betrays a guilty self-accusation which undermines that very detachment.

Thus love is thwarted by intense self-consciousness. 'Love by ambition' is a poem that ostentatiously does not go in fear of abstraction:

> Love by ambition
> Of definition
> Suffers partition
> And cannot go
> From yes to no.

Fuller paraphrases: 'only our efforts to understand love taunt us with the possibility of its perfection and finality. We define it into yes and no – into, that is, reciprocated and unreciprocated love – as though these clear alternatives solved anything. ... love can destroy itself, whatever the circumstances' (Fuller, p. 38). The need to find expression frames love in past modes of feeling and perception: 'definition' necessarily entails established ways of thinking; self-awareness destroys the experience even as it is taking place. Thus the poem evokes unreciprocated love by what sounds like deliberate near-cliché: 'The shutting of a door / The tightening jaw'. This is 'A *conscious* sorrow' (emphasis added), aware of itself being sorrowful, incapable of spontaneity. And reciprocated love is likewise evoked by knowing near-cliché: 'Views from the rail / Of land and happiness, / . . . / cheek to cheek / And dear to dear'. It is not important whether the 'voices' that 'explain / Love's pleasure and love's pain' are external or internal, past or present: the point is that they represent intervening conscious-ness, the voices of inherited behaviour precluding spontaneity. So love moves on: 'Love is not there / Love has moved to another chair'. The present cannot offer happiness because even as love begins it knows that it will come to an end, that it will die as it has done before; the present turns ghostly: love 'Designs his own unhappiness / Foretells his own death and is faithless'.

4

The style of 'Love by ambition' inclines towards the very ratiocination it wants to eschew; it has an air of seeking definitions. The word 'definition' itself is pointedly flanked at the outset by rhyming words that are likewise abstract nouns: 'ambition' and 'partition'. The speaker is evidently suffering from the disease he is diagnosing. He longs for the 'assurance' of 'expression' (in the words of 'The strings' excitement'). The style is characteristic of a number of the early poems in short lines, some other examples being 'Before this loved one', 'Sentries against inner and outer', 'This lunar beauty', 'Between attention and attention' and 'To ask the hard question is simple'. Fuller calls it 'lyrical-didactic', and notes that it owes something to the influence of the contemporary American poet Laura (Riding) Jackson. (See Fuller, pp. 36–8.) The influence can be regarded as symptomatic: Auden's poetry sounds as though for a short period he was in thrall to a style that did not quite suit, that, in his use, is fascinatingly in danger of not getting beyond mere style. Taken with an 'ambition of definition', he adopted a voice that in Riding's best poetry works acutely at the level of abstraction, its sinewy syntax mirroring the act of cerebration, but which in his own poetry verges on mimicry. This is not to belittle Auden's achievement in these poems. The style he took from Riding became one weapon in his arsenal. The method is typical of his ironizing sensibility.

Riding's poetry, however, is characteristically unironic. It is ambitious of definition to a degree that would purge utterance of its variousness so as to attain what in the Preface to her *Selected Poems* she calls 'the general human ideal in speaking'; it eschews language's particularizing and expressive potential; it aspires to the abstract:

> Come, words, away from mouths,
> Away from tongues in mouths
> And reckless hearts in tongues
> And mouths in cautious heads –
>
> Come, words, away to where
> The meaning is not thickened
> With the voice's fretting substance . . . [7]

The view of the function and possibilities of language implied here accounts for the attitude to poetry indicated by the titles of Riding's volumes of poems: the suspicion of *Poems: A Joking Word* deepens with *Poet: A Lying Word* (also the title of a kind of prose-poem in the volume). As the Preface to her *Selected Poems* and other prose writings by her attest, her disappointed ambition for what poetry might do led her to abandon it: 'what compatibility can there be between the creed offering hope of a way of speaking beyond the ordinary, touching perfection, a complex perfection associable with nothing less complex than truth, and the craft tying the hope to verbal rituals that court sensuosity as if it were the judge of truth?'[8] If Riding eventually felt unable to do as Auden did, and mine poetry out of the rich disparity between that 'perfection associable with . . . truth' and 'verbal rituals', what is arresting about her stand is not that she took it, but that she seems to have thought she was the first to experience the tensions that led to it.

The relationship between language and meaning underlies her distinguished poem 'Death as Death':

> To conceive death as death
> Is difficulty come by easily,
> A blankness fallen among
> Images of understanding,
> Death like a quick cold hand
> On the hot slow head of suicide.
> So is it come by easily
> For one instant. Then again furnaces
> Roar in the ears, then again hell revolves,
> And the elastic eye holds paradise
> At visible length from blindness,
> And dazedly the body echoes
> 'Like this, like this, like nothing else.'
>
> Like nothing – a similarity
> Without resemblance. The prophetic eye,
> Closing upon difficulty,
> Opens upon comparison,
> Halving the actuality
> As a gift too plain, for which
> Gratitude has no language,
> Foresight no vision.

The poem presents an absolute, Death, being sensually courted in verbal rituals. 'A blankness fallen among / Images of understanding' wittily conjures up the theft suffered by Death ('fallen among thieves') in the attempt to find similitudes for it. The poem ends by purporting to give up the struggle to find words: since Death is beyond the language of the living, all we can do is talk about it in comparative terms. The language we commonly use to describe Death ('furnaces' that 'roar', 'hell' that 're-volves', etc.) turns something for which we should be grateful (so the poem wants to argue) into an object of fear. Never-theless, the poem itself is obliged to strike its bargain with language by going through the motions of 'opening upon com-parison'. It was Riding's unwillingness, eventually, to make such compromises that led to her abandonment of poetry. Like the best of her poems, 'Death as Death' is remarkable for its single-minded tracking of thought, and – a quality that would have been immediately apparent to Auden – for its ability to make the reader aware of its language as language even as it unfolds: 'Like nothing – a similarity / Without resem-blance' takes the words 'Like nothing' and holds them up for inspection.

It is arguable that Auden's poetry gets its energy, as well as its elusiveness, largely from precisely such compromise, which makes itself felt in a rich tension between abstraction and image. Behind both his poem 'It was Easter as I walked in the public gardens' and Riding's 'The World and I' is a concern with the approximation between language and experience, self and the world, ultimately truth and art. Riding's poem begins 'This is not exactly what I mean / Any more than the sun is the sun', that is, any more than the idea of the sun, the sun as appre-hended, is the same as the sun itself. It ends, with 'thickened' and 'fretting' meaning, by trying to acquiesce in the approxima-tions of knowledge and language: it is best to be 'sure / . . . exactly where / Exactly I and exactly the world / Fail to meet by a moment, and a word'. Similar anxieties inform 'It was Easter as I walked in the public gardens', but section 1 of Auden's poem comes up against the recognition of a delight in 'An altering speech for altering things, / An emphasis on new names', an attitude that does not recognize, in Riding's words, any 'general human ideal in speaking' and which indeed gets close to 'courting sensuosity as if it were the judge of truth'. Both poems are concerned with the relation between mind and nature, inner and outer worlds, but whereas Auden's wants to bridge the gap between the two, Riding's ends by emphasizing it. Better, Riding argues, for 'the world and I' to acknowledge our differences than to ignore them, which would merely result in 'A sour love, each doubtful whether / Was ever a thing to love the other'. Section 4 of Auden's poem, by contrast, gestures towards a new sense of what 'love' is: 'You whom I gladly walk with, touch, / ... / We know it, we know that love / Needs more than the admiring excitement of union'.

Auden's lines about 'an altering spech' are brought up short by a realization of the contrast between the speaker's inner world and the world outside: 'But *thinking* so I came at once / Where solitary man sat weeping on a bench, / ... / Helpless and ugly as an embryo chicken' (emphasis added). The effort of the poem to find new life, to bring that 'embryo' to birth, entails reconciling the inner and the outer, thinking and living, consciousness and experience, the individual and society. Section 2 expresses the effort in an idiom strongly reminiscent of Riding's urgent abstractions: 'Coming out of me living is always thinking, / Thinking changing and changing living, / Am feeling as it was seeing – '. The combination of abstraction and urgency is arresting; this is felt thought. But even as the poem borrows Riding's style, it contradicts her attitude towards the relationship between language and experience. 'Living' is both a participial adjective referring back to 'me', and a gerund governing the ensuing verb 'is'. When the speaker is fully alive there is a dynamic interchange between self and other: thought and experience cannot be separated. The implication is that if you do separate them, 'thinking' becomes mere static knowledge and the self no longer 'living'. The ideas conform with those of D. H. Lawrence in *Fantasia of the Unconscious*, which influenced the early Auden. (Chapter 4 will investigate what was to become of Lawrence's influence on Auden in *The Orators*.) Man's condition is divided: existence entails consciousness of experience; consciousness therefore forms experience even as it defines it. Our thinking nature belongs to the reality we inhabit. Experience is modified by our awareness of it; having an experience entails defining it. Man cannot be like the ducks, which, at one with nature, unconsciously 'find sun's luxury enough'. Birth is a falling into consciousness of otherness, and the necessary fear of it:

> Is first baby, warm in mother,
> Before born and is still mother,
> Time passes and now is other,
> Is knowledge in him now of other,
> Cries in cold air, himself no friend.

In such passages Auden does not go in fear of abstractions, but in Ridingesque fashion generates a dynamic relationship between them, bringing them to life. The interplay between 'now' and 'other' is an example. The line 'Time passes and now is other' brings abrupt life to a string of unremarkable abstract words. That said, at times ratiocination runs away with the poem, as in section 3:

> So, insecure, he loves and love
> Is insecure, gives less than he expects.
> He knows not if it be seed in time to display
> Luxuriantly in a wonderful fructification
> Or whether it be but a degenerate remnant
> Of something immense . . .

To read such lines as ironic caricature of the insecurity which is their subject does not improve their quality. After this the notably uncerebral idiom of the impressive section 4, 'It is time for the destruction of error', comes as a relief: the diseased old life collapses in a style that revels in the destruction it depicts. It is significant that divided man succumbs with verbal panache: 'To destroy the efflorescence of the flesh, / The intricate play of the mind'. As for the new life, that is fleetingly conjured up in the unironic and mysteriously inexplicable concluding image: 'deep in clear lake / The lolling bridegroom, beautiful, there'. Like the similar underwater image for 'the future' in *Paid* ('with prolonged drowning shall develop gills'), this gestures beyond language. To end the poem with such a phrase, suspended, with no verb and no statement, the enticingly inconclusive concluding word pointing to a definite but indescribable beyond, 'there', outside the poem, is a 'beautiful' escape from 'the intricate play of the mind'. The bridegroom's presence is incontrovertible, but enigmatic. If the word 'lolling' is suggestive of a drowned body's posture, it implies, too, a wilful indolence, a passivity that could, if it chose, become active.

Riding's influence on Auden was not simply stylistic. The argument, central to her poetry, that present action is stalled because identity is inherited, must have impressed itself on Auden, especially as one of her poems, 'The Map of Places', expresses the idea in terms of maps and ships: 'The map of places passes', in time becomes irrelevant to our new terrain, where 'Now on naked names feet stand, / No geographies in the hand, / And paper reads anciently, / And ships at sea / Turn round and round'. Mapped experience is no guide to the territory of the future; it only leads back to the meaningless past: 'Holes in maps look through to nowhere'. In *Paid* 'maps upon the whitewashed wall / The hand put up to ask' are associated with the 'single old past' that must be left behind. In Auden's poem 'Who will endure' increasingly useless navigational maps wittily imply a blocked, mysteriously uncertain future: 'Conjectures on the maps that lie / About in ships long high and dry / Grow stranger and stranger'. In the 'Prologue' to *The Orators* 'mapping' is a metaphor for psychological deadlock, for the grip of past on present, of memory on action.

Like Auden's 'Love by ambition' Riding's poem 'The Definition of Love' concerns the dangers of the 'ambition of definition'. In both poems consciousness of love interferes with the experience itself. Indeed, Riding's poem could be read as a blueprint for the state in which love finds itself in Auden's early poetry. 'Ghost's adversity' haunts 'The Definition of Love', and Everett's remark about the lover in Auden's poetry being 'an uneasy ghost' who is 'pursued by a past but pursuing a present' could equally well be applied to Riding's poem, which ends: 'And we remembering forget, / Mistake the future for the past, / Worrying fast / Back to a long ago / Not yet tomorrow'. Auden seems to have been echoing Riding's 'remembering forget' conundrum in his poem 'To ask the hard question is simple': 'And forgetting to listen or see / Makes forgetting easy; / Only remembering the method of remembering, / Remembering only in another way . . .': as Mendelson explains, 'the mind . . . knows only the fact of its own consciousness' (Mendelson, p. 92). Actions are merely cyphers out of our evolutionary past: 'Till, losing memory, / Bird, fish, and sheep are ghostly, / And ghosts must do again / What gives them pain'. But in this poem Auden attempts to break out of the deadlock by entering that 'long ago' which Riding spurns. Her poem declares that 'Speech invents memory', but Auden's concludes with a prayer that 'memory restore' the evolutionary past, that 'love recover / What has been dark and rich and warm all over'.

That concluding line epitomizes the unRidingesque pole of Auden's early poetry, not only in sentiment, but in expression: it is rich with the various 'sensuosity' of human utterance; it does not quite know how seriously to take itself, it pleads, it questions, it offers itself as a half-comprehending prayer, it toys with the jocular. The echoes of Riding in Auden's early poetry indicate admiration, and resistance. Even as his poetry echoes her univocal voice, it resists it, as if to proclaim that human 'meaning' needs 'the voice's fretting substance'. Even, perhaps especially, the poems that echo Riding most loudly are, arguably, memorable for lines that most diverge from her style, lines such as 'Touching is shaking hands / On mortgaged lands', 'Or shaking hands / With snub-nosed winner', 'And leaning asking from the car / Cannot tell us where we are'. These lines, memorable for their metaphoric life, their 'thickened substance', containing images of life lived 'Between attention and attention', of the life not fully lived, have a verbal life, and satiric inflection, all their own. The poems in which they occur are not single-minded in the Riding way, as if to say that unequivocal utterance is misconceived, if not impossible.

5

The voice of 'Consider this and in our time' demonstrates to a marked degree the unstable utterance of Auden's early poetry. As a gestural tour-de-force its purport is inseparable from its rhetoric, its 'way of happening' (from 'In Memory of W. B. Yeats'). The first verse-paragraph unnervingly mingles confidence with confusion, urgency with disorientation, the diagnostic with the atmospheric. 'Consider this and in our time': that 'and' unsettlingly yokes deliberation and urgency. The reader is then projected out, or rather up, 'As the hawk sees it or the helmeted airman'. Perspective 'rifts suddenly': the panoptic eye homes in on the 'cigarette-end smouldering on a border' with its air of sinister significance. The mysterious is constantly on the verge of the merely mystifying, the spoof. Is the 'border' only an innocuous flower-border after all? – this is a 'garden party'. We are propelled from detachment to identification; but what are we being implicated in? The commands are tonally unidentifiable: 'Look there' may be more exclamation than command; 'Pass on, admire the view' could be out of a film travel documentary. No sooner have we been commanded – or is it invited? – to 'Join there the insufficient units' than these entities are seen as from an observatory, 'constellated at reserved tables'.

One might paraphrase the first verse-paraphrase as being about an irresponsible, privileged class whose social malaise is infecting everyone from the playboy set to the farming community. But what compels and disturbs is our relation to this account, to the poetry's unsettling manner of intimating, of raising our suspicions uncertainly. The military metaphors seem to contain sexual overtones. The lines 'smoulder' not only with guerrilla but also with sexual warfare. The lines 'Dangerous, easy, in furs, in uniform / And constellated at reserved tables' imply the fearfulness and fascination of sex, its secretive game. 'Reserved tables' flickers with military and sexual hints: forces in reserve, reserved for someone else. The sinister 'Supplied with feelings by an efficient band' has personal and political overtones: as in 'Control of the passes', to be 'supplied with feelings' is to be out of touch with your emotions; the word 'relayed' intimates musical brainwashing, so to say, the 'efficient band' recalling not only guerrilla units but also waveband and musical band.

In the second verse-paragraph uncertain syntax increases the oracular mystery of the address. The Antagonist is potentially the subject of the first four lines, but then seems to turn into the vocative at 'Your comments'. The all-inclusiveness of 'You talk to your admirers every day' has the effect of conflating the Antagonist and the poem's addressee, so that we become our own enemy – rather like John Nower containing the spy within himself. When the poem enters Auden's familiar terrain of psychological stalemate ('silted harbours, derelict works, / . . . strangled orchards, and the silent comb'), the journey inward is reinforced by elusive syntax. About the series of ensuing injunctions, 'Order the ill', 'Visit the ports', 'Beckon your chosen out' and 'Summon', Stan Smith comments that they 'may just carry over the indicative of the earlier sentence ("You talk"). But if they are orders, who is it that is addressing us now. . . . Are we . . . agents of his authority, or is his address that of an accomplice or, with irony, that of an enemy . . .?' (Smith, p. 44). This

disorientation, in which we do not quite know which side we are
supposed to be on (to adapt the title Auden later gave to one of
the Odes of *The Orators*), allows for a remarkable suppleness of
voice and attitude. The poet is able to empathize even as he
indicts; so, for instance, his rhythms briefly idle with the idle rich
when describing 'The leisurely conversation in the bar / Within
a stone's throw of the sunlit water'.

The poem encompasses contrasting moods with masterful
rhetorical agility; it is as much symptomatic as diagnostic:

> Seekers after happiness, all who follow
> The convolutions of your simple wish,
> It is later than you think; nearer that day
> Far other than that distant afternoon
> Amid rustle of frocks and stamping feet
> They gave the prizes to the ruined boys.
> You cannot be away, then, no
> Not though you pack within an hour,
> Escaping humming down arterial roads:
> The date was yours; the prey to fugues,
> Irregular breathing and alternate ascendancies
> After some haunted migratory years
> To disintegrate on an instant in the explosion of mania
> Or lapse for ever into a classic fatigue.

Those 'convolutions' are persuasively articulated by the convoluted syntax: 'Later', 'nearer', 'far other', 'distant', precipitate
the reader forward – 'nearer that day' – into an obscurely
sinister future to recall past times which somehow hold the key
to present malaise: the 'otherness' of the crisis to come and the
'distance' of that 'afternoon' uncannily merge. Youth has been
'ruined' before it sets out on its journey of ruination. In the last
five lines 'disintegration' and 'fatigue' are conveyed by a verbal
rush that is, none the less, expertly paced. The lines have an
'irregular breathing': two lines that 'explode' polysyllabically
('Irregular breathing and alternate ascendancies', 'To disinte-
grate on an instant in the explosion of mania') alternate with
lines that sound as though they are 'lapsing' away.

In an essay on the development of language Auden wrote that
'At some time or other in human history ... man became self-
conscious; he began to feel, I am I, and you are not I; we are shut

inside ourselves and apart from each other. There is no whole but the self'. The development of language was in response to a 'need to bridge over the gulf' between self and community. That there is buried deep in 'Consider this' a concern with language as community maker, as communicator, is borne out by this essay: arguing that communication depends on the relationship between speaker and listener, Auden adds in an illustrative parenthesis that 'It is always difficult to understand what people are saying at another table in a restaurant. We are outside the group' – which recalls the beginning of 'Consider this' with its 'insufficient units', its isolated groups 'constellated at reserved tables' (*An Outline for Boys and Girls and Their Parents*, ed. Naomi Mitchison, *EA*, pp. 303 and 304). Much of the early poetry is an attempt to break out of that sense of isolation, of being a 'stranger', 'cut off'. 'Consider this' is an invigorating failure to build the bridge: it begins in groups, and ends in foiled migration. And the notorious obscurity of the early poetry is no wilful perversion; it is, so the poems imply, a condition of the times. Yet even as 'Consider this' enacts this failure, one inclination of its rhetoric is to pull in the opposite direction: by the end, any feeling of us-and-them has dissolved; 'you' is addressed to poet and reader, speaker and society. Self and other have merged into a common, though fearfully unstable, identity.

2
Spender (1)
'The sense of falling light'

1

Anyone who wishes to make substantial claims for the poetry
which Stephen Spender wrote in the 1930s confronts a wide-
spread misconception and a practical problem. The misconception is the view of the poems as little more than footnotes to an
unusually interesting literary life. Spender himself has partly, if
inadvertently, encouraged this view, describing himself as 'an
autobiographer restlessly searching for forms in which to express
the stages of my development' (*WWW*, p. 138). But both his
autobiography, *World Within World* (1951), and his critical
study, *The Destructive Element* (1935), explore issues which
preoccupy Spender as a practising poet. Unfortunately, the
clarity and candour of Spender's prose have distracted attention
from his more demanding poetry: poetry such as that contained
in *Poems* (1933; second edition 1934) on which this chapter will
concentrate.

The practical problem is the inaccessibility of texts. The major
volumes of poetry that Spender published in the decade (*Poems*
(1933, 1934) and *The Still Centre* (1939) are no longer widely
available. A good proportion of the thirties poetry discussed in
this book appears (often in only slightly revised form) in
Collected Poems 1928–1953 (1955). But the contemporary
reader is most likely to turn to *Selected Poems* (1965), or to
Collected Poems 1928–1985 (1985). Both volumes contain selections of Spender's thirties poetry, but sometimes poems from the
period appear in revised versions, especially in the 1985 *Collected*

Poems. Sometimes the poet's changes are merely local in effect. At other times the changes present the reader with what amounts to a new poem: a striking example is the transformation of 'How strangely this sun reminds me of my love', seventeen lines long in *Poems*, 1933, into 'The Photograph', nine lines long in *Collected Poems 1928–1985*. Even more drastic is the treatment meted out to the sixty-five lines of 'Exiles from their Land, History their Domicile' (*SC*); omitted from the *Selected Poems* the poem makes a shorn reappearance in *Collected Poems 1928–1985* where it takes up a mere six lines and is called 'The Exiles'.

Spender's view of revision is divided. On the one hand, he argues that a poet can continue to 're-invent' a poem 'because he does not ever forget the complete intention behind the incomplete failure'. On the other hand, he is opposed to 'technical tidyings up', fearing that 'something which had the rough quality of a flaw in a semi-precious stone' might be turned 'into a superficial preciosity' (*CPS(1)*, p. 15). But in later statements Spender stresses the poet's right to alter rather than his duty to keep faith with the poetic self he once was – indeed, he feels that such faith may best be kept by revising: 'I sometimes remember, when I look at a poem, what I had originally meant to say: and I have another shot at saying it' (*SPS*, p. 9); 'In re-working poems I have always done so with the sense that in writing a poem I have certain intentions which I very rarely forget' (*CPS(2)*, p. 13).

Through such statements Spender implies a myth of the poet as explorer, the life of each poem paradoxically guaranteed by the fact that it is likely to be, as the title of one of his best post-thirties pieces has it, 'One More New Botched Beginning' (first published in volume form in *SPS*). This myth has attractions, but it blurs rather than sharpens one's sense of Spender's poetic achievement in the thirties. Urgently needed, then, is a Collected Poems which either prints poems as they were published in the major volumes of the thirties or includes textual apparatus which allows the reader access to these early versions. Such a work has still to appear; in the meantime, this study quotes from the early versions. Many of these poems initially appeared without titles, but were later given titles. Where appropriate, cross-references to titles in the more widely available *Selected Poems* and the two *Collected Poems* are supplied. We also indicate when discussing a poem originally published in the thirties whether it, or a version of it, appears in the volumes mentioned in the last sentence.

2

'When the muse first came to Mr. Spender he looked so sincere that her heart failed her, and she said: "Ask anything and I will give it to you," and he said: "Make me sincere."'[1] Randall Jarrell raises a central issue prompted by Stephen Spender's poetry, the vexed question of 'sincerity'. This chapter will consider whether his mockery is justified. 'Moving through the silent crowd' (*SP33*; included in *CPS(1)* and, under the title 'Unemployed', in *CPS(2)*)) is one of the few poems by Spender that Jarrell regarded favourably. 'The poem seems true and puzzlingly immediate,' Jarrell writes, 'touches me without reaching out to touch me'.[2] That 'puzzlingly' acknowledges the way the poem catches itself and its reader off-balance. What could have been 'sincere' but conventional, its display of pity merely rhetorical, is made 'true' by the poet's language. From the start, a quasi-documentary impulse wrestles with the admission of subjective involvement:

> Moving through the silent crowd
> Who stand behind dull cigarettes
> These men who idle in the road,
> I have the sense of falling light.

'Moving through the silent crowd', the poet is a distant heir of Blake's visionary wandering through the chartered streets of London; in both poems, the drama of experiencing matters as much as the content of what is experienced. 'Moving' propels itself past 'silent' to the 'I' of line four, Spender stressing a quietly restless 'movement' that applies as much to the poet's consciousness as to his body. That the 'crowd' is 'silent' may suggest it is subdued but potentially insurrectionary; more crucially for the poem, the adjective also suggests that the crowd has been stilled into an 'image' (see the poem's last stanza), its silence the product of the poet's need to see the unemployed in collective terms. These are, admittedly, the terms in which the unemployed are often seen; what distinguishes Spender's poem is the way he compels scrutiny of the cliché of the unemployed as a 'crowd'. Their silence allows the poet his 'sense of falling light'; the phrase is a fine shade away from turning the unemployed into 'flowers, / For poets' tearful fooling'.[3] From Owen Spender learned about the possibilities of pity as a poetic emotion; he also learned that it was an emotion beset by pitfalls, chief of which was the tendency, spelled out by Owen in 'Insensibility', to exploit suffering for the sake of a poetic effect. 'The sense of falling light' is such an effect – 'falling light' is moved by its own dying fall – and yet it knows that it is nothing more than a 'sense', a subjective intimation. The poet also knows (and fears) that intimations of this kind may mean more to him than attention to the circumstances of the unemployed.

The remainder of the poem confronts this knowledge and fear. Indeed the first stanza suggests economically that the poet is already 'haunted', as his final stanza has it, by the 'images' his poem mediates and by their ultimate 'emptiness'. That said, the reference to 'dull cigarettes' seeks to bully the poem out of sentimentality, to avoid conferring on the unemployed a spurious glamour; in this respect, it anticipates the later, would-be unillusioned reference to 'The cynical gestures of the poor'. Were that last-quoted phrase Spender's final word on the unemployed, the reader would feel the poet himself was being too easily 'cynical'. But the phrase belongs to the unfolding drama of the poem; through it the poet admits the class difference which prevents him from seeing the 'the poor' as other than alien. He duly produces a diagnostic phrase, but its tone is self-incriminating: 'a cynical gesture from this poet' is the line's unspoken sub-text.

Again, the side of the poem which searches after neutrality of tone gives the next lines ('Now they've no work, like better men / Who sit at desks and take much pay') that 'puzzling' quality Jarrell touches on. Are the unemployed 'like' the well-off in that both groups have 'no work', the well-off (or a particularly privileged section of the well-off) having sinecures that involve only a fiction of 'work' so that both groups 'sleep long nights and rise at ten'? 'Better', too, seems to want to be spoken ironically; the well-off are 'better' only in that they occupy more fortunate social positions, a fact which allows them to consider themselves the 'betters' of those who are poor. But, for a second, the reader may wonder whether the poet wishes 'better' to be taken – on a different level of irony – at face value, a word applicable to those who prosper in a world from which morality has been banished.

These flickers of ambivalence trouble and attest to inner trouble: are the unemployed 'better'? are the well-off 'worse'? do both groups share a common humanity despite being placed at loggerheads by a particular economic system? In the same breath, however, these flickers are smoothed into impassivity by the ballad-like simplicity of rhyme and rhythm: a simplicity which in turn is held open to the poem's complex self-awareness. Gone is the more transparent irony of the poem's first version whose opening stanza is clearer, yet less intriguing:

> Now you've no work, like a rich man
> You'll sleep long hours and rise at ten;
> And stand at corners of the street
> Smoking continual cigarettes.[4]

By contrast with the easy indignation experienced on behalf of 'You' here, 'sincerity' in the later poem involves much emotional and technical sophistication. Indeed, the poem does not assume, as Jarrell implies Spender too often does assume, that it knows exactly what 'sincerity' is; instead, it moves, vigilantly and powerfully, towards a first-hand discovery of what 'sincerity' might involve.

As Lionel Trilling observes, being 'sincere' means that we have to 'play the role of being ourselves, we sincerely act the part of the sincere person'; the result is that 'a judgement may be passed upon our sincerity that it is not authentic':[5] precisely the judgement made by Jarrell about Spender. Yet Spender's attempt to remain faithful to individual perception regardless of social opinion comes close to Trilling's account of 'authenticity'. In his autobiography,[6] Spender's self-consciousness about sincerely acting the part of the sincere person leads to interesting convolutions. He discusses the differences between his poetic sensibility and Auden's, focusing especially on his inability to share Auden's view that ' "The subject of a poem is a peg to hang the poetry on" ' (*WWW*, p. 59); then he qualifies the impression that he is 'trying to say . . . that my poetry is more "sincere" than that of other poets'. Yet in accepting 'the limits of . . . personal experience' and putting himself 'outside a very general movement amongst modern poets to develop philosophies, embrace creeds, join movements' (*WWW*, p. 60), Spender articulates what amounts to a diffident manifesto: one which helps to explain the authority of 'Moving through the silent crowd'.

What has been referred to above as the poem's 'complex self-awareness' surfaces in the fine last stanza. Here the sense of the unemployed as a class for whom the poet can feel improving pity is decisively banished:

> I'm jealous of the weeping hours
> They stare through with such hungry eyes.
> I'm haunted by these images,
> I'm haunted by their emptiness.

The stanza anticipates, confronts and outflanks the amusing if unfair description of Spender as 'the Rupert Brooke of the Depression': that is, a poet who sought, as Brooke did in poems written at the outbreak of the First World War, to cut an uncritically self-romanticizing figure at a time of crisis; the Depression, a period of severe economic recession (in Britain there were well over three million unemployed by 1932), was ushered in by the Wall Street crash of 1929, and began to affect Britain by 1930.[7] Spender frankly admits his indulgent, guilty jealousy of the suffering of the unemployed, or the suffering he fantasizes them as enduring ('the hours that drain away' at the end of the third stanza have been heightened into 'weeping hours'). This is not to say that the unemployed do not suffer; but there is an implicit recognition on Spender's part that his involvement with the subject is wrapped up with needs of his own such as the longing to get in contact with 'real' suffering, a desire generated by his own privileged detachment from poverty. The next two lines point up this recognition. Spender twice says that he is 'haunted', a tactic which avoids the clumsiness it appears to court. For one thing, the two uses of 'haunted' describe different hauntings: the first confesses the poet's obsession with 'images', received and constructed; the second his awareness of their 'emptiness'. For another, the words, and the self-consciousness they convey, may be head-on, but the feelings are dexterous. The final 'emptiness' that the poet locates at the heart of his 'images' – 'empty pockets' (stanza two) and the rest – renews a 'sense' of the sufferings of the unemployed. Beyond all the poem's 'hauntings', the reader is led to realize, lies a fullness of social experience which the poet bears witness to by conceding his poem's 'emptiness'.

The poem can be seen as Spender's reworking of T. S. Eliot's

'Preludes', particularly of the lines from the last section of Eliot's poem which Spender quotes in *The Destructive Element*:

> I am moved by fancies that are curled
> Around these images, and cling;
> The notion of some infinitely gentle
> Infinitely suffering thing.[8]

Arguably, Spender's 'I'm haunted by these images' came into existence by way of these lines. Yet his remarks on the kind of 'pity' he finds in Eliot's lines suggest his poem's distance from 'Preludes':

> It is not altogether the same pity for human suffering as one finds in James, and that in Wilfred Owen's poetry is so all-sufficient that he could write of them 'the poetry is in the pity'. It is an extension of this pity; humanity is not pitied because it suffers, but because it exists at all, and resembles, in its totality, this gentle and suffering thing. The pity is in the notion of a humanity without humanity. (*DE*, p. 135)

Both Spender and Eliot explore the gap between self and world; but 'the notion of a humanity without humanity', starkly present in 'Preludes', gives way in 'Moving through the silent crowd' to a sense of humanity's undiscovered humanity. Both poets rebuke the 'images' that fascinate them. In 'Preludes', however, the subsequent 'Wipe your hand across your mouth, and laugh' suggests a second self standing apart from the poem's 'I', mauling its vulnerable 'fancies'. For the Eliot of 'Preludes', the self is dispersed, multiple, overwhelmed by 'worlds', as the poem's penultimate line has it; for the Spender of 'Moving through the silent crowd', the self comes up against the ultimate 'emptiness' of its own creations, but, exiled from reality as it may be, consciousness is all the poet has. Eliot's fear of 'worlds' outside the self – even, or especially, if these 'worlds' consist of 'images' projected from other consciousnesses – is accompanied by greater attention to imagistic detail than Spender displays.[9] But this should not be made the basis for undervaluation of the younger poet's achievement; each poem explores, in its different way, the subject of 'pity' without succumbing to mawkishness or insensitivity.

Bernard Spencer (poet and contemporary of Spender at Oxford), doubtless reflecting on poems written during the thirties, commented in 1942:

> The capacity for pity and the capacity for scientific detachment may both be valuable to [the poet] in the rest of his life but they are dangerous to him as a poet. Pity and disgust and the scientific attitude are all attitudes of separation, not of joining. (Though pity or disgust might provide the necessary impulse to begin writing.) True poetry is a dance in which you take part and enjoy yourself.[10]

This version of 'True poetry' is drawn from Spencer's own practice; his best poems seek to move beyond, even as they acknowledge, the political pressures of the period. 'Allotments: April' is the most famous example, with its concluding image of 'Two elms and their balanced attitude like dancers, their arms like dancers'.[11] Yet this poem's delicately 'balanced attitude' reconciles less powerful stresses than those experienced by Spender's finest poems; in such poems 'pity' is allowed its place, even though its potential for 'separation, not . . . joining' is recognized and its tendency 'to become negative, exhausting, sentimental, masochistic' (*DE*, p. 218) taken on board.

3

'Moving through the silent crowd' is the only poem from Spender's early volumes (up to and including the second edition of *Poems*) that Jarrell exempts from his criticism. Other poems, however, persuade one that the poetry's emotions are often explored rather than asserted. Before looking at such poems, it is worth noting that 'Moving through the silent crowd' solves, by highlighting, a perennial problem in Spender's work: the relation between the poet's subjectivity and external circumstance. A. Kingsley Weatherhead remarks that 'Ubiquitously in Spender's work we find the poet covertly or overtly using the outside world for inward symbolic purposes'.[12] A strength of 'Moving through the silent crowd' is the poet's awareness of this impulse in himself, an awareness which prevents the plight of the unemployed serving 'inward symbolic purposes' in any trite or unfeeling way. The view of poetry as 'a use of language which revealed external actuality as symbolic inner consciousness' (*WWW*, p. 95) that Spender formed at Oxford underpins his practice. But his poetry is most achieved when 'symbolic inner consciousness' allows, as in 'Moving through the silent crowd', for the claims of 'external actuality'.

Spender was writing at a time when these claims were pressed upon poets with propagandist vigour. One indication of the pressure they exerted on Spender, and of the variousness of his response, is the recurrent appearance in his poetry and prose of the word 'real' (or of words akin to it). Spender's dealings with the 'real' are inseparable from, and frequently as exploratory as, his approaches to 'sincerity'. A probable influence on his use of the word is, once more, T. S. Eliot, whose use of 'Unreal' in *The Waste Land* passes a damning judgement on modern secular experience, a judgement which, in the form of prophetic vision, reaches its climax in 'What the Thunder said': 'Falling towers / Jerusalem Athens Alexandria / Vienna London / Unreal'. Spender does not share Eliot's anti-Utopian, apocalyptic feelings (though apocalyptic feelings of a sort find expression in his poetry of the thirties). But his questioning of experience, its value and meaning, was undoubtedly coloured by his awareness of Eliot's vision of unreality.

In the first seven lines of 'Rolled over on Europe: the sharp dew frozen to stars' (*SP33*; included in *CPS(1)* and, under the title 'Cornet Cornelius Rilke', in *CPS(2)*) he evokes a universe indifferent to human beings:

> Rolled over on Europe: the sharp dew frozen to stars
> Below us: above our heads the night
> Frozen again to stars . . .

Lines 8 to 11 endorse, yet counter, this vision, locating reality in the individual and his feelings:

> Only my body is real: which wolves
> Are free to oppress and gnaw. Only this rose
> My friend laid on my breast, and these few lines
> Written from home, are real.

Though the 'wolves' and 'rose' strike immature symbolist

postures, there is a quiet force here: clear and terse, the last line and a half in particular impress as being 'Written from home', from the centre of the poet's being, a centre under threat in the first part of the poem. By associating the 'real' with the subjective, Spender foreshadows his comment that Yeats's poetry 'shows how realism is not inconsistent with a certain romanticism, especially when it is self-dramatizing' (*DE*, p. 121).

Such, at any rate, was one direction pointed to by 'real'. However, in 'An "I" can never be great man' (*SP33*; included in *CPS(1)* and, under the title 'Trigorin', in *SPS* and *CPS(2)*) Spender uses 'real' with a more debunking emphasis: 'His only real pleasure fishing in ponds, / His only real desire – forgetting'. And yet these 'real' impulses, incontrovertible as they are, have nothing to do with the mysterious force that makes such a man 'great'. In this poem highfalutin notions of genius are both subjected to, and affirmed in the teeth of, homespun Freudian scepticism. If the poem fails, it does so because it relies too doggedly on unadorned (if congested) statement. Again, 'Who live under the shadow of a war' (*SP33*; included in *CPS(1)* and, under the titles 'The Shadow of a War' and 'Shadow of War', in *SPS* and *CPS(2)*, respectively) presents its Lawrentian theme (the clash between consciousness and instinct) with programmatic woodenness, genuflecting towards what it calls 'the realer passions of the earth'. Here, though, the yearning to be in touch with the 'real', often felt in Spender's best poetry, is evident.

In the sonnet, 'At the end of two months' holiday' (*SP34*; included in *CPS(1)* and, under the title 'The Sign *Faerhe nach Wilm*', in *CPS(2)*), Spender uses 'real' and 'unreal' to magnetize the poem's diverse feelings. As the poet comes to the end of his holiday his sense of what is 'real' and 'unreal' shifts. So, too, does the reader's. H. B. Kulkarni offers this scenario, 'A soldier is going in a train to the war';[13] but the poem works less straightforwardly than this implies; the reader is made to share a dislocating state of anxiety. Paradoxically, the 'real' manifests itself to Spender through what can be construed as an imagining, a reverie; on this reading, the poet, lying awake at night, imagines he 'was in a train'. It is improbable that the poet was lying awake in the train, given that the sights subsequently described would not be visible at night. Nor is it likely – though it is possible – that we are asked to make a simple temporal jump

in line five, given that the line's assertion, 'I was in a train', has
the air of clarifying the opening as much as what follows. At any
rate, the opening's preparation for the ensuing dislocations is
handled impressively:

> At the end of two months' holiday there came a night
> When I lay awake and the sea's distant fretless scansion
> By imagination scourged rose to a fight
> Like the town's roar, pouring out apprehension.

'Scourged' implies the imagination inflicting suffering on the
natural as it turns the sea into an emblem of human trouble, an
echo of 'the town's roar'. The poet is both culprit and spectator:
his imagination projects distress onto the natural, but he is
condemned to watch 'hasten away the simple green which can
heal / All sadness'. The subsequent shift of perspective is
conveyed with assurance:

> Abruptly the sign *Ferry to Wilm*
> And the cottage by the lake, were vivid, but unreal.
>   Real were iron lines, and, smashing the grass
> The cars in which we ride, and real our compelled time:
> Painted on enamel beneath the moving glass
> Unreal were cows, the wave-winged storks, the lime:
> These burned in a clear world from which we pass
> Like *rose* and *love* in a forgotten rhyme.

The division between the 'real' and 'unreal' could have been
crude. That it persuades stems from Spender's ability to realize
the 'realness' of his abrupt intuition. Most real is the unrealness
of what had been taken for granted; the 'signs' that represent the
holiday have become 'vivid, but unreal'. 'Vivid' does a good deal
of work, suggesting the way that objects make an impression in
the split-second of leavetaking; suggesting, too, that, in some
mental form, the experience of happiness remains 'living' (the
etymological sense of 'vivid'), waiting to be drawn upon should
the exigencies of the time ever permit. In this sense the 'sign' and
'cottage' are poor relations of the 'truly great' of Spender's most
famous poem who 'left the vivid air signed with their honour'.
(Certainly, the undercurrent of loss at the end of 'I think
continually of those who were truly great' (*SP33*; included in

CPS(1) and, under the title 'The Truly Great', in *SPS* and *CPS(2)*) points to the poet's fear that the truly great are 'vivid, but unreal'.)

Another reason for the success of Spender's sestet is the pressure he exerts on, and expresses through, the phrase 'our compelled time': broader implications (about the nature of the age) make themselves felt. The train journey may be a cliché of thirties poetry, but a sense of juggernaut-like force is itself forcefully conveyed. This is owing partly to the rhythmic quickening in the first two lines of the poem's sestet; partly to the surprising shift into the present in 'The cars in which we *ride*' (emphasis added): an effect thrown away by Spender's revision of 'ride' to 'rode' in his two *Collected Poems*. And, as is often the case in *Poems*, 1933 and 1934, the poet's self-consciousness helps, binding together the experience and the process of writing about the experience; 'the clear world from which we pass / Like *rose* and less *love* in a forgotten rhyme' is mimicked by the formality of the sonnet we have been reading. Throughout, this formality has been open to what threatens it. The 'rose' of the last line bids farewell to the symbolic trappings (and, by implication, the trust in personal experience) of 'Rolled over on Europe: the sharp dew frozen to stars': 'love', in this 'compelled time', is 'forgotten'. The appeal of a Romantic or Georgian union with the natural is felt (as the 'waverwinged storks' testify) but set aside.

The poem's self-reflexiveness extends to the rhyme of 'time' and 'rhyme' itself which yokes together two words whose relationship is adversarial. In Spender's sonnet the rhyme is telling, though (because of the interposed 'lime') not too telling – as it risks being at the end of Bernard Spencer's 'A Cold Night' where the poet longs to 'not always think of winter, winter, like a hammering rhyme / For then everything is drowned by the rising wind, everything is done against Time'.[14] Spencer's insistence, however, is justified by the fact that in his lines 'rhyme' has gone over to the side of 'Time', bludgeoning home the message from which the poet seeks temporary escape.

In his meditations on the 'real', as an undergraduate, Spender was governed by class guilt. 'We thought', he writes, 'that perhaps being a working man, or perhaps even making love with a prostitute, was to be *real*.' (*WWW*, p. 42: Spender's emphasis.) Spender's most impressive poems in the thirties accept the 'realness' of his experience, even as they suggest the distorted view of 'reality' this 'real' experience may buttress. 'My parents kept me from children who were rough' (*SP33*; included in *CPS(1)* and, under the titles 'Rough' and 'My Parents', in *SPS* and *CPS(2)*, respectively) is a much-anthologized example. The poem is at once confessional and generalized; there is little particularizing detail of the sort familiar after *Life Studies* (and which, with considerable success, Spender supplies in 'Diary Poems' or 'Auden's Funeral' (*CPS(2)*)). Rather, the voice the reader hears in 'My parents kept me from children who were rough' is both personal and archetypally that of the over-privileged child. To praise as 'sincere' a poem that so clearly (if quietly) knows what it is up to would be to risk selling short its achievement. And yet the poem bears out Donald Davie's point that 'the measure of a poet's sincerity is, it must be, *inside his poem*'.[15] Spender's use of the past tense implies the re-experiencing adult even as he focuses on the experiencing child. Yet the poet refuses to moralize, doing justice to the child's mingled feelings: envy and fear of 'rough' children, who seem to the child to thrive on their lack of comfort: 'Their thighs showed through rags. They ran in the street / And climbed cliffs and stripped by the country streams'. The lines call up a longing for a certain wild freedom: one buried implication is that the 'rough' children will never again experience freedom so completely.

The poem was untitled on its first appearance; its subsequent titles, 'Rough' (*SPS*) and 'My Parents' (*CPS(2)*), highlight different facets of the poem's total experience, the poet being concerned to convey the otherness of the other children and to lay bare the effect of his parents' protectiveness. These feelings come across rawly but skilfully, sinewy rhythms and scarcity of adjectives giving the first stanza its power to arrest. Here as elsewhere, Spender's rhythms overrun tidy pentameters; the less regular movement is vigorous and expressive.

In the second stanza fear ('feared' is repeated) seems to dominate. Self-lacerating comedy hovers at the edge of the writing, however, and Spender verges on clowning masochism in the line about the boys 'Who copied my lisp behind me on the road'. Yet the tonal risk is worth taking, since it keeps at bay the sentimental. If the lines caricature, they are about caricaturing. They catch the way memory has rigidified, even stylized, class hostility; subsequent attitudes of mind, the poem hints, are reinforced by the physical attitudes in which the poet's memory has frozen himself and the 'rough' children (he as taunted victim, they as 'coarse' aggressors).

The last stanza brings to a focus the poem's ability to render sharply and to imply underlying assumptions. Such an assumption is suggested by 'our world' ('our' was later revised to 'my') in the lines: 'They were lithe, they sprang out behind hedges / Like dogs to bark at our world'. The phrase speaks volumes about the separation of the boy's world from that of the other children. The conclusion sees the hostility as unremitting as ever, for all the boy's wish that it might stop:

> They threw mud
> And I looked another way, pretending to smile.
> I longed to forgive them, yet they never smiled.

There is latent self-mockery in that final line. The speaker's assumption that it was his right to 'forgive' should not be mistaken for complacency on Spender's part. On the contrary, what he offers is re-entrance into the child's way of seeing and feeling; to the child, it seems that he is both morally superior, in a position to 'forgive', and yet compelled to 'pretend', in some sense less true to his feelings than the other children (whose feelings are, of course, conveyed only as they are perceived by the child). 'They never smiled' caps and deflates the wavering gesture of 'pretending to smile'; the quasi *rime riche* of 'smile' and 'smiled' falls with a disappointed thud. 'They' are given an uncomplicated emotional integrity denied to the poet as a boy, confused by warring feelings. The poem has a representative importance in that it voices the feelings of guilt which prompt, in part, Spender's demands for a new social order. Without invalidating a more politically assertive poetry, the poem speaks out of Spender's grasp of the roots of social identity; in doing so, it shows him putting into practice what he preached in an important essay, 'Poetry and Revolution', published the same year as *Poems*, 1933:

> The majority of artists today are forced to remain individualists in the sense of the individualist who expresses nothing except his feeling for his own individuality, his isolation. . . . But by making clear the causes of our present frustration they [artists] may prepare the way for a new and better world.
> (*The Thirties and After*, p. 53.)

4

This 'feeling for his own individuality, his isolation', at the heart of Spender's best poetry in the thirties, is uncomplacent; it is alert to what lies outside, makes demands on and even calls into question the self. It is, arguably, apparent as the impulse behind comradely exhortation in, say, 'Oh young men oh young comrades' (*SP33*; included in *CPS(1)* and, under the title 'Us', in *CPS(2)*): other poems make clear that for Spender as a young poet the abiding pronoun is the first person singular, not plural. 'Van der Lubbe' (*SP34*; included in *SPS* and *CPS(2)*), a poem voiced for the man found guilty of burning down the Reichstag in 1933, is an extreme example. Van der Lubbe's manic laughter during his trial (partly occasioned by efforts to prove he had accomplices) is a central theme and a tonal catalyst of the poem: Spender ranges between snatches of doggerel ('I am glad I am glad that this people is mad') and something more bitterly dignified ('I laugh because my laughter / Is like justice, twisted by a howitzer'). This latter register suggests the poem's quasi-metaphysical dimension; Van der Lubbe's isolation is viewed as a case of possession by 'the outside world' that has 'Into the grave of the skull rolled'. The metaphor of the skull as grave is typically bold, and flickeringly prompts thoughts of potential resurrection. However, there are 'no stars riding heaven' and the speaker must 'die with the dead and slobber with fun'; if the world rises again from the grave of the skull, it does so in the form of manic hysteria. This 'I' has lost the power to judge, to hold itself apart from the madness of the 'outside world'; all it can do is vocalize through laughter its sense of usurpation by outer emptiness. Spender does not ask us to sympathize with his speaker; rather, he sees him as symptomatic of, yet victimized by, political chaos.

Isolation in early Spender is frequently experienced (and occasionally suspended) in the pursuit of relationship: whether with a person, past cultural achievement or future Utopia. In 'How strangely this sun reminds me of my love' (*SP33*; included in *CPS(1)* and, under the title 'The Photograph', in *CPS(2)*), the opening line's adverb is borne out by the remainder of the poem. Memory does, indeed, work with compelling strangeness in this piece. Spender combines what sounds like rapturous lyricism –

> Expansive sheets of blue rising from fields
> Roaring movements of light observed under shadow –

with cool acceptance of aloneness. 'Light observed under shadow' is a phrase that ramifies: literally descriptive, it is also applicable to the workings of memory and in turn to the process of writing a poem about memory. Superimposed upon the memory of the day spent walking with the friend is a second memory, a memory 'Of my walk alone at evening, when like the cottage smoke / Hope vanished, written amongst red wastes of sky'. This occurs in the poem before the 'identification' of the (chronologically earlier) morning spent in the company of the friend. In other words, awareness of loss leads into recall of an emotion which was not exactly happiness ('I remember my strained listening to his voice'), but which achieves 'completeness' (see the last line of the first section) in the process of being remembered. Accepting that the relationship was damaging for the friend whose 'hand will show error' henceforward, the poet concludes with lines whose very serenity is disquieting:

> That is for him.
> For me this memory which now I behold,
> When, from the pasturage, azure rounds me in rings
> And the lark ascends, and his voice still rings,
>   still rings.

Recompense for emotional loss comes, then, in the shape of 'this memory which now I behold', the 'now' pressing close to the 'now' of composition. The poet accepts his own self-centredness, seen as the basis of poetic achievement. The recognition accounts for the 'strange' force of what, at its outset, seemed to be just another love poem.[16]

'For T. A. R. H.' (*SP34*; included, under the titles 'To T. A. R. H.' and 'Remembering' in *CPS(1)* and *SPS*, respectively) is equally preoccupied with love and memory. And if 'How strangely this sun ...' ends with disquieting serenity, 'For T. A. R. H.' moves no less deceptively. In the first paragraph Spender discusses, and enacts, the blending of present and past; a moment of loving perception in the present acts, simultaneously, as a remembrance:

> Even whilst I watch him I am remembering
> The quick laugh of the wasp gold eyes. . . .
> Even while I see I remember, for love
> Is soaked in memory . . .

Spender has recourse, as in many of his poems, to a language that analyses as well as evokes; here 'soaked' brings 'love' and 'memory' to life, and implies their immersion in one another. Misleadingly clear in its change of direction ('At night' picking up, but not straightforwardly fulfilling, the promise of 'a night that knows and sees / The equable currents'), the second paragraph describes a different sense of living in a perpetual present: not a present that richly and happily compresses all time into itself, but a present in which meaning is temporarily suspended:

> At night my life lies with no past nor future
> But only space. It watches
> Hope and despair and the small vivid longings
> Like minnows gnaw the body. Where it drank love
> It lives in sameness.

A. Kingsley Weatherhead cites those 'small vivid longings / Like minnows' as an example of Spender's 'destructive device of elaborating a metaphor or a simile to the point where it becomes ludicrous'.[17] It is true that the 'minnows' swim up from the poet's consciousness rather than from some objective reality (as, say, Keith Douglas's 'logical little fish' do);[18] but, emotionally, the phrase conveys the poet's sense of his 'life' as somehow separate, a spectator of the 'small vivid longings' which both make it up and feed off it. The 'sameness' described here teeters between a limbo state and an affirmation of constancy. Only in the concluding lines, recording 'Gestures indelible', does Spender recapture the confidence of the opening; even so, the terse clutching at the 'indelible' betrays the anxiety it seeks to overcome.

Two other love poems, facing one another in *Poems*, 1933, illustrate Spender's skilful dealings with relationship and isolation. The first, 'Not to you I sighed. No, not a word' (included in *CPS(1)* and, under the title 'Not to You', in *SPS* and *CPS(2)*) is a poem which communicates quickly. Yet the poem's clarity, though real, is not its only virtue. A good deal is going on in the language. The opening line (just quoted) gets away with its 'poetic' inversion by means of its unstiltedly muttered second half, and prepares the ground for the eruption of suppressed feeling in the second stanza. The poem depends for its effect on the contrast between the 'monumental' calm of the first stanza and the anguish of the second. Both the calm and the anguish are adroitly conveyed. In both cases the 'outer' is called upon to mirror an 'inner' state: 'Any feeling was / Formed with the hills', Spender says in the first stanza, while in the second, 'empty walls, book-carcases, blank chairs / All splintered in my head and cried for you'. Though 'Formed' is emphasized, 'Any feeling' is curiously undecided, as if the search for what the fourth line calls a 'sign' were being evoked. By contrast, 'book-carcases' is less sign than symbol, the external bookcases having been metamorphosed by the internal strength of feeling. What intrigues is the way consciousness suspends awareness of its operations in the first stanza and sharpens such awareness in the second. This makes possible Spender's rare unity with the 'you' in the first stanza, 'We climbed together'; it also explains the pain behind 'I knew' in the second, which heralds the return of consciousness (of isolation, of the fact that the speaker's intensest emotions, in this case his realization of the intensity of the relationship, take place 'in [his] head').

The second poem, 'Acts passed beyond the boundary of mere wishing' (included in *CPS(1)* and, under the titles 'Wishing' and 'Acts passed beyond', in *SPS* and *CPS(2)*, respectively), celebrates an unexpected moment of apparent understanding between Spender and the poem's 'you' ('Marston', the subject of a number of early love poems: see Spender's account of this tortuous (non)relationship in *WWW*, pp. 64–8). The poem is of interest for two reasons: first, the relish, even playfulness, with which it exploits Auden's technique of writing about the personal in terms borrowed from the public world – like Auden, Spender draws metaphors from war and industry; secondly, the fact that, for all its exuberance, the poem remains confined to Spender's consciousness. This second point follows on from the first in that the metaphors of 'desertion' and 'mutiny' which Spender uses express his sense of inner division, as though Marston's response mirrored some generous impulse in himself which he 'feared' as well as desired:

> When we touched hands
> I felt the whole rebel, feared mutiny
> And turned away,
> Thinking, if these were tricklings through a dam,
> I must have love enough to run a factory on,
> Or give a city power, or drive a train.

There is humour here: of a boisterous yet quietly desperate kind. Spender's sensing in himself of an immensity of 'love' is sent up and deflated. Is this 'love' that admires itself so amusedly nothing more than solipsistic 'overflow'? If so, where does that leave this, or any other, relationship? The short line, 'And turned away', suggests an intensity too strong to be borne, but also a 'turning away' from the 'you' to the self. What makes the poem affecting, however, is the way the questions just raised are prompted by the poet's glimpse of an escape from selfhood, 'When we touched hands'.

5

An equally urgent question which haunts Spender's poetry is this: 'In a situation that seems to demand action, can any poem be a sufficient act?' (Hynes, p. 67). *Poems*, 1933, grapples with the issue of poetry's sufficiency by exhibiting the young poet's fears of insufficiency. The construction of heroes in whom to believe is a symptom of this fear; an example is the 'he' of 'He will watch the hawk with an indifferent eye' (*SP33*; included in *CPS(1)* and, under the titles 'Icarus' and 'Airman', in *SPS* and *CPS(2)*, respectively). This figure sheds his Audenesque indifference in the second line's 'Or pitifully', which makes him both Spender's opposite and other self. In fact, the reader realizes that the authoritative cadences mask the hero's ineffectuality now that he is 'like Icarus mid-ocean-drowned'. The indifference of his stare is now the indifference of non-being; its pitifulness is passive not active (that is, he is regarded with pity).

It may be that the poem's more interesting strata of feeling are not fully excavated, that the writing is too muscle-bound for its own good. But the fine 'Beethoven's Death Mask' (*SP33*; included in *CPS(1), SPS* and *CPS(2)*) is powerfully in control of the ambivalences roused by writing about the great composer, an artistic hero for Spender throughout his career. The title, one of the few titles in *Poems*, 1933, suggests the poet's task will be that of reviving a sense of the creative achievement borne witness to, yet veiled, by the composer's death mask. The opening, with its strenuous rhythm, brings out how much work the task involves: 'I imagine him still with heavy brow'. The labour of re-imagining Beethoven's achievement runs parallel to a vision of Beethoven's achievement as itself involving immense spiritual struggle and anguish. Beethoven is allied with and distanced from the young Spender. He is 'prisoned, masked, shut off from being' much as Spender in the next-but-one poem in *Poems*, 1933, is 'always at the edge of Being' ('Never being, but always at the edge of Being'; included in *CPS(1)* and, under the title 'Never Being', in *CPS(2)*). Yet the composer's achievement scales heights the young poet can only wonder at. 'He moves across my vision like a ship. / What else is iron but he?', Spender writes, yet the sense of the composer as a non-human force passes in the last two stanzas into a recognition of his humanity. Making this recognition is Spender's own achievement, and reminds the reader that 'Never being, but always at the edge of Being' concludes with the assertion, 'I claim fulfilment in the fact of loving': a claim both queried and sustained by *Poems*, 1933 and 1934.

Beethoven's heroism lies in his responsiveness to the 'Life' he 'sees leap – outside' his skull: 'Yet, in that head there twists the roaring cloud / And coils, as in a shell, the roaring wave'. As so often in Spender, the artistic process involves an interiorizing of experience. Here, though, the transformation wrought by Beethoven involves neither loss of vitality (the composer's 'head' becomes a thoroughfare for natural forces) nor sacrifice of control (the roaring wave only coils '*as in* a shell': emphasis added).

The poem has presented the composer in a variety of forms. From 'this hanging mask transfigured' (stanza 1), Spender moves on to imagine 'The beast squat in that mouth' (stanza 2) before the just-quoted comparison with a ship (stanza 3). If in stanza 4 the terms in which Beethoven is presented are still elemental, they are also bruisingly human: 'bending to the rain / The April rises in him, chokes his lungs / And climbs the torturing passage of his brain'. The wording is tensely balanced. Renewal hurts ('chokes his lungs') even as it energizes; it prompts, and is subjected to, 'the torturing passage of his brain'. 'Torturing' suggests 'tortuous' without confining itself to that suggestion: the word may derive from Shelley's *Adonais* where the 'one Spirit's plastic stress' is described as 'Torturing th'unwilling dross that checks its flight / To its own likeness, as each mass may bear'. Certainly for Spender, as for Shelley, the ultimate vision is of some quasi-Platonic essence; in Shelley's poem, famously, 'The One remains, the many change and pass';[19] in Spender's less eloquent (and more tentative) variation, 'the mystic One / Horizons haze', that is, horizons haze, in the sense both of veiling and outlining, the mystic One. The poem finishes on a note of hard-won transcendence: 'Peace, peace ... Then splitting skull and dream, there comes, / Blotting our lights, the trumpeter, the sun'. The internal slant-rhyme of 'splitting' and 'Blotting' mimics a clash out of which emerges a light that eclipses 'our lights'. In *The Destructive Element* Spender compares the 'extraordinary conjunctions of mood' in Beethoven's late Quartets with effects in Eliot's 'Ash Wednesday' (*DE*, p. 151). Lightness of touch does not distinguish his own tribute to Beethoven, but its moods are surprisingly integrated. 'Beethoven's Death Mask' is best glossed by Spender's own account of the composer's last works: 'They are simply the expression of a unique personality, one man's isolated experience in a world that seems almost beyond pleasure and pain, and that can only be heard; it cannot in any way be described' (*DE*, p. 150). The poem is more than a statement of ideas about Beethoven's life and music; it is a vivid, muscular, intelligent, empathic meditation on the nature of, and difficulty of coming to terms with, artistic genius.

6

Spender's labour of imagining is intensely but unself-regardingly present in 'Beethoven's Death Mask'. In the poem, 'I think continually of those who were truly great', the poet's sense of his vocation is overtly the subject of his work; the poem, 'In railway halls' (*SP33*; included, under the titles 'In railway halls, on pavements near the traffic' and 'In Railway Halls', in *CPS(1)* and *CPS(2)*, respectively), combines consideration of the troubled issue of pity in poetry with assertion of the explicit

political vision which pervades many later poems in *Poems*,
1933. Chapter 5 will begin by looking more closely at a number
of these poems.

'I think continually of those who were truly great' is something of a test-case in weighing the worth of Spender's poetry.
For Randall Jarrell the fact that the poem 'should ever have been
greeted with anything but helpless embarrassment makes me
ashamed of the planet upon which I dwell'. Jarrell continues:
'Part of the time he is fighting against his softer self, and the rest
of the time he just lets himself go'.[20] 'I think continually of those
who were truly great' is an example for Jarrell of soft-headed
thinking and writing, of a deliquescent romanticism that leaves
him in a state of 'helpless embarrassment'. One disagrees with
Jarrell at one's peril, but the violence of his response is in itself
significant (much as Byron's outbursts against Keats tell the
reader about the older poet's blind spots). Spender's poem, it is
fair to say, courts the 'embarrassment' which Jarrell speaks of;
what Jarrell fails to allow for is the way this response is
accommodated, and overcome, in and by the poem.

Indeed, 'I think continually of those who were truly great'
offers further evidence of that 'inner war between innocence and
irony, vision and form' which Helen Vendler finds chronicled in
Spender's journals.[21] Such a war is thematized in 'What I
expected' (*SP33*; included, under the titles, 'What I expected,
was' and 'What I Expected' (twice) in *CPS(1)*, *SPS* and
CPS(2), respectively). Samuel Hynes sees the poem as the
companion-piece to 'I think continually of those who were truly
great' (see Hynes, pp. 67–70), and its trust in 'Some final
innocence' is called into question in the act of being declared
(since the expectation of 'innocence' is couched in the pluperfect
tense: 'For I had expected always'). Yet, as the stanza continues,
the persistence of trust is implied by the concluding simile: 'Like
the created poem / Or the dazzling crystal'. The poem has been
'created', its clarity and coherence as crystalline as anything in
Poems, 1933.

'What I expected' blazons its self-awareness: this is what I
expected, the poem tells us, but this instead is what – disconcert-
ingly – turned out to be the case. No reader could overlook the
interplay between innocence and experience in the poem; subtly
balanced as this interplay is, it is also advertised. By contrast, 'I
think continually of those who were truly great' seeks to assert

'innocence' in the teeth of 'experience'. It throws down a
rhetorical gauntlet to those who would prefer self-protective
irony; but it does so with a serenity, grace and understated
awareness of loss that make 'helpless embarrassment' an inadequate response. For all its assertiveness, the famous opening line
('I think continually of those who were truly great') has a fine
absence of insistence; a rhythm at once singing and conversational is set up; the reader registers the implication in 'were' that
the present is a time in which heroism is both wanted and
wanting, but the implication communicates quietly. Much of the
poem combines rhapsodic desire with attention to detail. The
lines, 'Who, from the womb, remembered the soul's history /
Through corridors of light where the hours are suns / Endless
and singing', find an unexpected context for that thirties buzz-
word, 'history', here applied, with something like defiance, to the
'soul'. Moreover, the collection's obsession with time and remembrance is recalled yet transformed by these lines with their
imagining of an alternative to 'our compelled time'. If the reader
dislikes idealist alternatives to an existence drained of value, so
much the worse, this poem suggests, for him or her; to that
degree the poem could, *pace* Hynes, 'be called polemical'
(Hynes, p. 70). It is no accident that in *Poems*, 1933, the poem
followed, and was positioned opposite, the overtly polemical 'Oh
young men oh young comrades', which concludes, albeit more
aggressively, with another exhortation to remember: 'remember
what you have / no ghost ever had, immured in his hall'. 'I think
continually of those who were truly great', however, seeks to
revivify a sense of what is possible in the present by meditating
on the achievement of those who are now 'ghosts'. This respect
for what Spender wishes to claim as a living tradition prompts
him to draw resonance from major writers such as Gerard
Manley Hopkins and Shakespeare. Their influence works be-
nignly in lines like 'Whose lovely ambition / Was that their lips,
still touched with fire, / Should tell of the Spirit clothed from
head to foot in song': 'lovely' recovers an unprettified meaning
much as 'lovelier' does in 'The Windhover', while 'ambition' is
redeemed from the 'bad' sense of the word its use in *Macbeth*
memorably exemplifies.[22]

In the second paragraph polemic grows explicit: 'What is
precious is never to forget . . .', Spender begins, and his first item
to be remembered ('The essential delight of the blood drawn

from ageless springs / Breaking through rocks in worlds before
our earth') may prompt a less flattering application of 'precious'
than the poet intended. Lawrentian dogma is served up too
glibly. Yet the poem recovers its poise in the rest of the
paragraph, where Spender attends to matters closer to home;
when he writes of the need 'Never to allow gradually the traffic
to smother / With noise and fog the flowering of the spirit', he
persuades by dropping his voice. The words allow the reader
gradually to realize how easy it is to allow the flowering of the
spirit to be smothered. Part of the poem's distinction is that it
rehabilitates the shopworn 'spirit': we cannot afford not to
believe the word has significance – or so the poem convinces the
reader by means of symbolic promptings ('noise', 'fog', 'flowering') which link with, and play against, 'spirit'.
     The last paragraph mingles rhapsodic idealism with the tacit
admission that such idealism is founded on hope:

> Near the snow, near the sun, in the highest fields
> See how these names are fêted by the waving grass
> And by the streamers of white cloud
> And whispers of wind in the listening sky.

'Another Shelley speaks in these lines': Herbert Read's description of *Poems*, 1933 (quoted in Hynes, p. 99) could be applied to
the lines just quoted. Like Shelley, Spender has suffered from the
persistent and mistaken notion that passionate feeling excludes
the operation of intelligence. 'See where she stands!' (1.112),
Shelley exclaims in *Epipsychidion*, his words insisting on a seeing
that goes beyond the visual. So, too, Spender's lines do not aim
for descriptive accuracy; rather they encourage themselves to
'see' a symbolic landscape animated by the poet's desire. In
addition, the animistic detail is significantly elusive: 'waving
grass', 'streamers of white cloud' and 'whispers of wind' share a
fugitive quality, as though the poet were hard pressed to
substantiate the continuing presence of the 'truly great'. This
suggestion is checked, then quietly reinforced by the conclusion.
'The names of those who in their lives fought for life' abandons
imagery for resolute statement that makes the reader look hard at,
and sense the valuation implied by, Spender's use of 'life'.
Spender's use of 'life' has revolutionary suggestions of a kind
spelled out in the following passage from *Forward from Liberalism*:

To die is easier than to live. For to live, in the fullest sense, in our society, requires not merely the ability to exist, whilst the conditions that will make even existence possible for our children are being removed or violently destroyed; whilst half the population of capitalist countries lives in a state of semi-starvation; but also the will to remove material evils that are at present choking civilized life.[23]

'Whilst half the population of capitalist countries lives' uses 'lives' to mean merely lives; 'civilized life' uses 'life' sardonically to suggest how imperfectly we now live; both uses are set against the paragraph's ideal, 'to live, in the fullest sense'. Likewise, 'The names of those who in their lives fought for life' distinguishes between 'lives' and 'life', the latter drawing to itself what is meant by 'to live, in the fullest sense'.

The end of the poem complicates, without abandoning, this positive stance. The final line, 'And left the vivid air signed with their honour', brings out the poem's strain of elegy, for all the up-to-dateness of its sky-writing image (see Cunningham, p. 167). With its coupling of suggestions (of a bequest and a departure), 'left' does much to communicate this elegiac strain. The line is more than a fine flourish. However subliminally, it is about making fine flourishes that may evaporate. The sureness of 'signed', asserting identity, must contend with the nebulousness of 'honour'. The word proclaims its unworldliness. Spender's poem is far from casting a sceptically Falstaffian glance towards 'honour', but it does glimpse the word's vulnerability to such a glance.

That said, 'I think continually of those who were truly great' celebrates more than it elegizes; it is free from the conscious anxiety often found in *Poems*, 1933. It is a confident poem, its more troubled feelings coming through at a subliminal level: a subliminal pressure which turns it from rhetoric into poetry. More commonly, Spender's poetry is troubled in a conscious way. True, 'The Prisoners' (*SP33*; included in *CPS(1)*, *SPS* and *CPS(2)*) relaxes its guard, the poem's pity for its unspecified sufferers close to self-indulgence. Spender is aware of pity as a debilitating emotion in the poem, but only shapes debilitated poetry out of the awareness: 'No, no, no, / It is too late for anger, / Nothing prevails / But pity for the grief they cannot feel'. 'In railway halls' challenges comparison with 'The Prisoners'; it too is a poem about pity; it too refers to those less privileged than the poet as 'they' and claims to know what 'they' are in a way which risks condescension. But while the poem pursues a different route from that taken by, say, 'Moving through the silent crowd' it repays attention and brings to a head many of the critical issues discussed in this chapter.

Where 'Moving through the silent crowd' was 'haunted' by the 'emptiness' of its 'images', 'In railway halls' is angered by the suffering of those obliged to 'beg, their eyes made big by empty staring / And only measuring Time, like the blank clock'. The writing employs that refusal of fluency which serves express-ive purposes in early Spender: 'beg' and 'big' jostle assertively; the spondaic weight of the phrase, 'blank clock', underscores mood and meaning; the final simile makes apparent the primacy of feeling over description. The natural object is not, for Spen-der, the adequate symbol until informed, coloured or even wrenched by the workings of consciousness. 'Time' assumes abstract shape in the poet's mind as he considers the lives of those reduced to beggary: the abstraction, 'Time', is then related to the 'blank clock' which records it. That there is a relation between idea and image allows Spender's analytical impulses scope without turning the poem into a solipsistic desert of abstraction. The balance between inner and outer falters in some poems he wrote in the thirties. Here, just enough specific detail is suggested by the first line's 'railway halls' and 'pavements near the traffic' before 'the drama of experiencing' (to re-employ a phrase used earlier in this chapter) unfolds.

This drama centres on two things: the poet's dissatisfaction with poetry's tendency to console falsely and the poem's use of the word 'Time'. These concerns intertwine. In the second stanza the poet makes vocal a desire to wring the neck of rhetoric which the timbre of the opening three lines had already sug-gested: 'No, I shall weave no tracery of pen-ornament / To make them birds upon my singing-tree'. That the second line succeeds, despite itself, in offering an example of 'pen-ornament' is a calculated effect, a twist of self-disgust, the poet recognizing that writing involves rhetoric even as he hopes to short-circuit customary fluencies. Arguably the following lines only substitute a different kind of 'pen-ornament': 'Time merely drives these lives which do not live / As tides push rotten stuff along the shore'. Yet this is more than booming rhetoric. Spender articulates a determinist view of history which regards 'Time' as a force working through lives; the lines seem an outburst, not a settled conviction, a way of putting things that shocks poet and reader into greater awareness of the difficulty of adequate response, building towards the last stanza's onslaught on 'This Time'. Admittedly, the second stanza ricochets from the potentially sentimental into the unintentionally condescending, and it may be that in this poem Spender is less in control of his tones than he was in 'Moving through the silent crowd'. But his readiness to work out, and through, feelings impresses.

The third stanza voices guilt about 'the curving beauty of that line / Traced on our graphs through history'. Here, 'curving beauty' is both allowed and rejected. Initially, Spender might seem to have in mind some exquisitely modelled painting or sculpture before the next line's 'Traced on our graphs' casts a colder eye on the relationship between high culture and oppression. 'There is no consolation, no, none', the stanza begins, and the line works as self-address as well as admonition, stifling its disappointment that no 'consolation' can be derived from 'curving beauty'. The stanza's conclusion, 'where the oppressor / Starves and deprives the poor', is an instance of thirties political shorthand failing to get beyond the merely heartfelt.

Generally, though, the poem stays upright on the tightrope it walks. It denies the efficacy of art, yet it wants to convey that denial as effectively as possible. The final stanza balances between describing what it should not attempt and trying to 'let the wrong cry out as raw as wounds':

> Paint here no draped despairs, no saddening clouds
> Where the soul rests, proclaims eternity.
> But let the wrong cry out as raw as wounds
> This Time forgets and never heals, far less transcends.

The poem comes face to face with 'This Time' – or with the problems of writing about it appropriately. In the first stanza 'Time' meant the procession of minutes and seconds which make up existence; in the second stanza it took on a more personified force; at the end it is not allowed to escape into the stratosphere, but is nailed down as 'This Time'. This triple sense in which 'Time' is used in the poem keeps at bay the vague sonority yielded to by, say, the conclusion of 'From all these events'

(*SP33*; included, under the title 'From all these events, from the war, from the slump, from the boom', in *CPS(1)*):

> Time's ambition, huge as space, will hang its flags
> In distant worlds, and in years on this world as
>   distant.

Some Utopian meaning can be abstracted from this, but the lines exist more as gesture than substance. By contrast, at the end of 'In railway halls' the word 'Time' succeeds in concentrating rather than blurring the poet's feelings.

Spender's final position takes the form of something desired rather than something achieved. To 'let the wrong cry out as raw as wounds' is, this poem knows, devoutly to be wished and hard to attain; the wry art of the concluding off-rhyme bears witness to the difficulty of 'raw' utterance. Yet such awareness and intelligence make for a 'sincerity' that rebukes Jarrell's dismissal. 'In railway halls' reminds the reader that, throughout *Poems*, 1933 and 1934, Spender wrote good poems out of, and about, the workings of an often hard-pressed consciousness.

3

MacNeice (1)
Turning the Music On

1

MacNeice praised Auden for being 'one of the few living poets whose poetry can walk in the street without falling flat on its face', and he wrote that 'language cannot be divorced from some sort of social world'. Out of this belief came his emphasis on everyday utterance, which is always potentially poetic: 'Ordinary conversation is nearer to lyrical poetry than to cold prose' (a statement which largely accounts for his admiration for the plays of Beckett and Pinter); 'the casual remark is unique in the way that a lyric is unique'; and again, 'the spoken word has, without any effort, that plasticity which the lyric aims at'. That 'without any effort' is to be taken with a grain of salt, however, for it is evident not that everyday language is already poetic but that it has poetic potential, that poetry is the spoken word heightened. Thus MacNeice praised the poetic 'economy' achieved by 'the *twist* of an ordinary phrase, the apparently flat statement with a double meaning'. Such effects demonstrate what he called the 'two-or-more-in-oneness' he valued in poetry (*SCM*, pp. 100, 142, 165, 163). Nor is this a mere relishing of verbal ambiguity, for his poetry is pervaded by doubleness, which he wanted neither to resolve nor to simplify: detachment from and love of life; a superior, de-haut-en-bas attitude and a need to make 'contact'; sympathy and distance; an urge to celebrate and a bleak vision of the future; delight in the ephemeral and a hankering for permanence; engaged vitality and an acute sense of an ending. Though his provisional cast of mind desired

63

certainties, he was able to live with contradiction and make a strength of it. He was attracted to philosophic speculation at the same time as he was suspicious of the human intellect, of its propensity to generalize and so nullify particulars, to iron out 'the incorrigibly plural' (from 'Snow') randomness of experience.

Ideally for MacNeice everyday language is the rhetorical bridge between divisions within self and within society. His view of the function of art can be inferred from 'An Eclogue for Christmas', even though in its entirety the poem comes over as irresolute, catching the poet off guard, so he confessed, in its attack on 'the excess sugar of a diabetic culture'. Uncertain how to accommodate division without falling prey to it, nevertheless the poem conveys delight in variousness and an acceptance of what is. The poetry hovers between celebration and dismissal when A, the town-dweller, reviewing contemporary metropolitan society, veers into metaphors drawn from art and aesthetics:

> Jazz-weary of years of drums and Hawaiian guitar,
> Pivoting on the parquet I seem to have moved far
> From bombs and mud and gas, have stuttered on my feet
> Clinched to the streamlined and butter-smooth trulls of the
>   élite,
> The lights irritating and gyrating and rotating in gauze –
> Pomade-dazzle, a slick beauty of gewgaws –
> I who was Harlequin in the childhood of the century,
> Posed by Picasso beside an endless opaque sea,
> Have seen myself sifted and splintered in broken facets,
> Tentative pencillings, endless liabilities, no assets,
> Abstractions scalpelled with a palette-knife
> Without reference to this particular life.
> And so it has gone on; I have not been allowed to be
> Myself in flesh or face, but abstracting and dissecting me
> They have made of me pure form, a symbol or a pastiche,
> Stylised profile, anything but soul and flesh:
> And that is why I turn this jaded music on
> To forswear thought and become an automaton.

This picture of modern life as divided and fragmented (the mention of liabilities and assets fleetingly suggests that economic malaise is the cause) hints at an ideal of the complete man,

where flesh and spirit, body and soul, intellect and experience,
are united. Abstraction implies incompletion: abstract art and
abstract thought are symptoms of the divided man. It works
against the 'incorrigibly plural' life of particulars. Abstraction is
a reaction to the unthinking physicality of war, the 'bombs and
mud and gas'; the implication is that the swing between abstraction and mere sensation is never-ending. Turning on the voice of
the 'automaton', the poet reacts scornfully to the modern
tendency to abstract dissection, and opposes pure cerebration
with unthinking sensation. Yet the poetry spoken by A takes on a
life of its own that belies the epithet 'jaded'. The voice takes over
in spite of itself. Alliterative scorn, 'pivoting on the parquet',
becomes participatory celebration; diction famously associated
with First World War 'bombs and mud and gas' carries over
onto the dance-floors of the jazz age where A has 'stuttered on
[his] feet' (recalling Wilfred Owen's 'stuttering rifles' rapid
rattle', from 'Anthem for Doomed Youth'). The comic rhyming ('gauze-gewgaws') and the helter-skelter syntax (it takes a
moment to realize that 'abstracting and dissecting' looks forward
not back) convey the effect of lively automation. In the act of
mimicking what it condemns, the voice allows itself to be won
over.

Even the reconciliation at the end of the poem admits a wry
note. What arrests in these lines is the gracefully passing verbal
gesture:

> Let all these so ephemeral things
> Be somehow permanent like the swallow's tangent wings:
> Goodbye to you, this day remember is Christmas, this morn
> They say, interpret it your own way, Christ is born.

It might be supposed that MacNeice's inner divisions would
incapacitate his art, and some have felt this to be the case.
Graham Hough, for instance, makes an interesting remark about
MacNeice's poetry generally: 'The poet's own voice, if he has
one, is taken over by the voice he intends to parody' (quoted
from *Casebook*, p. 121). One can accept the accuracy of this
observation while questioning the negative evaluation. The
sense of the poetry being 'taken over' creates a self-conscious
awareness of division that gives the best of MacNeice's poetry its
vitality. As G. S. Fraser points out, the awareness shows in

MacNeice's propensity for oxymoron (see Casebook, p. 130): in the present instance 'tangent wings' deftly brings together abstraction and image, the timeless and the temporal. But framing it between the tentative 'somehow' and the take-it-or-leave-it 'interpret it your own way' underlines the momentary nature of this resolution.

MacNeice's consciousness of internal division does not, admittedly, always yield such poetry. At times the result can be too discursively self-conscious. Finding it difficult to free his mind from the attempt to reconcile the 'ephemeral' and the 'permanent', in poetic terms the concrete and the abstract, and at the same time conscious of selling short 'this particular life' – for whatever alternatives, philosophical or political, ideal or Utopian – he is liable in some of his thirties poems to fall back on propounding a philosophy of the impermanent, an inherently contradictory enterprise. Thus 'Train to Dublin' and 'Ode' lose direction among opposing impulses. They want both to make important-sounding statements and to live for the moment. There is an improvisatory air about their generalizing: statements come across as happened upon in the act of writing; one verbal event spirals out of another. It is as if MacNeice does not want to relinquish the prerogative of standing back from experience and uttering home truths, but is aware also that such utterances run the risk of freezing experience in a way that violates its flux. The difficulty is that a philosophy of the impermanent debars him from giving the impression of speaking once and for all.

Consciousness of division informs 'Train to Dublin', which, in the words of Edna Longley, 'explores perhaps the fundamental metaphysical paradox that troubles the conscience of Mac-Neice's poetry: how can pattern be achieved without stasis, without falsely systematizing, without doing violence to what a letter of 1930 calls "Lots of lovely particulars"? The poem contrasts "gathering my mind up in my fist" with life's own fluid "repatterning".' Longley goes on to argue that 'in a sense poetry was itself the answer to the problem' (Mac, pp. 143, 144). This is persuasive: when MacNeice is writing at his best the poetic act itself constitutes a unifying mode of perception. But Longley does not consider the quality of the writing in 'Train to Dublin'. It begins well. The first stanza, for all its abstracting tendencies, depicts the sensations of a train journey so that the argument becomes urgent and realized. Rhythmic and syntactic drive holds the imagery together to surpass 'the way that animals' lives pass', the automatic, unthinking way that both fascinated and appalled MacNeice. But the poem does not consistently achieve such fusion of thought and experience. The repetition of the 'I give you' formula half way through is too easy a method of holding together a series of disparate facts, thoughts, impressions and personally haunting memories. At times argument is limply applied to the central metaphor of the train, as in the line, 'For during a tiny portion of our lives we are not in trains'. But one phrase does articulate precisely a reconciliation between concrete and abstract: the oxymoron 'the sea's / Tumultuous marble' not only states the conjunction of fluidity and stasis, flux and permanence, but also demonstrates it with an impressive conjunction of the visual and the conceptual. The phrase conjures up MacNeice's poetic endeavour to reconcile the liquidity of experience with the permanence of artistic form. Like 'the swallow's tangent wings' the image works on both impressionistic and cerebral levels, and so demonstrates what it is talking about.

'Ode' is in danger of merely juggling with paradox: the 'automaton' voice can sound too much like cerebral rambling. The diurnal round of the first verse-paragraph, 'the wheel / Of work and bearing children', spawns, in the second, imagery of circles, of enclosure and limitlessness: 'bounds', 'horizon', 'limit', 'rim'. Later the bounded-boundless paradox of circularity returns with the cumbersome imagery of boomerangs ('May his good deeds flung forth / Like boomerangs return / To wear around his neck / As beads of definite worth'), with the alliteratively willed 'regular and rounded sea', and with the – more compelling – image, 'The pedals of a chance bicycle / Make a gold shower turning in the sun'. One can see the point of all this: the poem attempts to reconcile the contingent and the absolute, the finite and the infinite. But the way of proceeding comes over as too random. One word or image triggers another: 'Limit' sparks 'my love, my limit'; 'islanded hour' at the end of the third verse-paragraph generates the island-shore opposition in the next. This is not so much felt thought as an uneasy shifting between thought and feeling.

2

Many of the shorter lyrics MacNeice wrote in the thirties triumphantly demonstrate what 'Ode' and 'Train to Dublin' are about. They enact momentary resolutions of the kind that appear intermittently like crystallizations in the to-and-fro of those poems, resolutions such as 'the sea's / Tumultuous marble', and the 'gold shower turning in the sun'.

'Snow' teems with imagistic and prosodic life, bursting the bounds of any vestigial form in rhythm or rhyme, enacting 'the drunkenness of things being various', capturing itself in the act of spontaneous and mystified enjoyment. The awed delight in snow and roses coming together is mirrored in the coming together of sound between two words that pull in opposite directions: 'collateral' and 'incompatible'. Though abstractions, the two words are swept up into the poem's swirl of images. The same sort of effect is achieved by the abstract phrase 'incorrigibly plural', which, in the context, takes on the force of sensory impression. This mercurial movement between abstract and concrete comes from the alliterative rush: 'Incorrigibly *p*lural. I *p*eel and *p*ortion / A tangerine and s*p*it the *pips* . . .' (emphases added). The notion of receptivity to immediate impressions may help to explain the final line, 'There is more than glass between the snow and the huge roses': that is, we do not view the world through a transparent medium, we sense it on the pulses. 'Between' is tricky, though, seeming to have two, 'collateral' and 'incompatible', meanings: 'between' as in 'in common', and 'between' as in 'gulf between'. The line does not so much *mean*, as evoke a feeling of spontaneous plenitude and 'plurality'. It is impossible to paraphrase the poem, just as it is impossible to pin down the 'variousness' of experience: 'World is crazier and more of it than we think'. Yet that is an abstract statement about life: in the poem thought and experience maintain a risky balance. The result is to throw weight on the verbal pattern: 'All we know is the splash of words in passing', as the poem 'Entirely' says. The discursive is brilliantly absorbed into the enacting.

MacNeice's divided nature, tugged between flux and permanence, movement and stillness, change and permanence, makes him a poet much possessed by time. Ideally art would transcend such divisions, although MacNeice's thirties lyrics invariably betray, in ways that become their saving grace, a sense that art's attempt to arrest time is a beautiful illusion, ready to shatter: 'The moment cradled like a brandy glass' (from 'The Brandy Glass'). This is the effect, and the buried theme, of 'The Sunlight on the Garden', which achieves an exhilarating poise between fear at the passing of time and the desire to 'cage the minute / Within its nets of gold'. That image intimates the precious fragility, the vulnerability – this is a love poem – of the moment. The poem is itself a net of gold, an intricately patterned cage of sound. Its construction is tense: the skilful internal rhyming unashamedly draws attention to itself, as if to declare the precarious nature of the poem's artifice. Written two years before the start of the Second World War, it captures the sense of an ending with MacNeice's most engaged sang-froid, an elegantly tight-lipped bravado: time cannot be prevented, but, as in Antony's death-speech in Shakespeare's play ('We are dying, Egypt, dying'), despair can be kept at bay by the almost self-indulgent ability to express it extremely well. Hence the covert and not so covert references to writing in the second stanza:

> Our freedom as free lances
> Advances towards its end;
> The earth compels, upon it
> Sonnets and birds descend.

We can stave off desperate thoughts of the end by writing beautifully arresting poetry about it, the punning (on 'freelance' and, after a fashion, on 'descend': 'alight' and 'die') being a tonally adroit reminder of the humanly verbal, unstable material out of which the artifact is created. Such effects, even in such a delicately wrought lyric as this, show MacNeice's skill at bringing everyday language to the point of art; they prove his demotic inspiration.

3

Demotic inspiration is responsible for MacNeice's frequent deployment of cliché, which, perhaps surprisingly, is closely involved with the vitality of his poetry, especially of poems that treat urban society, such as 'Birmingham', 'Bagpipe Music', 'Christmas Shopping' and the significantly titled 'Homage to

Clichés'. These poems especially bear out Michael Longley's comment: 'The gaudy paraphernalia of MacNeice's poetry, the riot of imagery, the dizzy word-play add up finally to a reply to death . . .'.[1] His way with cliché is part of the word-play. Cliché plays an essential part in his ability to move out into society, to make contact, to get beyond himself. It enables the poetry to take on the language of the people depicted, to move into their circle of communication.

The point comes over in 'Homage to Clichés', which demonstrates that cliché has for MacNeice a much wider significance than its merely verbal form, or rather that its verbal form manifests an experiential context. Discussing the poem in his essay 'Experiences with Images', he wrote that by clichés he 'meant the ordinary more pleasant sense-data of the sensual man' (SCM, p. 163). The poem hallows everyday social ritual. Its colloquialism comes over as the verbal equivalent of living for the moment. The automaton voice that speaker A thinks of taking on in 'An Eclogue for Christmas' is vivaciously assumed in 'Homage to Clichés' with its headlong rush of language:

> With all this clamour for progress
> This hammering out of new phases and gadgets, new trinkets
>   and phrases
> I prefer the automatic, the reflex, the cliché of velvet.

'Phrases' grows out of 'phases' with smooth verbal automation. The clichés that follow, 'fish coming in to the net', are automatic actions and responses in the arena of love and sex, as that phrase hints:

> I can see them coming for yards
> The way that you answer, the way that you dangle your foot
> These fish that are rainbow and fat
> One can catch in the hand and caress and return to the pool.

The familiar atmosphere of a bar has become rich and strange; social ritual has taken on a slight air of mystery. But a note of desperation grows louder as the poet's voice takes on those of the barflies and barmaid in the clichéd phrases, 'This is on me' and 'What will you have now? The same again?'. These are repeated more and more frenetically in the course of the poem, until the

voice shifts into hysterical bagpipe music in an attempt to fend
off 'the final music' (of 'the Bell'), ringing the changes on the
familiar 'this year next year sometime never' until it begins to
sound dislocated and crazy.

Significantly, however, the poem ends with a retreat to the
everyday world of sanity, apparently endorsing

> This whole delightful world of cliché and refrain –
> What will you have, my dear? The same again?

– and the delightful world of the poem is composed of such
refrains. But the tone of these last two lines is inscrutably
slippery. In the penultimate line the voice speaks as the poet *in
propria persona*, but then in the last line slides into the role of
barmaid again, though by this time the 'apparently flat' questions ('What will you have, my dear? The same again?') have
become 'twisted' to produce 'a double meaning': an insouciant
ending both sympathizing with the blinkered bar-life attitude of
giving no thought for the morrow, and gently sending it up with
a note of bathos. To what extent the poet ventriloquizes the
barmaid's voice, and to what extent he identifies with it is
enticingly open. One could object with Graham Hough that 'the
poet's own voice, if he has one, is taken over by the voice he
intends to parody', but it is this wavering register that gives the
poem its emotional resonance, lifting it above simple satire. The
poet stands at a distance, but implicates himself at the same
time. Intriguingly both without and within, he tries to gather his
own life up as much as he does the lives he ventriloquizes.

The voice of 'Birmingham' is similarly elusive, although the
poem comes over, albeit interestingly, as less in control of its
effects and more uncertain of its sympathies – and its anger. It is
an early instance where the poet assumes an 'automaton' voice,
though only intermittently and with less assurance than in the
later 'Bagpipe Music', which 'turns the music on' with aplomb.
Edna Longley regards 'Birmingham' as an unequivocal condemnation of modern industrial society, which it undoubtedly is:
'MacNeice not only accuses capitalism of breeding injustice, he
accuses materialism of short-changing the spirit'. But the question remains how far the poet is implicated. Longley notes the
difficulty when she writes that 'In one sense MacNeice's powers
of observation and absorption relish what he condemns', but

then dismisses it with the statement that 'this is the inherent paradox of poetic subject matter rather than any suspect attraction to surfaces' (Mac, p. 48). But the overall effect of the poem is a good deal more complex and less consistent than this statement implies. In the first place, it is not so easy to separate subject-matter and attitude: the poet, after all, chooses his matter, what details to emphasize. In the second, the statement ignores the poem's voice, which moves in and out of different roles, sympathetically attitudinizing in a way that reveals the tensions endemic to modern industrial society, potentially representative. But does the spiritual emptiness of the people depicted correspond to something in the poet?

Revivified cliché can make for sympathy and understanding. 'There, unvisited, are Vulcan's forges who doesn't care a tinker's damn': the move from the classical smithy to the tinker of the cliché is movingly desperate in its comically satiric descent. By such vocal means MacNeice achieves flashes of sympathy for those reduced to empty-headed automatons in the service of mindless industrial society. Similar means are used in the presentation of the apparently vacuous shopgirls of stanza three, where the exfoliating diction mirrors the onlooker's wavering, constantly readjusting attitude. There is a striking instance in what may at first sound like the careless repetition of a word. The action of 'emptying' in the first line ('the shops empty') triggers the loaded epithet 'empty' in the next ('empty as old almanacs'). 'Relaxation' spirals into inanity: 'the shops empty, shopgirls' faces relax / Diaphanous as green glass, empty as old almanacs'. Then the de-haut-en-bas tone is suddenly diminished by the sideways move to the 'Burne-Jones windows': 'As incoherent with ticketed gewgaws tiered behind their heads / As the Burne-Jones windows in St. Philip's broken by crawling leads'. 'Incoherent' captures a deep ambivalence. The girls are incoherent because 'empty', but they are also eyecatchingly out of place and so arrest the poet's sympathy: on the one hand associated with 'diaphanous green', on the other with that odd locution 'crawling leads'. And what are we to make of the fleeting but striking identification with the shopgirls' point of view in this stanza's last three lines, with their bold assumption of the first-person voice? – 'the gutter take our old playbills, / Next week-end it is likely in the heart's funfair we shall pull / Strong enough on the handle to get back our money; or at any rate it is possible'. Is this mocking mimicry, or sympathy? The lurking presence of the proverbial 'the devil take the hindmost' merely reinforces the Janus-faced tone: a hard-bitten attitude plays off against the sense of what makes such an attitude necessary.

What 'coherence' the poem possesses lies in the consistency with which it refuses to stay put emotionally, precisely in its resistance to a coherent attitude that might falsify truthfulness to impressions as it pans out across the scene. The rapid tonal withdrawal of 'or at any rate it is possible' is remarkable for its conjunction of sympathy, stoicism and plain flatness. It prepares the way for the shift at the start of the next stanza to an apprehension of endings, an apocalyptic flavour peculiar to MacNeice. The trams usher in a gaudy technicolour version of the decline of 'the West'; this sweeps up the urban scenery of car, traffic-signal and engine into a fiery ritualized panorama which, with the phrase 'Pentecost-like', momentarily hints at spiritual release, a brief glimpse of divine grace, and then moves on to bleaker horizons. The opening up at the end of the poem to a wide and threatening Audenesque perspective of spiritual and economic torpor – the 'factory chimneys on sullen sentry' 'like black pipes of organs' capturing both dimensions – is remarkable. But even more remarkable is the quick narrowing of focus in the final line to convey the plight of those caught in the economic machine: 'To call, in the harsh morning, sleep-stupid faces through the daily gate'. The vacuity of the populace earlier in the poem has here, in a sharp access of sympathy, become '*sleep*-stupid'; and the plight of the workers has assumed dignity with the flickering tonal elevation of the factory gate in the final phrase 'the daily gate' (in conjunction with those 'sleep-stupid faces', possibly intimating Virgil's gates of sleep at the threshold of the Underworld in *Aeneid* VI). But in the end it has to be said that the poem works best as a series of rich impressions. If it is asked where the poet stands, the answer seems to be nowhere: he moves too fast, seemingly carried along by the verbal and imagistic flood, on the one hand sympathizing with the plight of those caught in industry's web, on the other rubbing his hands before the fire of apocalypse.

But 'Birmingham' can be heard as preparation for the more assured voice of later thirties poems, pre-eminently 'Bagpipe Music' and 'Christmas Shopping'. In such poems MacNeice's response to the surface of life at times approaches nihilism, a sceptical despair revealing a terrifying void not only in society but at the centre of self. This is the dark side to the vitality that 'Snow' captures in its celebration of 'the productions of time' (the phrase by Blake that MacNeice quotes more than once in his prose, on the authority of Yeats).

In taking on society's propensity to 'forswear thought', the devil-may-care voice of 'Bagpipe Music', however satirical, builds a bridge between self and the world. A mood of despair is simultaneously indulged and kept at bay. Terror and exhilaration combine in the poem's frenzied music. The apparent stance is disdain for an empty, valueless society. There are no distinctions, all walks of life are satirized: the vulgar nouveau riche, the upper classes, the get-rich-quick, the unemployed ('All we want is a packet of fags when our hands are idle'). Yet by virtue of the poem's rhythmic vigour its voice participates in the couldn't-give-a-damn ethos it outwardly condemns. Thus, like much of MacNeice's poetry, 'Bagpipe Music' exposes the speaker's possible vacuity as well as that of the culture satirized: the speaker merges with his culture, and the satirical stance collapses. As with 'Homage to Clichés', the difficulty and fascination is to perceive, in the mounting hysteria, where reader and writer stand in relation to one another: the voice may reveal the hollowness of the times, and yet the poem gets a kick out of reproducing that voice. Its vigour belies the message of a world running down. William Empson's jaunty line 'Waiting for the end, boys, waiting for the end' (from 'Just a Smack at Auden') understands this perfectly.

Sympathy for the satirized emerges most powerfully at the end of 'Bagpipe Music', with the angrily defiant implication of man's tragic lot:

It's no go my honey love, it's no go my poppet;
Work your hands from day to day, the winds will blow the
   profit.
The glass is falling hour by hour, the glass will fall for ever,
But if you break the bloody glass you won't hold up the
   weather.

There is an access of colloquial sympathy ('my honey love', 'my poppet') as the rumbustious rhythm teeters over into the frenzy of despair. The effect reads now, and must have read then, as perfectly in tune with the mood of the times, and yet its near-tragic defiance raises the poem breathtakingly above its occasion: its timelessness grows out of its timeliness. It is the sort of achievement MacNeice considered the age demanded, as some sentences from the concluding paragraph to his book on Yeats testify. In the long dialogue which MacNeice, Auden and Spender had with the figure of Yeats, the sentences are testimony to the potency of his example. For MacNeice at the end of the thirties Yeats has gained a new franchise. He speaks to the needs and anxieties of MacNeice's generation with more urgency than for a previous generation of poets:

> He can serve us ... as an example of zest. Much modern poetry has inevitably a gloomy content; so had much of Yeats's poetry, but whether it is nostalgic, love-lorn, cynical, darkly prophetic, angry over politics, or embittered over old age, there is nearly always a leaping vitality – the vitality of Cleopatra waiting for the asp. The poet kicks against life but that is because his demands from life are high.[2]

The leaping vitality of 'Bagpipe Music' kicks with the life that it is kicking against. Its manic dance rhythm becomes a dance of death.

'Christmas Shopping' has one of the most finely tuned voices amongst MacNeice's thirties poems of metropolitan malaise. The 'dizzy word-play' is more controlled than in 'Birmingham' and even 'Bagpipe Music'. Like 'Birmingham', 'Christmas Shopping' moves outward from a peopled urban scene, beyond the 'slumward vista', beyond 'the margin / Blotted with smoke-stacks', to an extensive view ('fading zone / Of the West', 'Further out on the coast') that dwarfs the scene, rendering it pathetically helpless. But this development is more artfully plotted in 'Christmas Shopping' than in 'Birmingham', and controlled by more dexterous rhythms. The occasional fade-out (as in 'or at any rate it is possible') which impedes the onrush of 'Birmingham', becomes the rhythmical pattern of 'Christmas Shopping', stanza by stanza and even line by line. Metrical bathos prepares for the 'blank momentum' of the future. Falling trochees are the norm, creating a dwindling, 'maundering music' in every line, an effect repeated in the truncated last line of every stanza, so that even the phrase 'Salaries rising' falls away. These effects prepare for the terrifying bathos of the final 'Mind is a vacuum'. Mimicry is also artfully controlled, as compared with the apparent happenstance of 'Birmingham'. The descriptive third person pronoun of the first line, 'Spending beyond their income on gifts for Christmas', which sounds a slightly derisory note, rapidly gives way before the more sympathetic first person as the poem takes on the voice of those derided: 'What shall we buy for our husbands and sons / Different from last year?' – or at any rate derision mingles with something more plaintive as the poem suddenly puts itself in the shoes of the wives and mothers oppressed by trivia. In the poem's first half the voice shifts intermittently in and out of the first person, becoming sympathetically if unobtrusively ventriloquial: 'Here go the hours of routine, the weight on our eyelids', and 'once we're / Started who knows whether we shan't continue, / Salaries rising'. When the first person reappears in the last stanza, with 'the fog that wads our welfare', it does so with a more bleakly prophetic, representative air.

In 'Christmas Shopping' the twist of the ordinary phrase and the cliché revivified capture a mood and attitude peculiar to MacNeice's kind of social protest: it is not verbal wit so much as verbal clowning, conveying hang-dog despair. It flirts with the danger of 'falling flat on its face', but it is just this element of risk that, at its best, gives tonal edge. A vein of self-mockery runs through the diction, as if to admit the inadequacy of social anger, that fiddling while Rome burns is an inadequate but the only honest response. The way the diction exfoliates has more sustained control than in 'Birmingham':

> Foxes hang by their noses behind plate glass –
> Scream of macaws across festoons of paper –
> Only the faces on the boxes of chocolates are free
>   From boredom and crowsfeet.
>
> Sometimes a chocolate box girl escapes in the flesh,
> Lightly manoeuvres the crowd . . .

Literal and metaphorical are jumbled as the lines move from 'macaws' to 'crowsfeet' and the faces pictured on the chocolate boxes trigger the clichéd image of the 'chocolate box girl' in flesh-and-blood actuality. In the next stanzas metaphors of war and death spiral out of one another ('The great windows marshal their troops for assault on the purse', 'Down to the sewers of money – rats and marshgas', 'the weight on our eyelids – / Pennies on corpses", 'weighted in the boots like chessmen') with their submerged analysis that warmongering is at the root of social collapse and that history, with 'hoodwinking logic', is repeating itself in this time between wars – all this cast in a hysterical-sounding syntactic spiral in which anger and sympathy combine. The opposition between the words 'down' and 'rising' captures the false hopes of the unemployed who are up against the downward spiral of consumer society. Sympathy and disdain combine in the rising hysteria of the relentless repetition of those two words.

This combination is achieved by the voice's shifting register:

> ... Starting at a little and temporary but once we're
> Started who knows whether we shan't continue,
>   Salaries rising,
>
> Rising like a salmon against the bullnecked river,
> Bound for the spawning-ground of care-free days –
> Good for a fling before the golden wheels run
>   Down to a standstill.

The verbal play on 'starting-started', as if words are frenziedly running away with the poet, mocks the shallow aspirations of the unemployed even as it evokes them. Then the salmon and the bullnecked river, sparked off by the word 'rising', image forth all that the unemployed arc up against, condemning the society that has turned them into spiritually hollow automatons. Such shifts enable the poem both to evoke empathically the state of mind of society's participants and victims, and to satirize it. The image of the salmon develops into the mordantly mocking line 'Bound for the spawning-ground of care-free days'; but even as this derisive tone is established, it slides back into sympathetic justification with the *carpe diem* 'good for a fling' as the voice becomes doomladen and invokes time running out, 'down to a standstill'.

Even when the three final stanzas move out to take a distant view of the society in a terrifying, uncannily surreal vision that transcends both sympathy and derision, they get there by deft verbal play and ironic juxtaposition. With a 'blank momentum' the assonantal phrase 'through the tubes' rushes into an image that, with the phrase 'the dead winds blow the crowds', adds infernal dimensions to the 'conduits', the 'sewers of money', earlier in the poem. Those winds and crowds seem to recall the London Underground underworld of Eliot's 'Burnt Norton' III – although, whereas Eliot's lines have the effect of dismissing 'this twittering world', MacNeice's momentarily elicit sympathy for the crowds who are blown 'like beasts in flight'. The 'fire in the forest', from which they are fleeing, dwarfs suburbia's Christmas celebrations with an apocalyptic image of the end of time: that fire alliteratively and ironically gives way to little palpitating Christmas 'firtrees' with their candles; and the phrase 'chattering households' is poised between sympathy and dismissal. If the minds of the people are vacant, so too is the mind of the terrifyingly imagined prime mover who moves nothing, the 'giant at Swedish drill' of the final stanza, who embodies a nihilism in which we all, including the poet, so his automaton voice intimates, participate. 'Mind is a vacuum': the terror is in response to the poet's inner world as much as to the world he inhabits. 'Christmas Shopping', 'Birmingham' and 'Bagpipe Music' take on a vitality of their own even as they want to expose society's spiritual vacuity; but in giving voice to that society, they sound as though they are giving voice to something in the poet himself.

4

The mirror-image of MacNeice's desire for contact, of his responsiveness to dizzying particulars, is his sense of himself as an outsider. His relation to the demotic is symptomatic: an acute ear for everyday speech brings the poet near to 'ephemeral things' and common culture, while the attempt to find poetic life in the demotic demands a scrutinizing frame of mind that stands outside language even as he turns the music on – just as in life MacNeice felt himself simultaneously within and without, an outsider with loyalties to examine, who at times hankers to belong but cannot, at times resists the pressure to belong.

   This sense of himself comes over powerfully in 'Carrickfergus' with its 'economical notation of alienation', in Robyn Marsack's

phrase,[3] with its engaged scrutiny, distant but involved, of his
Anglo-Irish inheritance, of feeling a Protestant outsider in
Ireland and an Irish outsider in England. Ireland is the arena in
which MacNeice's personality and contemporary events most
obviously reflect on one another. Immediately, in the first line ('I
was born in Belfast between the mountain and the gantries'),
'between' intimates division as well as connection (as it does also
in 'Snow'), not belonging and belonging. The falling of stress on
open vowels, the full open-vowel masculine rhyme at the end of
the second and fourth line of every stanza, and the feminine
(unrhymed) ending of every first and third: together these effects
convey a nostalgia which belies the muted bitterness of the personal and historical memories recorded in the poem. Nostalgia
and an air of defeat come together in haunted phrases: 'the
hooting of lost sirens', 'The yarn-mill called its funeral cry at
noon', 'Under the peacock aura of a drowning moon'. Personal
and historical elements intertwine:

> I was the rector's son, born to the anglican order,
>   Banned for ever from the candles of the Irish poor;
> The Chichesters knelt in marble at the end of a transept
>   With ruffs about their necks, their portion sure.

Here alienation mixes with guilt. There is savage irony in
'portion', the Chichesters' portion in Heaven being at the
expense of the portion extorted from the Irish Catholic poor.
This sense of exclusion gives way to another when MacNeice
goes to England to be educated, when he 'thought that the war
would last for ever' and that 'never again' would

>   people not have maps above the fireplace
>   With flags on pins moving across and across –

> Across the hawthorn hedge the noise of bugles,
>   Flares across the night,
> Somewhere on the lough was a prison ship for Germans,
>   A cage across their sight.

The repeated 'across' captures Northern Ireland's frustrations
and thwartings, as well as MacNeice's acute sense of being
thwarted and hemmed in by his past and his childhood, unable

to escape that past, but remote from it. The double note concludes the poem: confinement and escape, belonging and not belonging, regret and relief:

> I went to school in Dorset, the world of parents
> Contracted into a puppet world of sons
> Far from the mill girls, the smell of porter, the salt-mines
> And the soldiers with their guns.

MacNeice is often described as reticent, which is right when not applied in a spirit of accusation. It is reticence in such poems as 'Carrickfergus' – although so much is implied – that produces the pressure behind its tensed emotions.

'Epilogue: For W. H. Auden' (the title of the poem as published in *Letters from Iceland*, an account of the trip MacNeice and Auden made in 1936; later, the poem was titled 'Postscript to Iceland') is another reticent poem, 'free from over-emphasis', though its reticence manifests itself in a different way. It is haunted by the emotionally Janus-faced state of aloneness. Fear of loneliness, isolation, plays off against self-protective aloofness: the phrase 'lonely comfort' in the second line elicits the double feeling at once. Whereas in 'Carrickfergus' the pressure of external events acts as a powerfully submerged theme, in 'Epilogue' it is the overt subject. The poem fends off even as it seeks to face up to the outside world. 'Carrickfergus' is an autobiographical lyric, whereas 'Epilogue', as befits its place at the end of *Letters from Iceland*, is cast in the form of a poem for a public occasion, as one poet addressing another in a postscript to a series of open 'letters'. Indeed it does all the things expected of a thirties poem so comprehensively as to teeter on the verge of self-caricature – which is itself characteristic of the poetry of the period. But by the end it has transcended itself with great authority. At its core is private suffering, buried and yet painfully exposed. It uses all the tonal stops and tricks of diction at MacNeice's command.

In the second stanza the self-ironizing diction of 'fancy turn, you know' prepares for 'graver show', which, albeit stiff-upper-lip and public-school, sounds a deeper irony. Private and public concerns support and play off against each other in thirties fashion: civil war breaks out in Spain, world war looks imminent ('Down in Europe Seville fell, / Nations germinating hell'), and

MacNeice returns home to face life without his recently estranged wife:

> Here in Hampstead I sit late
> Nights which no one shares and wait
> For the 'phone to ring or for
> Unknown angels at the door;
>
> Better were the northern skies
> Than this desert in disguise –
> Rugs and cushions and the long
> Mirror which repeats the song.

'Unknown angels at the door' – the flip despair disguising real personal anguish – anticipates the universal fear of the last line, the forthright terror of 'The gun-butt raps upon the door'. The poem manipulates the familiar thirties method of psychological landscape with great deliberation. In the lines just quoted the real Iceland blurs into symbol on being recalled to register emotional states. The Iceland the poet visited was a real desert, exhilarating because under no pretence, whereas in Hampstead the desert is disguised; civilized life merely cushions the desert within, emotional sterility. Psychological landscape is purposefully and 'donnishly' signalled earlier in the poem, when MacNeice correctly gives it Audenesque authority: 'And the don in you replied / That the North begins inside'. The poem ironically recognizes the attractions and dangers of escape into thirties Utopianism – 'Not for me romantic nor / Idyll on a mythic shore' – and deflates the clichéd contemporary dream of a simple, whole life on an island, in lines evoking a thirties chumminess:

> So we rode and joked and smoked
> With no miracles evoked,
> With no levitations won
> In the thin unreal sun.

The linguistic knockabout of 'rode', 'joked', 'smoked', 'evoked' moves on to something more telling with the phrase 'the thin unreal sun', though what it tells is significantly ambiguous: did that islanded hour afford the opportunity to step back and take stock, or was it a guilty evasion of responsibilities?

The 'fancy turn' turns ominous as the assonantal jingle of 'So although no ghost was scotched' gives way to the ravens two lines later, which 'cruise around the rotting whale' and start to smell of the rot of Europe from which the travellers made their escape. Willy-nilly, the symbolic imagination gets to work and will not let the poet relax. There is insouciant acknowledgement of what he escaped: 'While the valley fades away / To a sketch of Judgment Day' makes the day of doom seem pleasantly distant, although the word 'sketch' shows more than a trace of guilt. The poet's fellow letter-writer was good at sketching doom. 'Unreality' became a welcome relief, but was it a neutral ground or an evasive one? Poker-faced mockery flickers across the vacant lines 'No great happenings at all' and 'Holidays should be like this'.

The poem encompasses a very wide tonal range, in large part the result of the adept handling of its tricky metre, trochaic tetrameter, which is made to accommodate such suavely banal lines as 'Drinking coffee, telling tales' as well as the high-sounding Yeatsian 'Through that forest of dead words / I would hunt the living birds'. The result is a complex of emotions, none of which has quite the last word even when the last word comes:

> Our prerogatives as men
> Will be cancelled who knows when;
> Still I drink your health before
> The gun-butt raps upon the door.

The straight-spoken last line, which demands to be taken at face value (partly as the result of the slight rhythmic jolt in the change from trochees to iambs), declares its fear and determination as the outside world forces itself upon the attention of the poet. But this conclusion is hedged about by equivocation all the same. 'Who knows when' and 'Still I drink your health' hover between the careworn and the carefree, between fatalism and pulling oneself together.

A sense of responsibility lurks painfully in the poem. Isolation is at the heart of its stricken conscience. Personal isolation mirrors and plays off against historical isolation. The poet would break through it with his poetry; but is that poetry in danger of becoming a further means of isolation, of keeping the world at bay? 'Lonely comfort walls me in' is both defiant and guilty. Loneliness can provide the comfort of burying one's head. Self-

protection can turn into denying the self. The first stanza's
insulating walls of loneliness anticipate these lines:

> Rows of books around me stand,
> Fence me round on either hand;
> Through that forest of dead words
> I would hunt the living birds –
>
> Great black birds that fly alone
> Slowly through a land of stone,
> And the gulls who weave a free
> Quilt of rhythm on the sea.

The poet's responsibility is to use language not as a means of
evasion and false comfort, blithely sketching in Judgment Day.
Such a reaction to the pressure of events is to take up the
embattled position of loneliness. The contrast is an exhilarating
isolation, imaged, with a deliberate grandeur reminiscent of
Yeats, in the 'great black birds' flying through their stone
landscape. The 'quilt of rhythm on the sea' has the feel of a
'comfort' more genuine than the 'lonely' sort at the start of the
poem.

The poem thus addresses an issue of paramount importance to
MacNeice and his contemporaries: how to write poetry in an age
that demands so much, while remaining true to the self and to
poetry, to the poetic self. Conversely, there is the guilt attendant
on burying oneself in words while the world is going to the dogs.
The loneliness that engulfs the poet towards the end of the poem
is different from the searching and independent aloneness of the
'great black birds' and gulls weaving free: 'the fear of loneliness'
comes with the fear of failing to make verbal contact, and the
unwieldy word 'uncommunicableness' jolts the reader into an
awareness of the terror of incoherent psychic isolation that lurks
beneath the witty surface of this poem:

> . . . the fear of loneliness
> And uncommunicableness;
> All the wires are cut, my friends
> Live beyond the severed ends.

The chumminess has deepened into something unfathomably

other here. A frayed relationship, severed nerves, the cut wires (telegraph wires?) of a disintegrating Europe: all means of communication, whether with the psyche, within personal relations, or in the world at large, have been sheared. Yet mingled with the fear is a certain exhilaration, the isolation of the adventurer beyond the frontier as opposed to the man fenced in with himself; the friends at any rate *live* beyond the severed ends, and the 'death-wish' mood – a not uncommon mood in MacNeice's poetry – has changed by the end of the poem to courage, even if at a low ebb. In working its way towards this state of mind the poem moves from the wit of some of the earlier lines to something more biting and emotionally deadly accurate in those lines 'All the wires are cut, my friends / Live beyond the severed ends'. The phrase 'my friends', poised between comma and line-ending, seems to hesitate despairingly, but then 'lives beyond' itself into the next line; because there is no conjunction at the comma (for example 'but'), the change of emotional direction, from despair to daring, is unexpected, and all the more convincing for being so. The poem evinces supremely well the combination of qualities for which Spender came to admire MacNeice: 'Ultimately he is a poet of temperament, of gaiety and melancholy cultivated by wit, taste and learning, and held together by courage: the virtue he most admired' (Casebook, p. 50). The combination was to work on a much more extensive scale in *Autumn Journal*, a poem of temperament and courage in the face of the 'death-wish'.

4
Auden (2)
The Orators: 'They stole to force a hearing'

1

Disorientation is essential to the experience of reading *The Orators*.[1] Everett's confession to finding the work 'almost impenetrably obscure' (Everett, p. 27) is truer to its nature than Mendelson's demonstration that there is a 'hidden key' (a paper by Auden's friend, the anthropologist John Layard), and that it is 'possible to reconstruct the original conception that was blurred in the finished work'; for such an approach is in danger of letting the conception displace the work. Nevertheless, as this chapter will show, Mendelson has some crucial insights, especially when he writes that the work's 'bafflingly elusive tone emerged in part from the divisions Auden recognized in himself only while he was writing it' (Mendelson, pp. 104, 106, 94). And when Everett asks such questions as 'does Auden know that there is no difference between the Airman and the Enemy, or not?', she hits on the text's indeterminacy, although to expect answers is to sell such insight short. For all her evident frustration at finding *The Orators* indecipherable, her comment that it 'appears to be an account of an attempt to come to terms with – and finally break free from – the voices and attitudes, within and without a man, which prevent him from coming to maturity', gets near the mark, except that the work is not 'an account of an attempt', but the attempt itself (Everett, pp. 31, 29). Fuller does not like 'a good deal of what looks like automatic writing' (although his final verdict is that *The Orators* 'is still surely the most significant and disturbing long poem of its era') (Fuller, pp. 66, 74); but such automatism is part of the text's 'way of happening' and cannot be divorced from its essential nature – as Auden himself was to imply, however disparagingly, when he wrote in the Preface to the 1966 (third) edition: 'My guess today is that my unconscious motive . . . was therapeutic, to exorcise certain tendencies in myself by allowing them to run riot in phantasy'.

The Orators contains every topos familiar from Auden's earlier work: frontiers, exile and escape, the new start, ancestor worship, feud, matriarchy, the public-school ethos, social malaise and diagnosis, the leader, the group, consciousness and self-consciousness. The text is a voicing forth, an acting out – and thus an exorcizing – of the instabilities of the earlier poetry. The first part of 'Argument' (which comprises the second section of Book I, 'The Initiates') recycles lines from poems that appeared in the privately printed *Poems* (1928) but did not survive into *Poems* (1930). The opening, 'Lo, I a skull show you, exuded from dyke when no pick was by pressure of bulbs', recalls lines from an abandoned eight-part poem: 'In Spring we saw / The bulb pillow / Raising the skull' (an image out of Eliot's 'Whispers of Immortality'). The sentences, 'The dew-wet hare hangs smoking, garotted by gin. The emmet looks at sky through lenses of fallen water', recall lines from the concluding part of the same poem: 'The dew-wet fur of the dead hare / Smokes as light sparkles on the snare. / / The grass looks upward at the flower / Through lenses of a fallen shower'. These phrases, from 'Argument', 'At the frontier getting down, at railhead drinking hot tea waiting for pack-mules, at the box with the three levers watching the swallows', recall the opening of another such abandoned poem: 'On the frontier at dawn getting down, / Hot eyes were soothed with swallows'.[2] The spoof air given these lifted phrases and sentences by their new context is symptomatic of how *The Orators* takes off earlier Auden. In the first part of 'Argument' the tone in which the coming of the Leader is announced, and in which the mysteriously secret ritual unfolds ('Speak the name only with meaning only for us, meaning Him'), constantly veers into the pseudo-prophetic, as is immediately signalled by the farcically exaggerated syntactic inversion of 'I a skull show you' and by the near-comedy of 'exuded'. The skull and bulb image of the abandoned poem has found a different, parodic context. Similarly, the alteration of 'snare' to 'gin' (i.e. gin trap) in the process of transferring the hare image enables much horseplay to be got out of the pun on 'gin': cigarettes and drink do for the hare ('smoking, garotted by gin'). The frontier railway station of Auden's abandoned poem acquires a farcical air in *The Orators* with the addition of the would-be mysterious circumlocution 'at the box with the three levers' (signal-box?). When, later in the first part of 'Argument', 'Poetry of the waiting-room' flashes up on the screen, it is as if the self-referential irony of the writing is being signalled.

But the relationship between 'Argument' and the abandoned poems is not simply parodic, for the earlier poetry can sound as though it is already parodying itself, sometimes flickeringly so, at others more deliberately. The eight-part poem from which 'Argument' borrows twice, ends on a loud note of self-parody: 'Gargantua – the race is run – / Kicks the view over, pisses at the sun'. This may have something to do with the spoof victory gesture in the first part of 'Argument': 'one writes with his penis in a patch of snow "Resurgam" .' *The Orators* foregrounds, in a spirit of exorcism, what had been going on in Auden's poetry from the beginning. Another notable example occurs in the third section of 'Argument'. The sentence 'Love, that notable forked one, riding away from the farm, the ill word said, fought at the frozen dam, transforms itself to influenza and guilty rashes' is lifted from the last verse-paragraph of 'Because sap fell away', another poem that did not get further than *Poems* (1928).[3] In this poem love and feud coincide in Audenesque fashion with guilt-ridden illness, but in the borrowing the topos of the 'diseased youngster' verges on public-school silliness. Presumably Love 'transforms itself to influenza and guilty rashes' because of what happens in the next sentence, 'seduction of a postmistress on the lead roof of a church-tower', and presumably it is because of the 'guilty rashes' that there is 'an immature boy wrapping himself in a towel, ashamed at the public baths'. But the abandoned poem already contained the seeds of its own parody: the first verse-paragraph, with its dubious team-spirit and changing-room goings-on ('we sit lax, / In close ungenerous intimacy', 'a snub-nosed winner', etc.), ends 'Open a random locker, sniff with distaste / At a mouldy passion'. Even as the team-spirit rugby mode began to appear in Auden's poetry, as early as 1927, he was camping it up, as he was to do in a more thoroughgoing, though also more complicit, fashion four years later in *The Orators*.

Nor were Auden's borrowings from earlier work confined to abandoned poems. As poetry of departure, the first part of 'Argument' recalls 'Doom is dark and deeper than any sea-dingle'.[4] In 'Argument' departure for the new life ('Going abroad to-day?') is apparently hampered by what the earlier poem calls 'restraint of women': 'Sound of horns in the moist spring weather, and the women tender. I feel sorry for you I do. Girls, it is His will just now that we get up early'. Parodic deflation marks the tone, or tones, here in a way not typical of 'Doom is dark', although even that poem flickers with something other than the straight-faced. Is there deflation in the portentous-sounding Anglo-Saxon alliteration of the first line? The balance between the precise-seeming and the vaguely suggestive in such lines as 'Of new men making another love' is beautifully poised; but when the poem goes on to pretend to pin the vagueness down, it becomes even more teasingly precise-cum-vague: 'Converting number from vague to certain'. And just how is one to take the word 'lucky' in the last line, balanced as it is against the high poetry of 'with leaning dawn'?

In the orations which make up *The Orators* the author is nowhere and everywhere, nowhere as a central perspective, a univocal presence, everywhere as the medium through which the orators' voices sound, voices which become exaggerated, deflected, amplified, attenuated in their passage through the medium. *The Orators* demonstrates to a marked degree the symptoms it pretends to diagnose. Many critics point out that 'Address for a Prize-Day' (the first section of Book I) presents an analysis of social neurosis and disease recognizable from Auden's earlier poems and from *Paid on Both Sides*. Everett comments: 'An element in Auden's own outlook, a tone in his own voice, is exaggerated till it becomes farcical, insincere, and dangerous'. In fact what Everett calls this 'undermining complexity' has been present in Auden's poetry, at however unconscious a level, from its beginnings (Everett, p. 29). In the Address the exaggerated public-school idiom of the speaker, an old boy, is from the start in 'intonational quotation marks', to use Mikhail Bakhtin's phrase (from his essay 'From the Pre-history of Novelistic Discourse'):

Commemoration. Commemoration. What does it mean?
What does it mean? Not what does it mean to them, there,
then. What does it mean to us, here now? It's a facer, isn't it
boys? But we've all got to answer it. What were the dead like?
What sort of people are we living with now? Why are we here?
What are we going to do?

What Heaney, in describing the poem 'Since you are going to
begin to-day', calls 'the gradual accession of a fast tone over a
solemn occasion', is not a gradual accession here, but the
consistent idiom.[5] The tone is evident in the parodic examination of first and last things, in the stiff-upper-lip movement from
'It's a facer' to 'What were the dead like?', in the culminating
bathos of 'What are we going to do?' Parody and spoof are
fundamental to the Address. By the end the voice is ridiculing
itself so comprehensively that even Mendelson's phrase 'black
comedy' takes the effect at a level of seriousness the language
seems to want to ward off (Mendelson, p. 99): 'Time's getting on
and I must hurry or I shall miss my train. . . . All these have got
to die without issue. Unless my memory fails me there's a stoke
hole under the floor of this hall, the Black Hole we called it in my
day. New boys were always put in it. Ah, I see I am right. Well
look to it. Quick, guard that door. Stop that man. Good. Now
boys hustle them, ready, steady – go'.
    Auden's way with other writers and literatures in *The Orators*
resembles his way with his earlier poetic self. Each borrowed
idiom frequently teeters over into self-parody. This is particularly
the case with Saint-John Perse's *Anabase*, with its inscrutable
rituals and mysterious leader, the 'Stranger', founder of a new
civilization.[6] (Saint-John Perse is the pseudonym of the French
diplomat-poet Alexis Saint-Léger Léger; *Anabase* was published
in 1924 and, in English translation by T. S. Eliot, in 1930.) Auden
obviously responded to Perse's nomadic world of unspecified
frontier, mysterious destiny and augured exile; and the theme of
'the City of your dreams' in *Anabase* would have caught the eye
of the author of John Nower's soliloquy in *Paid on Both Sides*
about a dream city ('There is the city, / Lighted and clean once,
pleasure for builders'). As Fuller remarks, 'much that is oblique,
exotic and liturgical' in the first two parts of 'Argument' seems
'inspired' by *Anabase* (Fuller, p. 56). The effect is disturbing, for
Auden borrows the mysteriously prophetic tone while frequently

turning it into comic grotesquerie. 'A schoolmaster cleanses himself at half-term with a vegetable offering' sounds like a take-off of the sort of activity in *Anabase* practised by the 'Stranger', who 'is offered fresh water / to wash therewith his mouth, his face and his sex', or by the 'widows' who undergo 'purification . . . among the roses'. *Anabase* begins 'I have built myself' and ends '*Who talks of building?*'; the voice of 'Argument' says in arch archaism, 'I waken with an idea of building'.

The second part of 'Argument' consists of spoof Anglican responses. Imitation Anglo-Saxon poetry in the first two parts of 'Statement' (the third section of Book I) is disorientatingly followed by a pastiche of Gertrude Stein's experimental style at the start of the third part: 'An old one is beginning to be two new ones. Two new ones are beginning to be two old ones', etc. This collapses into farce with 'Nothing is being done but something being done again by someone', as do the imitation Anglo-Saxon *Maxims* in the next paragraph: 'Jelly fish is laziest, cares very little. Tapeworm is most ashamed; he used to be free'. *The Orators* parodies these and many other literary influences even as it draws poetic strength from them.[7]

2

Voices in *The Orators* turn in on themselves and self-destruct, disintegrating in caricature and exaggeration. The result is a fascinating stylistic narcissism: one can hear each voice listening to itself and turning hollow. This syndrome is at the heart of *The Orators*. Near the start of 'Journal of an Airman' occur these sentences: 'Self-care is not to be confused with self-regard. Self-care is carefree. Self-regard is the treating of news as a private poem; it is the consequence of eavesdropping'. Much of Auden's early poetry sounds as though it is treating news as a private poem. This is the effect of its landscapes of psychological impasse, of the 'dismantled washing-floors, / Snatches of tramline running to the wood' in 'The Watershed', of the 'silted harbours, derelict works' and 'strangled orchards' in 'Consider this', of the whole topography of 'Control of the passes'. Narcissism hears what it wants to hear in its eavesdropping on the world. Hence the early poetry's intriguing blur of the diagnostic and the symptomatic. For all their rhetorical display and gestural air, many of the early poems remain secretive – but enticingly so, as if the reader is being let in on something. One way of reading and hearing *The Orators* is as the culmination and exorcising of this syndrome, poetically and psychologically.

This is the range of emotions knowingly tapped by 'Letter to a Wound' (the fourth section of Book I), which is a brilliant acknowledgement and exposé of self-regard, implicitly recognized as a source of power even as it is sent up. Like all the voices in *The Orators*, that of the Letter is self-divided, mocking itself in the act of defining itself. It finally accepts that narcissism is a condition of its existence; it sees that 'the really fascinating subject is one's personal abyss' (Mendelson, p. 103) – and on a personal level this is Auden coming to terms with his homosexuality. But the self-mockery is two-edged, for in sending up the style of the intimate love-letter, the Letter undercuts its admission of narcissism. The deadlock is absolute. 'The unnerving conceit . . . of a man outrageously addressing his own, carefully guarded, wound' (Everett, p. 31) denotes narcissism to excess. Self-regard has become synonymous with identity: 'You are so quiet these days that I get quite nervous, remove the dressing. No I am safe, you are still there. . . . But I am calm. I can wait. The surgeon was dead right. Nothing will ever part us. Goodnight and God bless you, my dear. Better burn this'.

In the course of arriving at this acceptance the Letter goes through a series of rhetorically posed emotions, the intonational quotation marks much in evidence: 'Outside I saw nothing, walked, not daring to think. I've lost everything, I've failed. I wish I was dead. And now, here we are, together, intimate, mature'. The letter writer trumps himself by relating with juvenilely sinister delight how 'Once I carved on a seat in the park "We have sat here. You'd better not"', and then admitting that 'Now I see that all that sort of thing is juvenile and silly, merely a reaction against insecurity and shame'. Awareness of your own obsession may make for awareness of others' obsessions, for sympathy: 'Thanks to you, I have come to see a profound significance in relations I never dreamt of considering before, an old lady's affection for a small boy, the Waterhouses and their retriever, the curious bond between Offal and Snig, the partners in the hardware shop on the front'. But, with that comically named couple Offal and Snig, the tone here slips into a knowingly coy self-mockery.

In his 1966 Preface Auden wrote that 'The central theme of *The Orators* seems to be Hero-worship', and, in a letter of 1931, that 'the theme [of Book I, 'The Initiates'] is the failure of the romantic conception of personality; that what it inevitably leads to is part 4 [i.e. 'Letter to a Wound']' (quoted in Mendelson, p. 97). It leads to the hero as sufferer, narcissistically unable to separate his sense of himself from his sense of loss: he is his wound. As Stan Smith points out, a useful gloss on *The Orators* occurs in *The Enchafèd Flood*, where Auden argues that Hamlet is the first example in literature of the suffering Romantic Avenger Hero who cannot exist without his grievance; it defines his being: ' "My injury," he says, "is not an injury *to* me; it *is* me. If I cancel it out by succeeding in my vengeance, I shall not know who I am and will have to die. I cannot live without it" '.[8] This is the situation of the Airman, the romantic hero who comes to a recognition, which is his moment of crisis and fulfilment, that the Enemy is himself. But the recognition does not lead to the self-congratulatory complacency of 'Letter to a Wound'; it leads to suicide. The Airman sometimes sounds like Hamlet. He sees himself as the avenger of the death of his Uncle Henry, who, in the matrilineal version of personal development and inheritance which underlies *The Orators* (as it does *Paid on Both Sides*), and which Auden borrowed in part from D. H. Lawrence's *Fantasia of the Unconscious*, represents the Airman's 'real ancestor'. In spoof Hamlet style he muses: 'Fourteenth anniversary of my Uncle's death. Fine. Cleaned the airgun as usual. But what have I done to avenge, to disprove the boy's faked evidence at the inquest? NOTHING (never reloaded since it was found discharged by your untasted coffee). Give me time. I PROMISE'. It is only later, three days before his final take-off, that the Airman understands the secret of Uncle Henry's words 'I have crossed it'. His crossing has been a suicide: the Airman must follow suit and act out the imperatives of his own divided nature. The only way out of his impasse is to see it through to the end:

My whole life has been mistaken, progressively more and more complicated, instead of finally simple.

My incredible blindness, with all the facts staring me in the face, not to have realised these elementary truths.

1.   The power of the enemy is a function of our resistance, therefore

2.   The only efficient way to destroy it – self-destruction, the sacrifice of all resistance, reducing him to the state of a man trying to walk on a frictionless surface.

3.   Conquest can only proceed by absorption of, i.e. infection by, the conquered. The true significance of my hands, 'Do not imagine that you, no more than any other conqueror, escape the mark of grossness.' They stole to force a hearing.

This desire for simplicity amongst all the complexity describes the impression 'Journal of an Airman' itself makes, before it resolves, or dissolves, into the breathtaking simplicity of the last day preparatory to take-off ('Wind easterly and moderate. Hands in perfect order.'). It also describes the encoded air of much of the early poetry, obscure yet direct, enacting the 'convolutions' of its 'simple wish', in the words of 'Consider this' – a poem which did indeed 'proceed by absorption of, i.e. infection by, the conquered', as the addressee became both subjected to and the disseminator of spreading malaise; the protagonist of 'Consider this' is an agent of the Antagonist, as the Airman is of the Enemy. Stylistically Auden writes himself out in *The Orators*, coddling, exaggerating and being infected by, the rhetoric of others; he can 'conquer' them only by being taken over, 'absorbed' by them, in a stylistic 'sacrifice of all resistance'. That is, in those words of Auden, the poetry is 'therapeutic, to exorcise certain tendencies in myself by allowing them to run riot in phantasy'. The Airman's hands, which usually represent self-regard in the Journal, the selfishness of kleptomania, the narcissism of masturbation, are also, by the end, the means of freeing himself through suicide ('Hands in perfect order'), the ultimately selfish act which brings about the ultimate freedom from self. The Airman's hands 'stole to force a hearing' because kleptomania can be a call for help; they are also about to steal his life in the ultimate call for help, suicide (and sexual death may be implicit too, for flying can be a metaphor for sexual intercourse). There is also a sense in which the poet steals voices, from his own and others' repertoires, in order 'to force a hearing'. Indeed, Auden's poetry has been forcing a hearing from the start.

3

Auden's later disquiet about the political implications of *The Orators*, as expressed in his 1966 Preface, is in keeping with the Airman's self-division: 'My name on the title-page seems a pseudonym for someone else, someone talented but near the border of sanity, who might well, in a year or two, become a Nazi'. Even so, this older Auden cannot think himself back into the divided self that must have generated *The Orators*. Nor could he quite do so even three months after its publication: 'the result is far too obscure and equivocal. It is meant to be a critique of the fascist outlook, but . . . I see that it can, most of it, be interpreted as a favourable exposition' (letter, quoted in Mendelson, p. 104). In fact the work is more thoroughly and consistently double-minded than this accusation of confused obscurity allows. Its very structure supports equivocation. Its perspective is plainly divided, between Book I, 'The Initiates', and Book II, 'Journal of an Airman'. Book I views the Hero from the outside, as he is rumoured among the 'initiates' in 'Argument', where he is a function of their desire for 'Him', the desire of 'Obedience for a master' (from 'To ask the hard question'). As Auden pointed out in a letter written while he was composing *The Orators*, Book II 'is the situation seen from within the Hero' (quoted in Mendelson, p. 103). By realizing the idea of the hero, the Airman eventually comes to recognize the sham nature of his own heroism; but he can only do so by acting out its imperatives, by performing, and thus exorcising, the romantic role of the isolated individual alone and above, 'As the hawk sees it or the helmeted airman' – and the poetic dimension to the political theme is never far away: is haughty panoptic authority suitable in either case?

The structure of *The Orators* bears some relation to that of T. S. Eliot's contemporaneous poem-drama *Coriolan*, the two parts of which were first published, separately, in the period when Auden was working on *The Orators*. Although Auden may not have read *Coriolan* until after he had completed *The Orators*, it is instructive to compare the two works, since *Coriolan* also explores the issue of leadership, and with a similar outcome.[9] Also, intriguingly, the works have two sources in common: *Anabase*, and General Erich F. W. Ludendorff's *The Coming War*.[10] Part I of *Coriolan*, 'Triumphal March', presents the leader as perceived from the outside by the 'press of people', part II, 'Difficulties of a Statesman', as perceived from the inside. Coriolan attempts to live up to the image his people hold of him ('What shall I cry?'), but the inner perception undermines the outer. What at the start of 'Triumphal March' sounds like a voice of impressed and impressive ritual ('Stone, bronze, stone, steel, stone, oakleaves, horses' heels / Over the paving'), a voice borrowed from *Anabase* ('Stone and bronze' occurs in part IV of *Anabase* with the 'Foundation of the City'), modulates into the voice of the thoughtless, excitable people, which, in moments of dramatic irony, betrays more about them than they suspect: 'We hardly knew ourselves that day, or knew the City'. The unreliability of the people's awed voice makes the status of their leader uncertain. Similar, though more radical, equivocation determines the style of 'Argument' in *The Orators*: 'The thrashing He gave the dishonest contractor who promised marvels in an old boy's tie. . . . His ability to smell a wet knife at a distance of half a mile. His refusal to wear anything but silk next to His skin'. If the voice of 'Triumphal March' mocks itself, it wants to come across as doing so unknowingly, whereas the credulity of 'Argument' teeters over into a knowing, public-school self-mockery.

From the leader's inner perspective in 'Difficulties of a Statesman' Coriolan reveals that his appearance of authority is a sham, that what from the people's point of view looks like lack of 'interrogation in his eyes' denotes vacancy, that what looks like 'indifference' is lack of sympathy, that what is 'hidden' from them is as much hidden from himself, and that he has faith neither in his own tired abilities nor in the outward signs of authority (the busts of his predecessors). He exemplifies the romantic conception of personality, the Hero as sufferer, goaded, if at all, by a sharp sense of loss, induced, as in *The Orators*, by separation from the mother: 'Mother / May we not be some time, almost now, together'. Like the Airman he is self-divided, and he ends by committing political suicide, for at the conclusion he is as much shouting himself down as being shouted down by his people: when for the last time he despairs 'What shall I cry?' the answer he gets, 'RESIGN RESIGN RESIGN', is a voice echoing as much from inner vacancy as from the crowd outside.[11]

But the differences between *The Orators* and *Coriolan* are as instructive as the similarities. *The Orators* subverts by radical mockery the very concepts of heroism, leadership and authority.

Coriolan explores the basis of leadership and the ground for authority, as it might be democracy (or, as Eliot implies, pretended democracy with all its pitiable limitations), and the fascist leader with his spurious spiritual authority. The contrast between the two works is underlined by the very different use they make of *Anabase* and Ludendorff's *The Coming War*. *The Orators* undermines by camping up Perse's ritualism. Eliot's borrowing of Perse's mysterious tones has the effect of questioning whether they are not merely mystifying, while still permitting the mystery to resonate. Auden's use of *The Coming War* is pure spoof. What Fuller calls Ludendorff's 'hair-raising' account of war mobilization, 'with its allusions to a Jewish-Jesuit-Freemason conspiracy' is deflated at the end of 'Journal of an Airman' by Auden's schoolboy medieval apocalypse: 'All menstruation ceases. Vampires are common in the neighbourhood of the Cathedral, epidemics of lupus, halitosis, and superfluous hair.' (See Fuller, pp. 67–8.) Here at least fascism gets a caricaturing come-uppance. The enumeration of military hardware in 'Triumphal March' comes almost verbatim from Ludendorff's book, but any satirical note in its recital is aimed more at the gullible populace than at their leader.[12] *The Orators* exposes by exorcising the contemporary prevalence of the fascist mentality, whereas *Coriolan* sounds like an apology for it as a lamentable necessity for the thoughtless times.

4

Everyone in Auden's early poetry 'is barred . . . from participating in the world beyond the frontiers of the self', writes Mendelson ('Introduction', *EA*, p. xvi). The prose sections of *The Orators* enact *in extremis* this self-enclosed, solipsistic world, stylistically, thematically, psychologically. Their hermeticism is symptomatic. Stylistically the voices are perpetually committing suicide as they fall into farcical exaggeration, caricature and self-mockery. How far the poems of *The Orators* move beyond therapeutic exorcism, 'the treating of news as a private poem', is another matter. The 'Prologue', the 'Epilogue' and the two poems 'We have brought you, they said, a map of the country' and 'There are some birds in these valleys', both in 'Journal of an Airman', represent a new movement in Auden's poetry towards accessibility. They are less inclined to 'force a hearing' than his previous poetry. The six Odes that comprise Book III are more problematic.

The metre of the 'Prologue', iambic pentameter with frequent anapaestic substitution and sparsity of caesura, achieves a mellifluousness new to Auden. But the effect is deceptive. The graceful sound of the consistently full-rhymed feminine line-endings gradually transforms into the insinuatingly sinister. The 'mother's figure' getting 'bigger and bigger' gains sway so that by the end 'fever' is made to rhyme with her 'giantess' accusation of 'Deceiver', feminine rhyme accompanying the accession of matrilineal power. The myth-making air of this poem, its approach to human experience through parable landscape, looks forward to the manner of the sonnets of *In Time of War*, to for instance 'Wandering lost upon the mountains of our choice', and even to 'In Praise of Limestone', which also has a maternal scenery. The 'Prologue' formalizes what occurs as if by happenstance in previous poetry, in for instance 'The Watershed' or 'From the very first coming down'.

From the start the 'Prologue' admits its propensity to turn landscape into symbol: 'By landscape *reminded* . . .' (emphasis added). The familiar theme of matrilineal and ancestral trammels finds expression in the equally familiar map metaphor, but with knowing deliberation:

> By landscape reminded once of his mother's figure
> The mountain heights he remembers get bigger and bigger:
> With the finest of mapping pens he fondly traces
> All the family names on the familiar places.

The artfully managed puns and double-entendres denote a meditated, even calculated style. 'Finest' takes on a manly air in the light of the phallic connotation of 'pen', a 'nonchalant' manliness of the sort associated with the protagonist of the poem 'Watch any day his nonchalant pauses, see', who, like the hero of the 'Prologue', is a failed conqueror ('He is not that returning conqueror'), a quester from the land of adolescence who assumes an 'accosting profile' but is caught in the web of the past, 'the inertia of the buried'. 'Fondly', in the lines just quoted, mingles foolishness with lovingness, with possible overtones of phallic fondling. 'Tracing', copying the 'family names', involves tracking them down: the double meaning points up how homing in on one's history reveals the ineradicable traces it has left on one's personality. Even the ordinary word 'familiar' quickens a little by virtue of its proximity to 'family'.

> Among green pastures straying he walks by still waters;
> Surely a swan he seems to earth's unwise daughters,
> Bending a beautiful head, worshipping not lying,
> 'Dear' the dear beak in the dear concha crying.

In this context, 'still waters' sounds significant: 'still waters run deep'. Moreover, as Fuller points out, the allusion to Psalm 23 (verse 2: 'He maketh me to lie down in green pastures: he leadeth me beside the still waters') lends the hero a status of 'a quasi-divinity', 'but he is no Jove, and his swan-like beauty is impotent, "worshipping not lying", whispering in girls' ears rather than going to bed with them'. Fuller further comments that 'sexual meanings of "beak" and "concha" reinforce what might have been', and that the hero 'does understand that life should be natural and instinctive, lying not worshipping, . . . but he does not put his knowledge into action. He tells others about it. He is, in fact, an "orator"' (Fuller p. 54). This is helpful, especially in highlighting the connection between oratory and leadership buried in the poem. But Fuller does not remark that 'lying' is surely a pun central to the poem: in not lying with 'unwise daughters' our hero turns himself into a liar with words. In his role of 'prophet' he sounds suspiciously glib: 'Carries the good news gladly to a world in danger, / Is ready to argue, he smiles, with any stranger'. Arguing, talking about it, self-consciousness, supplants action; taking thought incapacitates. He is 'Coward' and 'Deceiver': the genesis of the romantic hero is deception born out of cowardice. As 'The Initiates' is about to demonstrate, oratory is a lying power that leads to specious authority. *The Orators* enacts on a large scale the lies of verbal authority, which are capable of making 'worshippers' of a gullible people whose 'obedience [cries] for a master'.

The 'Prologue' itself, however, with its rippling mellifluousness, is far from 'oracular', and in this respect is significantly unlike D. H. Lawrence's highly strung, psychoanalytic treatise, *Fantasia of the Unconscious*, in which, nevertheless, Auden found much that affected his ideas about, and vocabulary of, the fall into knowledge and birth of consciousness.[13] *Fantasia* outlines a matrilineal version of the process of individuation. Consciousness in the individual comes with the growth of the 'idea of the mother': 'the figure of the mother' gradually develops 'as a conception in the child mind'. The cause of contemporary unhealthy 'self-consciousness, an intense consciousness', is an unnatural acceleration in this process. A child's sexual drives, aroused too early by the mother's possessiveness, can find no outlet, and 'this is how introversion begins'. The lineaments of this argument are clearly traceable in the 'Prologue'. Auden's hero, unable to take charge of his life and participate in sexual relationships, but nevertheless obsessed by sex and always 'ready to argue' and intellectualize it, is like Lawrence's introverted contemporary adolescent whose sensual and spiritual faculties get sundered, and who consequently suffers from 'sex in the head'. According to Lawrence, one symptom of this intense self-consciousness is masturbation, the complaint of the Airman, who, divining the enemy within himself, is acutely introverted (*Fantasia*, pp. 62, 105–16 *passim*).

But even as the 'Prologue' borrows Lawrence's thought, it mocks his strenuousness. The lines 'Under the trees the summer bands were playing; / "Dear boy, be brave as these roots"', he heard them saying' owe something, but not their suavity, to these sentences from *Fantasia*: 'A huge, plunging, tremendous soul. I would like to be a tree for a while. The great lust of roots. Root-lust. And no mind at all'. Auden's 'Dear boy' endearingly deflates Lawrence's egotistic oratory. Those tree-roots tap a dark world in *Fantasia*: 'The true German has something of the sap of trees in his veins even now: and a sort of pristine savageness, like trees, helpless, but most powerful, under all his mentality' (*Fantasia*, pp. 38, 39; and see Fuller, p. 54). If Auden was exorcizing the potential Nazi within himself, he would have sensed the incipient Nazism in Lawrence's psyche.

'We have brought you, they said, a map of the country' is another poem in the *paysage moralisé* mode. The sestina form, with its six repeated and re-patterned end-line words signalling encoded meaning, has a riddling air and cries out for allegorical interpretation. (Auden was to employ the form with increasing assurance throughout his career, notably in the poem 'Hearing of harvests rotting in the valleys', later titled 'Paysage Moralisé'.) The form stylizes the cryptic method of the whole of *The Orators* and epitomizes the quest of reader and Airman alike. The poem contradicts the desiderata at the opening of the Journal: 'Organisation owes nothing to the surveyor. It is in no sense prearranged. . . . The effect of the enemy is to introduce inert velocities into the system (called by him laws or habits) interfering with organisation'. The sort of organization provided by 'We have brought you, they said, a map of the country' owes everything 'to the surveyor' and its formal pattern is highly 'prearranged'. This is in keeping with the Audenesque preoccupation with 'mapped' experience, here deployed with a self-conscious poetic deliberation that mirrors the prescriptions of those who issue the 'map'. 'The heroic "He" is locked within a landscape donated by the false "They"' (Everett, p. 33). The poem contrasts the inherited view of experience, the territory where the elders 'lived for years', the mapped 'country' (with its 'inert velocities', its 'laws or habits'), with what happens when 'he arrived at last' in the territory itself, familiar but unknown, where he finds himself not acting according to plan.

The key to the poem's allegory, argues John Blair, is provided by the sentences which introduce it in the Journal: 'Of the enemy as philosopher. Talking of intellect-will-sensation as real and separate entities. The Oxford Don: "I don't feel quite happy about pleasure"'. 'The bay' corresponds to 'intellect', 'the clock' to 'will' and 'the wood' to 'sensation'.[14] The poem represents the attempt to integrate the three, to overcome the division between consciousness and being which, as we have seen Lawrence argue, bedevils the contemporary individual. In 'The Watershed' the wood (to which 'snatches of tramline' ran) conjured up the darknesses of the psyche. Here the forbidden wood in which the protagonist finally finds 'consummation' more surely asks to be decoded in this way, such is the effect of the formalized allegorical framework. Once again Auden seems to be reviewing his previous poetic self, bringing it into the conscious light of day.

'There are some birds in these valleys' is an equally composed poem. But, as with the 'Prologue', its 'intimate appeal' is sinisterly deceptive, in keeping with its theme of betrayal and duplicity. The persistent feminine line-endings, assonance, alliteration, the archly 'poetic' syntax ('By seeming kindness trained to snaring', 'They circle can serenely', 'Fingers on trigger tighten', 'Must smarting fall away from brightness'), all conspire to draw the reader in and seduce with suave phrasing and dying fall. We suspect we are being 'snared' by the poem's 'seeming' and 'tricky' effects: if we 'feel no falseness' at its sleights of hand, we ought to, it seems to say. The reader is in danger of being decoyed by the mannered art (the poem was later titled 'The Decoys'). The poem apprehends itself, moralizing its landscape too self-consciously. Even as Auden's poetry takes on a more formal air, it seems to warn us not to be overwhelmed by its poise. It is artful in both senses of the word.

5

The Odes likewise call attention to themselves, sometimes excessively. They parody a genre, for odes ought to be lofty and dignified, but these repeatedly drop from high to low within the space of a line or phrase. They have possibly attracted more bewildered and contradictory attention than any other work by Auden. Justin Replogle's argument is instructive. He takes the fifth Ode ('Though aware of our rank and alert to obey orders') as a 'notoriously unclear case' demonstrating one of 'the most striking features' of Auden's early work: to 'explode and collapse under pressure from the incompatible parts of Auden's temperament'. Replogle is anxious to distinguish what he calls Poet from Antipoet in Auden, the straight from the spoof. He is inclined to agree with Joseph Warren Beach that 'the speaker [of the fifth Ode] is not Auden, but one of the sick. Auden is outside the monologue, more knowing than the speaker, healthier, showing some contempt for him'. Beach wants Auden to be 'standing outside the poem laughing at the speaker's performance'. At the same time Replogle is worried by the uncertainty of all such readings: 'Apparently we are expected to discover, without external comment, that the speaker is unreliable, that the truth (or most of it) is the opposite of what he says. Yet his unreliability is so faint as to be scarcely discernible' (quoted from *Casebook*, pp. 113–14). This may be so if the Ode is read out of context. But in context its voice can be heard participating in the disorientation at the core of *The Orators*. On the other hand, must this distinction between Poet and Antipoet be insisted upon? It seems that the Odes were unique acts of composition, and that only after they were written did Auden intuit how they

fitted the larger work. As such, they do indeed reflect 'incompatible parts of Auden's temperament'. Tonally they refuse to be
pinned down. Their frequent mimicry of English public-school
lingo wavers between imitation and parody; ventriloquism slides
into ridicule. They give voice to that 'balancing subterfuge' which
is the subject of the poem 'Watch any day his nonchalant pauses,
see'. They 'Would drown the warning from the iron wood' with
their nonchalance. They mimic the knowing air in fear of the
unknown. Such effects are made possible by their forms, especially in Odes I, II, III and V, where the capacious stanzas can
accommodate long sentences that shift and change tack.

The first Ode is striking for its presentation of the poet *in
propria persona*. Beginning with what sounds like a parody of the
Audenesque panoramic view, it immediately throws the reader
into perspectival and syntactic confusion:

> Watching in three planes from a room overlooking the
>   courtyard
>   That year decaying,
> Stub-end of year that smoulders to ash of winter,
>   The last day dropping;
> Lo, a dream met me in middle night, I saw in a vision
> Life pass as a gull, as a spy, as a dog-hated dustman:
> Heard a voice saying – 'Wystan, Stephen, Christopher, all of
>   you,
>   Read of your losses'.

One suspects a take-off of the airman's vantage point in 'Consider
this' with its similarly uncertain perspective and shifting syntax,
an impression confirmed by the third line: the 'cigarette-end'
fleetingly homed in on at the start of 'Consider this' was only
hintingly metaphorical, but here it gets the full metaphorical
treatment, even to the 'dropping' of the ash from the 'stub-end of
year'. Seeing 'Life pass as a gull, as a spy, as a dog-hated
dustman' could be mockery of Auden's own diagnostic idiom.
The alliteration and the dream-vision framework owe something
to the medieval poet, William Langland, though with a poker-
faced air, for the words 'Lo, a dream met me in middle night'
jocularly misconstrue a line from the Prologue to *Piers Plowman*:
'Thanne gan I to meten a merueilouse sweuene' (Then I began

to dream a marvellous dream).[15] The portentously vague 'voice' sounds like a parody of the doom-laden voice of Auden's earlier poetry: like that one, this comes disembodied out of nowhere. In the earlier poetry it could sound truly commanding; when it utters again towards the end of this poem its 'command' turns, hilariously, into a cry for help: 'Save me!' The voice has lost its voice. At the same time the panoptic vision dwindles to a view from the sidelines, as the dream dissolves in bathos: 'I stood a spectator; / One tapped my shoulder and asked me "How did you fall, sir?" / Whereat I awakened'.

The host of voices in this poem is symptomatic of the Odes. Warnings framed by quotation marks mingle the portentous, the clichéd, the gnomic, the comic, the bathetic, to highly destabiliz-ing effect: night-nurse, 'We shall not all sleep, dearie'; Headmaster, 'Call no man happy'; Stephen [Spender], 'Destroy this temple'; Christopher [Isherwood], 'Man is a spirit'. The effect reinforces the tonal instability of the whole poem. How, for instance, does one 'say' the three-word sentence 'It did fall' at the start of the fifth stanza? Is it triumphant, bathetic, matter-of-fact, emphatic? Why or how is Africa 'superb'? The impatience detectable in Everett's description should not detract from its accuracy: 'The tone of the poem hovers between the heroic and the ridiculous; indeed, lines can hit a note which it is impossible to name with certainty as either' (Everett, p. 34).

'Yes, self-regarders', concludes the sixth stanza: the malaise of solipsism which infects all walks of society infects Auden's poetry, along with his set. 'Wystan, Stephen, Christopher, all of you, / Read of your losses': to be called to account in the chummy familiarity of Christian names is unsettling. The attempt to make the poem more generally applicable by later replacing these names with 'savers, payers, payees' runs counter to one of the poem's compelling impulses: to ridicule the Audenish impression of being in the know. 'Self-regard is the treating of news as a private poem' could be an epigraph to this Ode, which makes play of its cliquishness in a spoof re-enactment of *The Orators*' theme of the group in search of a leader. It makes private references with a nod and a wink. Spender as doom-watcher plainly turns ridiculous: 'Stephen signalled from the sand dunes like a wooden madman / "Destroy this temple"'. Does Isherwood suffer a similar fate? –

> And in cold Europe, in the middle of Autumn destruction,
> Christopher stood, his face grown lined with wincing
> In front of ignorance – 'Tell the English', he shivered,
>   'Man is a spirit'.

But even if Christopher's words sound like a faintly ridiculous *non-sequitur*, they preserve something of a high style. To collocate hospitalized Auden with the death of an influential figure behind *The Orators* runs the risk of treating news as a private poem:

> Shaped me a Lent scene first, a bed, hard, surgical,
>   And a wound hurting;
> The hour in the night when Lawrence died and I came
>   Round from the morphia.

Mendelson explains that 'Auden had suffered a real wound, an anal fissure, which was not in fact the result of sexual relations but which he explained psychosomatically to friends as "the Stigmata of Sodom"' (Mendelson, p. 111). As with many of the private references in *The Orators*, the reader feels teased into decoding while suspecting a vein of mockery. Alarming parallel and comic contrast between Auden's wound and Lawrence's death unsettlingly mingle.

The mixture of tones becomes even more audible towards the end of the poem. The seventh stanza moves uncomfortably from the scary to the farcical. 'I saw the brain-track perfected, laid for conveying / The fatal error': the consonantal scratch of 'brain-track perfected' chillingly renders perfection as death-wish. This is a not so fond tracing of family names. What Stan Smith calls 'the figure of oedipal anxiety, the castrating "father, / Cold with a razor"' (Smith, p. 63) is immediately followed by the deliberately silly line 'One sniffed at a root to make him dream of a woman'. It is not surprising that in the ensuing stanza the poet hesitates to step forward as leader. The 'healers' who do volunteer are parodic figures: 'granny in mittens, the Mop, the white surgeon'; and even John Layard, Auden's healer hero, is called 'loony'. But the beggar's voice, which enters the waking world at the end of the poem, outside the fantastical dream-vision, leaves the tonal whimsy behind, and in its address to 'the earth' – which at this late stage makes a powerfully enigmatic entry into the poem – reaches beyond Auden's private pantheon, the 'yelping' rabble of healers. Yet it solves nothing, reinforcing, rather, the ambiguity at the centre of *The Orators*, as the divergent critical reactions testify:

> 'Won't you speak louder?
> Have you heard of someone swifter than Syrian horses?
> Has he thrown the bully of Corinth in the sanded circle?
> Has he crossed the Isthmus already? Is he seeking brilliant
> Athens and us?'

Fuller interprets these words as welcoming social revolution; Mendelson senses threat behind them; Stan Smith writes that the beggar 'speaks of our deepest terror, that a conqueror is coming even now' (Fuller, p. 70; Mendelson, pp. 111–12; Smith, p. 63). The new conqueror could be either an even bigger bully than the Corinthian tyrant (this is Mendelson's view), or a true leader opposed to oppressive tyranny (Fuller's). The fact that the beggar speaks in questions allows for both possibilities. Are his words prophecy or riddle, prediction or conundrum? 'Deepest terror' certainly captures one feeling in the lines, but is there not deep longing also? The word 'seeking' calls up both emotions. And the last two lines, with their sibilants and 'Isthmus-us' echo, possess a strangely seductive music.

In the second Ode the spoof team-spirit replay of Hopkins makes for tonal quicksilver. Does the exclamation 'And how!' express emphasis or disbelief? Is there dubiety in 'conspire' in the lines 'Never did members conspire till now / In such whole gladness'? 'Currents of joy incalculable in ohms / Wind from the spine along the moving arms / Over the great alkali wastes of the bowel, calming them too': does this metaphorical medley represent high-spiritedness run riot, the poetic equivalent of adolescent exuberance? Or has deliberate over-writing crossed the boundary into bad writing? Is this electrical-cum-physiological landscape comically brilliant or hilariously bad? Such radical uncertainty in the first stanza prepares, or rather does not prepare, for the shifting tones of the rest of the Ode.

The erotic undercurrent, never far beneath the surface of this Ode ('members' in the first stanza implies limbs as well as club members), erupts in the ninth stanza:

> Heart of the heartless world
> Whose pulse we count upon;
> Alive, the live on which you have called
>   Both pro and con,
> Good to a gillie, to an elver times out of mind
> Tender, to work-shy and game-shy kind
> Does he think? Not as kind as all that; he shall find one fine
>   day he is sold.

'Religion is the sigh of the oppressed creature, the heart of a heartless world and the soul of soulless conditions. It is the opium of the people':[16] as Mendelson remarks, the phrase Auden takes from these famous sentences by Karl Marx has been 'rhetorically heightened from rigorous scepticism to theatrical exuberance' (Mendelson, p. 112). But the exuberance teeters on the edge of the absurd, with its exaggeratedly Hopkins-esque contortions, its self-conscious diction ('gillie', 'elver'), its jostling of the clichéd with the elevated. The poetry prompts questions about its seriousness, even as it seems to be promoting an alternative to Marx's view of a religion born out of despair. Yet when the next stanza makes fun of Hopkins's God, his 'sir', it breaks through to a convincingly exuberant, and erotic, rhetoric: 'Now about these boys as keen as mustard to grow / Give you leave for that, sir, well in them, flow, / Deep in their wheel-pits may they know you foaming and feel you warm'. Can Marx be made to square with a Lawrentian erotic life-force? The poem seems to want this, and yet it casts doubt. When John Cornford, who was killed in Spain in 1936 fighting for the Republicans, began a love poem written during the Civil War with that phrase by Marx, 'Heart of the heartless world', he gave it an intimate context that owed something to Auden's example, but with an appealing gravity that ignored the elder poet's horseplay – an ironic testimony to Auden's massive influence.

The whole of the third Ode 'hit[s] a note which it is impossible to name' (Everett, p. 34). Style, speaker, participants, location, situation are thoroughly undefinable. The two initial alliterated long lines in each stanza accommodate diverse tones: from the exuberantly schoolboy-epic ('What siren zooming is sounding our coming / Up frozen fjord forging from freedom'), the jovially chummy ('With labelled luggage we alight at last / Joining joking at the junction on the moor'), and the jingly expectant

('Picnics are promised and planned for July / To the wood with
the waterfall, walks to find'), to the forlornness of exile reminiscent of the Anglo-Saxon poems 'The Wanderer' and 'The
Seafarer' ('This life is to last, when we leave we leave all, /
Though vows have no virtue, though voice is in vain'), and hope
declining ('Watching through windows the wastes of evening, /
The flare of foundries at fall of the year'). The poem can be
regarded as an extended metaphor that 'describes life in terms of
arrival at a seaside hotel, barracks, school or sanatorium'
(Fuller, p. 70), but one soon relinquishes any attempt to pin the
poem down. What registers is the host of Audenish motifs, held
together by the relentlessly seductive wizardry of the half-rhyme.
'Freedom' is played off against 'exile' in a way familiar from
earlier poems: escape may represent imprisonment in self. 'The
junction on the moor' conjures up watersheds of decision. Past
battles and future feuds, hemming one in, offering challenges,
hover in the wings: 'Each new recruit', a 'fort for sale', 'Shut in
by wires / Surplus from wars', 'the blistered paint / On the
scorching front' (is this, fleetingly, a battle-front?). There are the
panoramic vantage-point, a coast to be scanned ('To climb the
cliff path to the coastguard's point'), comatose industry ('the
derelict dock deserted by rats'), mysterious messengers from a
world beyond ('then riders pass / Some afternoons'), a 'border'
which is 'for blooming of bulbs', but which of course conjures up
a frontier.

Mid-poem there is an uncanny change. Does the poetry
merely toy with the sinister? 'These grounds are for good': is this
flippantly or sinisterly ironic? Does the line 'This life is to last,
when we leave we leave all' hint at death, or doesn't it? 'In
groups forgetting the gun in the drawer' conjures up suicide in
cinema-cliché. And what, for instance, is the tone of 'We live like
ghouls / On posts from girls'? The poem seems to put its despair
into perspective:

> The slight despair
> At what we are,
> The marginal grief
> Is source of life.

'Marginal' is fascinatingly elusive, both confirming and denying
'slight': grief takes one close to the edge, but if this retreat is

turning into a mental asylum, it is also taking the occupants closer to the 'source'. But then again the line 'Is source of life' sounds duplicitous: 'goes deep' and/or 'is all we have to show for our shallow life'. This poetry is poised between insouciance and break-down. It has an unnerving way of 'Saying Alas / To less and less'. 'And nerves grow numb between north and south': the dying cadences of the short-line passages register emotional numbness and tight-lipped resignation with uncanny precision. 'Though we only master / The sad posture': the metre masters the sadness with a tactful art that acknowledges the need to maintain a 'posture' in the face of encroaching decline – and the pun in 'master' (the poem is dedicated to a schoolmaster) itself demonstrates such tact. The concluding lines maintain a posture:

> Hear last in corner
> The pffwungg of burner
> Accepting dearth
> The shadow of death.

The revision of the first two lines here to 'Grown used at last / To having lost' damagingly neutralizes a masterly comical-sinister note. The wry verbal life in the guttering decline of the original version mirrors the poem's stoical posture. If this Ode enacts a retreat from the grand Audenesque, the group ideology, the frontier mentality, the schoolboy heroics and hocus-pocus, it does so with fine quizzicalness. To quote the poem, it is 'peering through glasses' at Auden's 'own glosses' on life.

The third Ode quizzes the idea of the group, the fourth that of the leader. In his 1966 Preface Auden wrote of the fourth Ode: 'I express all the sentiments with which his followers hailed the advent of Hitler, but these are rendered, I hope, innocuous by the fact that the Führer so hailed is a new-born baby and the son of a friend'. The 'I hope' indicates, once again, Auden's only partial insight into his younger self. Most readers probably feel a similar hope, which means they also feel the need to deny that the poem makes fascism sound possibly attractive. Parody of the leadership theme is implicit in the Ode's highfalutin doggerel. The speaker pooh-poohs low and high, 'our proletariat' and 'our upper class', the whole set of present leaders including Mussolini, 'the ninny', and Hitler, 'the false alarm' (Fuller, p. 71, reminds us that the latter did not come to power until January 1933), a host of left- and right-wing social and political movements, as well as writers of the older generation. The indiscriminate laying about (MacNeice was to achieve a similar effect by different means and with far greater finesse in 'Bagpipe Music') renders the speaker attractively unreliable, in keeping with the comically hyperbolic praise of the infant John Warner (son of Auden's Oxford friend, novelist and poet Rex Warner), who is hailed not only as the conquering hero ('At every corner / News of Warner, / His march on London, / His enemies undone'), but also as the healer of social and psychological ills.

In this context it is difficult to take seriously, as some readers have done, the vision of society under Warner's future leadership:[17]

> See him [Warner] take off his coat and get down with a
>   spanner
> To each unhappy Joseph and repressed Diana, . . .
> The few shall be taught who want to understand,
> Most of the rest shall live upon the land;
> Living in one place with a satisfied face
> All of the women and most of the men
> Shall work with their hands and not think again.

As Mendelson remarks, this 'imaginary new order will display the primitive fascistic virtues Lawrence demanded in his *Fantasia*' (Mendelson, p. 114). As part of the knockabout encomium to the infant saviour, the Ode's hierarchical society comes over as a parodic version of this sort of vision in *Fantasia*: 'For the mass of people, knowledge *must* be symbolical, mythical, dynamic. This means, you must have a higher, responsible, conscious class: and then in varying degrees the lower classes, varying in their degree of consciousness'. Or later in *Fantasia*: 'At all cost, try to prevent a girl's mind from dwelling on herself. Make her act, work, play. . . . Anything to keep her busy, to prevent her reading and becoming self-conscious'. 'Leaders – this is what mankind is craving for', chants Lawrence in *Fantasia*; and the fourth Ode comes up with its spoof leader who instils, not loyalty, but smugness, the 'satisfied face' (*Fantasia*, pp. 68, 77–8, 78). But the mockery in Auden's version encompasses self-mockery; again the poet is exorcizing the Lawrence within

himself. Though he wanted to come to terms with what, writing
eight years later in an essay about Lawrence and education, he
saw as the basic Lawrentian tenet that 'Man fell when he
became self-conscious', he early on, so the indirections of *The
Orators* imply, felt apprehensive about the naively retrogressive
use to which Lawrence's ideas could be put. In that essay Auden
enunciates what *The Orators* seems to have been struggling to
articulate: 'the fact that the Fascist countries appear on the
surface to be putting [Lawrence's] theories into practice makes
their study extremely important to socialists'. In particular, the
essay takes issue with the sort of practical application of Lawrence's ideas gestured at in the lines quoted above: 'As a matter
of observation it is true that book-learning has a bad effect on
many people, and that manual work is viewed with horror. But it
is not true to say: 1. That you know that mental activity *must
always* be only suited to a few. 2. That you know who they are.'
(*Education To-day – and To-morrow, EA*, p. 385). One impulse
behind the fourth Ode may indeed have been to declare a Utopia
of manual labour, but the formula 'Shall work with their hands
and not think again' holds the impulse in check by means of its
ironically self-satisfied air.

Yet quite how far *The Orators* undermines Auden's Lawrentian vision – how far it has been exorcized – is impossible to tell.
In the fourth Ode's final verse-paragraph, immediately after the
lines quoted above, the poetry modulates into something more
evocative. For all the implausibility of the new life with its
'change of heart', its 'final keeping of the ever-broken vow' and
whatever is meant by 'The official re-marriage of the whole and
part', the concluding lines captivatingly move into what Fuller
calls an 'observed lyrical moment' (Fuller, p. 73):

> Falcon is poised over fell in the cool,
> Salmon draws
> Its lovely quarrons through the pool.
> A birthday, a birth
> On English earth
> Restores, restore will, has restored
> To England's story
> The directed calm, the actual glory.

The lines about the falcon and salmon, with their open vowels
and captivating diction ('quarrons' is an obsolete and rare word

for the body), conjure up a pristine natural harmony. Yet the impression that the lines are too obviously working for an effect is confirmed by the line 'Restores, restore will, has restored', where the syntactic archness looks forward to the contortions of the sixth Ode, a spoof hymn. And yet, again, the 'directed calm' of the last line comes over with powerful conviction as the poetry feels its way towards the compelling last phrase 'the actual glory'. The phrase 'directed calm' wants to reconcile spontaneous tranquillity with the notion of organization and leadership; 'actual glory' to reconcile the real with the ideal. Out of the fourth Ode's double-talk emerges a frustrated Utopianism that recognizes itself as such. It is significant that, though the 'earth' is invoked, as it is at the end of the first Ode, the restoration happens not to England, but 'To England's story', which is an equivocal wish-fulfilment.

The fourth Ode equivocates about leadership, the fifth about the led. Lawrence's declaration that 'men must be prepared to obey, body and soul, once they have chosen the leader' sounds like the point of departure: 'Though aware of our rank and alert to obey orders' (*Fantasia*, p. 79). The title 'Which Side am I Supposed to be On?', which Auden gave the poem in the 1940s, is an ironically superior comment on his earlier self, as if irony were not already present in the poem, and as if the poetic intelligence behind it was unaware of what it was up to. But self-awareness does not necessarily entail clearsightedness. Auden's title highlights what Mendelson calls the 'divided psyche' of the poem, but at the expense of the ambiguity, even confusion, which is essential to its divided nature (Mendelson, p. 115). The poem's doubleness can be felt early on, before it is revealed more openly half way through. It is tempting to speculate about the Ode's ambiguous setting, both school and barracks, but the very concept of a setting is beside the point. The poem's stage is the Audenesque, and it is filled with familiar properties, scenery and obsessions.

The poem begins on a note of false security, the tone of one who thinks he knows it all, cock-sure, blasé: even 'The youngest drummer / Knows all the peace-time stories like the oldest soldier'. The schoolboy idiom gives off a strong whiff of clichéd Auden: 'The pistol cocked, the code-word committed to memory'. The phrase 'Though frontier-conscious' betrays anxiety beneath its insouciant surface; it has a knowingness that hints at fear of the

unknown. The apparently secure tone of the opening is under-
mined by a wavering, uncertain syntax. The subordinate clause
at the start ('Though aware . . .') appears not to be resolved by
any main clause ('The youngest drummer / Knows' is a flickering, but awkward and unlikely, possibility). 'Though' in the
sixth line picks up the poem's first word, thus prolonging the
anticipation of a syntactic resolution. But no resolution comes
before the full-stop at the end of the second stanza, and
anticipation dissolves in a vague sense of unease and insecurity.
Insecurity is the feeling generated by the 'frontier-conscious'
second stanza, about which Fuller writes: 'the schoolmasters
[are] merely veteran pupils perpetuating the legends and secrecy
which maintain morale in their conflict against the "They" who
operate beyond the frontier' (Fuller, p. 73). Again one suspects
that this authoritative Auden is too automatic, that the pseudo-
precise definite article is beginning to sound glib through
repetition: 'the tall white gods', 'the working of copper', 'the
islands', 'the maned lion'. The 'open wishing-well' has a fairy-tale
aura which reinforces the sense that the stanza is all a tall tale.

Thus when the third stanza begins 'Perfectly certain, all of us',
on the contrary nothing is certain: the voice is mimicking the
false security of the poem's opening. That phrase's idiomatic
complacency is then disturbed by rumours, 'not from the
records', of activity beyond the frontier, the threatening and
repressed unknown, the enemy within, 'who returned to the
camp' and whom we don't want to acknowledge. But spoof
Auden is more than intermittently audible in these rumourings:
in 'the unshaven agent' who, 'clutching his side collapsed at our
feet' and says in camped-up English stiff-upper-lip style, 'Sorry!
They got me!'; in 'At night your mother taught you to pray for
our Daddy / Far away fighting'; and in lines such as these, where
Homeric bravado mingles with the schoolboy variety: 'To stand
with the wine-dark conquerors in the roped-off pews, / Shout
ourselves hoarse: / "They ran like hares; we have broken them
up like firewood"'. But the take-off of familiar obsessions –
feud, inherited antagonism, inculcated patterns of behaviour –
mingles with lines that move beyond the schoolboy idiom and
ask to be taken 'straight':

> Yes, they were living here once but do not now,
> Yes, they are living still but do not here . . .

Turning over he closes his eyes, and then in a moment
Sees the sun at midnight bright over cornfield and pasture . . .

Your childish moments of awareness were all of our world . . .

This Ode demonstrates to a marked degree how in *The Orators*
Poet and Antipoet, in Replogle's terms, go hand in hand. Its
long sentences move so rapidly between registers that any
attempt to locate a fixed position or persona is bound to fail. It
voices intonationally what becomes explicit at the tenth stanza.
This is Mendelson's helpful explanation of the poem thereafter:
'we . . . resemble the Airman in that our own division causes the
war we endure. Our fear of the other side is what gives the
enemy their strength. We "have made from Fear" their laconic
captain, and their avenging forces are our own repressed impulses transformed into seven deadly sins. . . . Our internal
barrier is too hidden and too dangerous for us to understand:
"They speak of things done on the frontier we were never told."
. . . We shall never be parted from our wound, we exist because
of our own conflicts' (Mendelson, p. 114). The divided psyche
which thus becomes the poem's focus makes itself evident, in this
poem and in much of Auden's early poetry, in a stylistic
doubleness. The poetry is self-reflexively 'frontier-*conscious*'
(emphasis added), which makes for an unstable register that
continually undermines itself. Even at the point where the poem
penetrates deepest behind the lines of the psyche, it cannot resist
the schoolboy risibility of 'squat Pictish tower' and 'Death to the
squealer'.

The enemy within 'are brave, yes, though our newspapers
mention their bravery / In inverted commas'; and the poetry
itself teems with inverted commas, visible and invisible. The
high incidence of directly quoted speech (there are eleven
instances) reinforces the sense of intonational quotation marks
throughout. The landscape of psychological impasse in the last
four stanzas glistens with refurbished cliché, with verbal cliché
and clichéd topoi: 'Passports are issued no longer', 'In a quiet
sector they walked about on the skyline, / Exchanged cigarettes,
both learning the words for "I love you" / In either language',
'Try it and see', 'you may shoot without warning'. In this
context the poem's last line is uncanny. Whether or not it
contains a (telling) pun, the statement 'We shall lie out there' is

not clichéd, and yet it has the ring of the familiar. It gains power from its monosyllabic ordinariness, its flat refusal to inflect a voice or bandy a tone. If it speaks of death it does so in an undertone, which is a triumph after all the gestural language that has preceded. It makes 'defeat' sound 'necessary'.

The final Ode prays, tongue-in-cheek, for 'Our necessary defeat', presumably as one way out of the cul-de-sac in which *The Orators* finds itself at its conclusion. Behind 'necessary' is perhaps the double implication of 'needed' (to effect a cure) and 'inevitable', but if so the Ode merely toys with a doubleness that will become more weighty in Auden's poem 'Spain', in the line 'The conscious acceptance of guilt in the necessary murder'. Replogle argues that in this Ode Auden's 'Poet steps across the border between high dignity and comic pomposity, and decorum is broken' (quoted from Casebook, p. 115). But decorum is something we have learned to do without long before this in *The Orators*, and the arresting discomfiture of the Ode reinforces the way in which the whole work subverts any such expectations. As a schoolboy parody of the quaint diction and syntax of the metrical renditions of the psalms, the Ode enacts a 'defeat' of language even as it prays for enlightenment: rather than 'illumine' it obfuscates. Mystification is of its essence. We are thrown at the start: is the 'Father, further' chime absurd? 'The numbing zero-hour' mingles stark fear with a strong whiff of the schoolboy heroics of the 'siren zooming' variety. 'Regardant' is so high-flown it stalls. 'Stubborn and oblique' sounds intelligent, but on inspection turns out to be jabberwocky, as does the contorted syntax of 'Our maddened set we foot', which sounds like an inversion of 'We set our maddened foot' but is not, in spite of this later revision. 'These nissen huts if hiding could / Your eye inseeing from / Firm fenders were' is only untanglable if 'could' is not an auxiliary verb. 'Your loosened angers' is an undeniably brilliant phrase for God's thunderbolts – if that is what it is. The circumlocution of 'Be not another than our hope' is comically pointless. 'Expect we routed shall / Upon your peace' awkwardly requires 'be' to be supplied from the previous line. In the light of all these inappropriate devices, 'disarm' in the penultimate line is a surprisingly appropriate pun that picks up the thread of military metaphors running through the poem. The ham-fisted style of this Ode is sustained with disarming skilfulness. It is a self-preening performance. Stylistically it suffers acutely from the Airman's complaint, self-regard, and is the poetic equivalent of his end, his 'airy sacrifice', as this Ode puts it. The poem commits a stylish suicide.

The 'Epilogue' is stylish too, but not self-destructively so. If the sixth Ode strangles the hymn, the 'Epilogue' breathes new life into the ballad. The ridiculous sound-patterns of the 'Father, further' variety are transformed into a compelling music of full rhyme, internal pararhyme and alliteration. The sixth Ode relies heavily on a reader's sense that it is written by an extremely knowing, and not merely incompetent, writer. The 'Epilogue' acknowledges the limits of such self-reflexivity, with the text of *The Orators* perpetually going beyond the reader's ken: ' "O where are you going?" said reader to rider'.[18] If the sixth Ode offers defeat, and the defeat of language, as one way out, the 'Epilogue' offers escape, and escape into a new idiom: 'As he left them there, as he left them there'. Mendelson writes that the 'Epilogue' is 'a memorable ending, but an empty one' (Mendelson, p. 115). But memorability is its essential quality. In enacting an escape, it has rescued from the vocal mêlée of *The Orators* a style that looks forward to Auden's more composed later poetry.

5
Spender (2)
'To will this Time's change'

1

'They were extremely non-political with half of themselves and extremely political with the other half' ('Background to the Thirties', in *The Thirties and After*, p. 18). Is Spender's judgement about the poets of the thirties relevant to his own work? This chapter attempts an answer; it begins by considering some of the more overtly political or programmatic pieces in *Poems*, 1933; it then briefly discusses *Vienna* (a long poem about the suppression of the Austrian socialist uprising in February 1934, the year the poem was published) and *Trial of a Judge* (a poetic drama published in 1938); finally, it looks at *The Still Centre* (Spender's last collection of the decade, published in 1939). Among other things, this last collection contains Spender's most important poems about the Spanish Civil War, poems considered in Chapter 8.

Spender's dealings with politics and history in *Poems* might be approached through a piece of contemporary critical writing by C. Day Lewis, whose critical study, *A Hope for Poetry*, was published in 1934, the same year as the second edition of *Poems*. In *A Hope for Poetry* Day Lewis describes the dilemmas facing the modern poet, 'acutely conscious of the present isolation of the individual and the necessity for a social organism which may restore communion' (quoted in Casebook, p. 36). Employing the central image of 'The Conflict', his most revealing (and arguably most satisfying) poem of the thirties, Day Lewis says of the poet:

116

'Standing as a man between two worlds, he stands as a poet between two fires' (Casebook, p. 37). In 'The Conflict', Day Lewis writes 'As one between two massing powers I live', and it is for the honesty with which he defines his position rather than his final injunction to 'Move . . . with new desires' that the poem has value. The poem concludes, 'For where we used to build and love / Is no man's land, and only ghosts can live / Between two fires', yet the admonition to support 'The red advance of life' carries less conviction than the poet's quieter recognition that he does, indeed, 'live / Between two fires'.[1] Similarly, *A Hope for Poetry* cites approvingly Yeats's famous remark: 'We make out of the quarrel with others rhetoric, but of the quarrel with ourselves, poetry' (quoted in Casebook, p. 39). But Day Lewis then shifts ground to argue that what matters is that 'the writer has emotionally experienced a political situation and assimilated it through his specific function into the substance of poetry' (Owen is referred to as 'the real ancestor' and Spender's 'In railway halls' praised as a poem which 'suggests the lines on which . . . writers must work for the present' (Casebook, p. 40)).

Day Lewis's grasp, then, of the problems faced by the modern poet sheds sidelong illumination on the conflicts visible in Spender's work. It also suggests the individual way Spender conceived of and presented these conflicts. His prose and poetry are more searching and more surprising than Day Lewis's. Certainly the more overtly political texts in *Poems* are rarely uncomplicated. The attempt to glorify a Stakhanovite ethos in 'The Funeral' (*SP33*; included in *CPS(1)*) seems wholehearted enough: 'Death is another milestone on their way', the poem begins; the dead man's comrades 'record simply / How this one excelled all others in making driving belts'. Yet Spender's poem is sophisticated. A clue to the poem's nature is the word 'simply': the poem is a version of pastoral, celebrating a simplicity in which the usual complications of existence drop away. Spender's language responds to the challenge, adroitly turning 'bourgeois' assumptions on their head:

> This is festivity, it is the time of statistics
> When they record what one unit contributed:
> They are glad as they lay him back in the earth
> And thank him for what he gave them.

Spender's tone is playfully solemn; a kind of serious fun moti-
vates the diction. 'It is the time of . . .' is a phrase one expects to
be rounded off with something grander than 'statistics'; the
poem works by serenely ignoring (while challenging) such
expectations. That is to say, Spender knows what his words are
doing; he is not merely mouthing catchphrases. Admiration for
the supposed collectivist idyll is apparent, but the impact of the
poem has to do with the author's and audience's cultural
distance from a world in which a life can be regarded as 'one
unit'. 'The Funeral' imagines a Utopia which is no less remote
for being approved, even though the poem behaves as though
remoteness belonged to the individualist culture to which Spender himself belongs. The sub-text (though not overt meaning) of
the final stanza is that individualism is hard to banish:

> No more are they haunted by the individual grief
> Nor the crocodile tears of European genius,
> The decline of a culture
> Mourned by scholars who dream of the ghosts of
> Greek boys.

'They' may not be haunted by the individual grief; but the
cadencing of the line suggests that the poet could easily be
seduced by such grief (one remembers the 'haunting' experienced at the end of 'Moving through the silent crowd'). *Poems*,
1933, as a whole subverts Spender's subversion in this poem of
his 'culture': 'European genius' is praised in two of the collection's strongest pieces ('Beethoven's Death Mask' and 'I think
continually of those who were truly great'). The reference to
'scholars who dream of the ghosts of Greek boys' scores a
palpable satiric hit, and yet the line also lingers sympathetically.
That the mourning scholars are given the poem's last word
might be seen as betraying the poet's uncertainty about the ideal
to which the rest of the poem is committed. Yet the poem is a
more controlled performance than such a reading suggests. This
control is shown by the way Spender manipulates both idioms:
the collectivist pastoral of the first four stanzas and what might
be called the individualist pastoral of the final stanza. The
former, dominant idiom is characterized by a buoyant, declarative confidence ('They speak of the world state', 'They think how
one life hums, revolves and toils'); the latter is nostalgic,

regressive and haunting, its syntax noticeably more dragging and self-qualifying.

'The Funeral', then, attests to inner division, but it does so with some stylishness and without fissuring helplessly. Its Utopian strain contrasts interestingly with the element of level-eyed realism about history in 'In 1929' (*SP33*; included in *CPS(1)*, *SPS* and *CPS(2)*). 'In 1929' celebrates peace as an impermanent respite from conflict: twelve years ago the 'new, bronzed German' and 'myself, being English' would have been at war, while in ten years time 'The communist clerk', the poem predicts, 'Builds with red hands his heaven; makes our bones / The necessary scaffolding to peace'. This latter conflict is glossed by Paul, Spender's surrogate in *The Temple* (that 'complex of memory, fiction and hindsight' (*T*, p. xii)), as 'a world revolution' (*T*, p. 152), and the poem's ambiguous acceptance of this prospect shows in the wording. The clerk's hands are 'red' with commitment but also blood, the 'heaven' is 'his', not ours, and our destruction is a 'necessary' stage before 'peace': 'necessary', there, is wryly conscious rather than rhapsodic in its nod towards Marxist dialectic.

Sonorous and opaque, explicit and terse, 'In 1929' is full of contesting suggestions. Its title tethers it to a specific moment when 'A whim of Time, the general arbiter, / Proclaims the love instead of death of friends'. The alertness to the chancy nature of 'Time' saves this opening generalization from portentousness: 'Proclaims' is both confident and conceivably hollow (that is, time's whims make it possible to conceive of a time when an opposite proclamation would have equal authority). In his Introduction to *The Temple* Spender uses 'hindsight' to spell out what is implicit in the poem: that is, a sense of 1929 as a time of precarious peace, 'the last, because pre-Hitler, summer' (*T*, p. xiii). And just as in the novel there is 'some sense of terrible events to come' (*T*, p. xi), so in the poem shadows make themselves felt even as their seeming absence is affirmed. 'The once-envious dead', the poet supposes, 'haunt us no longer'; 'Our fathers killed. And yet there lives no feud'; 'There falls no shade across our blank of peace' – these assertions seem troubled by the haunting, feud and shade they exorcize. 'Blank of peace', for instance, is curiously neutral, as though such peace were a vacuum, not quite believable.

When Spender goes on to articulate 'a philosophy' the poem

holds its meanings close to its chest: arguably a sign of its uncertainty about whether to emphasize the positive or negative aspects of its vision of history. So far as the section can be unravelled it appears to declare that any long view of history induces a sense of mankind's futility ('lipping skulls on the revolving rim') redeemed only by 'the posture of genius with the granite head bowed'. The lines clarify somewhat (are more clearly pessimistic) in their most recently revised form (*CPS(2)*). Yet the original version keeps its options open; the 'philosophy', after all, may not be that of the poet but his sense of what has been bequeathed by 'Our fathers' misery, the dead man's mercy, / The cynic's mystery'.

The poem is not fatally damaged by its refusal to choose between alternatives; indeed, its fine close is founded on such a refusal. It asserts that 'Lives risen a moment', whether 'Joined or separate', are, in the end, 'always separate'. Yet if the conclusion reinforces the feeling, derived from the poem's opening, that the lives of the three friends have come together only for 'a moment', it also challenges the pessimism promoted by geological or anthropological perspectives. These lives, and all they have experienced, form 'A stratum unreckoned by geologists'; their unavailability to later enquiry does not invalidate their import-ance. At least such is one, quite possible, interpretation; another reading, laying stress on the insistently physical last line, 'Sod lifted, turned, slapped back again with spade', might veer in a less hopeful direction. 'In 1929' is balanced between formal and thematic antitheses – eloquence and inelegance, hope and wari-ness, the clear and the unfathomable – and, though it may not fully answer the questions it arouses, it is a signal example of Spender's ability to delve more deeply as a poem unfolds.

In 'The Express' (*SP33*; included in *CPS(1)*, *SPS* and *CPS(2)*) Spender's achievement is to find a subject which works in its own terms while serving as a vehicle for more allegorical implications. By way of the word 'manifesto' the express is linked with revolutionary energy in the opening line: 'After the first powerful plain manifesto'. The poem memorably develops this link in what follows. After the first powerful plain manifesto what ensues is very far from 'plain' in any straightforwardly propagandist way.

The reader is struck, rather, by the relish with which the poem moves towards and holds at bay a point-by-point comparison between train and revolution. In the lines, 'She passes the houses which humbly crowd outside, / The gasworks and at last the heavy page / Of death, printed by gravestones in the cemetery', Spender does more than describe accurately the experience of leaving the station. His metaphors bring into play other associations: the houses, 'humbly' crowding round the 'queen'-like train, suggest courtiers, an association extravagantly at odds, yet ultimately compatible, with the half-shaping notion of the train as revolution (compatible because the new order is endowed with the majesty and authority of the old); the train is leaving behind 'the heavy page / Of death', suggesting both that it is journeying towards new life and, more self-reflexively, that it embodies or prefigures a new style of writing such as this poem manifests. This last suggestion is picked up later in the poem where Spender writes: 'And always light, aerial, underneath / Goes the elate metre of her wheels'. The phrasing here encourages the reader to take 'lines' in the next line, 'Steaming through metal landscape on her lines', as a further example of a self-awareness which contributes to the poem's exuberant immediacy (which in this instance implies that what is desired can be experienced now).

As the poem develops, its non-literal meanings emerge more clearly: the train 'plunges new eras of wild happiness' and the poem's Utopian momentum takes it 'Beyond the crest of the world'. The ending, however, returns to the world through a verbal arrangement favoured by Spender in other poems (such as 'The Pylons'). In this arrangement, the old order's merits are brought to mind even as the poem seeks to supersede them:

> Ah, like a comet through flame she moves entranced
> Wrapt in her music no bird song, no, nor bough
> Breaking with honey buds, shall ever equal.

These lines both vindicate their implicit claim to be offering a new 'music' and evoke the natural beauty explicitly rated as inferior. In fact, the newness of Spender's music has much to do with the adaptation of traditional lyrical devices – especially exclamation and hyperbole – to unfamiliar material. To the benefit of his poem Spender's wording in 'no bird song, no, nor bough' protests too much; it invites the reader to question rather than accept. As in 'At the end of two months' holiday' Spender

pits technology against nature, as though technology represented the politically (and poetically) progressive and nature the
politically (and poetically) conservative; in other poems, such as
'I think continually of those who were truly great' where the
truly great 'hoarded from the Spring branches / The desires
falling across their bodies like blossoms', natural images serve
progressive ends. In both cases what counts imaginatively is the
lyrical impact of Spender's use of natural imagery, its refusal to
serve a didactic purpose in any dutiful way. This may complicate, as it does at the end of 'The Express', where the reader
instinctively sides with the 'bough / Breaking with honey buds',
but it does not damage. Partly this is because 'like a comet
through flame', remodelling the hackneyed 'flaming like a comet',
ensures that the train is allied to, as well as contrasted with,
natural phenomena. The close of 'The Express' reaches towards
an ideal of synthesis between the new and the traditional. It does
so almost, but not wholly, despite itself.

2

Another well-known anthology piece from *Poems*, 1933, 'The
Landscape near an Aerodrome' (included in *CPS(1)*, *SPS* and
CPS(2)), is more riven by inner conflict. The result is a fascinating if troubled piece of writing. Whereas 'The Express' uses its
train to represent Utopian change, things as they might or
should be, 'The Landscape near an Aerodrome' uses its plane to
allow an overview of things as they are. Though placed immediately after 'The Express', the poem differs from it in mood and
has more in common – on a first reading – with the diagnostic
Auden of 'Consider this and in our time'. As the travellers in the
plane descend, the second stanza concludes, 'they may see what
is being done', and the attempt to 'see what is being done' helps
to propel the poem.

   That said, the opening picks up where 'The Express' left off,
the man-made machine being compared favourably to the
natural world. The plane is 'More beautiful and soft than any
moth / With burring furred antennae feeling its huge path /
Through dusk'. These lines 'feel' their path from word to word
and sound to sound with massive yet delicate assurance. The
generous syntax allows the second line to be read as applying

either to the 'air-liner with shut-off engines' of line three or to the 'moth' with which the plane is compared in line one. In fact, moth and plane coalesce in the adjectival pairing of 'burring furred'. Yet the lines are complex in a way that differs from the complexity of the previous poem's conclusion. 'The Express' may rouse the reader's protest on behalf of 'bird song' and 'bough / Breaking with honey buds', but it clearly proclaims the beauty of the train; 'The Landscape near an Aerodrome' is less programmatic in its coupling of technology and nature. The reader responds to its opening effect, but is left to wonder what purpose it serves. Is Spender asking for admiration of the plane as an emblem of some improved future? Or does the rest of the poem question the initial admiration for an emblem of affluent living subsidized by oppression and hardship, emblematized in turn by the landscape around the aerodrome?

These and other questions are legitimate yet fail to unriddle a surprisingly enigmatic poem. The poem is frequently criticized for the polemical note it finishes on, directing the reader to where 'Religion stands, the church blocking the sun'. And there is no disputing Spender's animus against institutionalized religion, or the opportunist way the imagery is manipulated to express it. But 'The Landscape near an Aerodrome' is a poem that never fully resolves itself into paraphrasable statement (despite Spender's own efforts in the concluding lines). Its metaphors and verbal designs pursue their own ends in ways that keep open a number of possible responses and meanings, and allow the poem to explore itself in the act of exploring an environment.

Two examples of this are the poem's use of sexual imagery and the vocabulary it employs for acts of observation. The sexual imagery is intermittent, insinuating, eddying. In the second stanza the travellers' 'watching' is provoked by 'feminine land indulging its easy limbs'; their eyes 'Penetrate through dusk the outskirts of this town', as though the travellers were at once lovers and voyeurs of the feminine land.

To 'see what is being done' (and here Spender's difference from the Auden of 'Consider this and in our time' makes itself felt) involves, in this poem, pleasure and guilt. The politicized observer's penetrating gaze is desired by Spender, yet there is the suggestion, too, that it is made possible by the travellers' aloofness. Here the point about the wording used for acts of observation is pertinent. The travellers owe something to

Auden's hawk or helmeted airman. At the same time they almost parody Audenesque detachment. In the third stanza 'they *observe* the outposts / Of work' and '*remark* the unhomely sense of complaint' (emphases added), both verbs capturing a condition of apartness which is itself 'unhomely'. By way of 'remark' Spender suggests, albeit briefly, the 'peculiar horror' (*DE*, p. 135) of Eliot's vision in 'Rhapsody on a Windy Night' (compare the lines, 'Half-past two, / The street-lamp said, / "Remark the cat which flattens itself in the gutter"'). The travellers have an ambiguous relationship with Spender, embodying his divided view of individualism. On the one hand, they have the freedom and vision of mental travellers who 'may see what is being done' (where 'may' itself is not free from the implication of possible indifference). On the other hand, their position with regard to the society they observe is equivocal. It seems an irony that the plane's coming in to land is described as 'the last sweep of love': the climax of the coupling between disengaged observer and exploited landscape is not fulfilment but the discovery of 'hysteria'.

Indeed, one reason for the poem's power is the split between the language of detached observation (used of the 'travellers') and the language of 'hysteria'. This language enters the poem overtly in the third stanza with its startling, Expressionist comparisons that beg the question, 'Who is making these comparisons, Spender or the travellers?':

> chimneys like lank blank
>   fingers
> Or figures frightening and mad: and squat
>   buildings
> With their strange air behind trees, like women's
>   faces
> Shattered by grief.

The short answer is 'Both'. These lines are governed by 'they observe', but what 'they' observe is filtered through the poet's consciousness. The point is worth attention because it helps to explain why the lines just quoted retain control despite depicting chaos. The lines still have the feel and movement of detachment, but the highly wrought comparisons concede their lack of interest in 'objective' description. The writing seeks to lay bare a psychic landscape, as though such a landscape were deducible from the physical landscape. The effect, however, is to suggest the disturbed state of the observer. In a hysterical world the sane observer will see signs of hysteria. This is one notion conveyed by Spender's calm inflections. Yet the lines also suggest the impossibility of remaining detached.

As a result, when disturbance fully erupts in the last lines, the moment – though clumsy – can be viewed with sympathy as betraying need: Spender's need to claim that his response fuses the subjective and objective, that he is right about this culture and feels his conviction passionately. But the difficulty of achieving such a fusion has been evident throughout. Spender should not be blamed for lack of coherence so much as praised for exploring an irreducibly individual vision, unsurenesses included. Significantly, this vision is communicated through figurative language (playing against statement); the moth image – often seen as an isolated felicity in an otherwise flawed poem – serves, rather, as a means of entrance for Spender. Its refusal to advance an extractable moral prepares the reader for a poem whose workings are tentative yet tenacious. Spender provides an apt gloss on these workings:

> the imagination suggests to the poet the undefined sensation of a metaphor which explains to him the quality of some experience. But to feel his way beyond this vague sensation to the exact image of the metaphor, to pursue it through solitude to places where it is hidden from all that has been put into words before, and then to mould it within all the hazards of language, reconciled with grammar and form, is extremely difficult. ... The writer who clings to his own metaphor is facing his own loneliness; in fighting to distinguish a new idea from similar ideas which have already been expressed, he may find that his most hidden experience brings him in conflict with current ideas among people surrounding him, and face to face with the terrifying truth of his own isolated existence.
>
> (*WWW*, p. 93)

In 'The Landscape near an Aerodrome' Spender's language reveals him in the act of 'fighting to distinguish a new idea from similar ideas which have already been expressed'. That idea defeats paraphrase, but it is bound up with his ambivalence about the possibility of objective diagnosis of civilization (such as Auden's early poetry seemed – to Spender and others – to offer). Yet the fact that the poem purports to describe an external world helps; subjectivity does not turn all it touches into abstraction or symbolic significance. The poem needs its 'charcoaled batteries', 'fields / Behind the aerodrome, where boys play all day / Hacking dead grass' and 'winking masthead light': details which, whatever their ultimate function, allow the reader to focus on a scene that is external to the poet's consciousness.

3

This balance, interplay or conflict between 'inner' and 'outer', consciousness and world, subjectivity and objectivity, is fundamental to Spender's achieved poems in the thirties. Estimation of his poetic success demands revision (though not abandonment) of the criteria apparent in the adverse reviews of Spender's work in *Scrutiny* (a literary journal, edited by F. R. Leavis, famous for its emphasis on evaluation). Certainly a good poem needs to be 'realized', but *Scrutiny*'s conception of the 'realized' was too circumscribed; it did not sufficiently allow for the dramatization of consciousness to be found in Spender. Moreover, readers should think twice before condemning Spender for 'clumsy' rhythms or 'blatantly manufactured' images.[2] There are lapses in the handling of rhythm and imagery in Spender's work, but also finenesses of a kind which demand more sympathetic reading than Leavis and his fellow-reviewers permitted themselves. Whereas Auden and MacNeice frequently rely on a virtuoso handling of traditional forms, Spender's stanzaic shapes and overall structures are held open to the often ragged mess of feeling; tentative and exploratory, they are concerned to mirror the emergence into words of consciousness. What may resemble clumsiness in Spender is often the badge worn by integrity.

In *Poems*, 1933 and 1934, this integrity is frequently tested as the poet seeks to embrace a vision of change. 'Without that once clear aim, the path of flight' (*SP33*; included in *CPS(1)*) records a mood in which the vision has gone, but the desire to embrace it remains. Though the poem risks melodrama, its phrasing skilfully mimics the confusions of nightmare. In the line 'This century chokes me under roots of night', the associations are controlled, suggesting both the nearness and intensity of the century's oppressiveness. The head-on confrontation between 'This century' and the individual speaks volumes about Spender's conception of the poet's role (and the burden of that role). The ending, with its confession of entrapped isolation, has genuine pathos:

> Nor summer nor light may reach down here to play.
> The city builds its horror in my brain,
> This writing is my only wings away.

Spender's 'horror' offers a momentary (and horrified) glimpse of nihilism from which the poet is saved by 'This writing'. Only 'This writing' allows refuge from 'This century'; the two 'This's' are pointedly opposed – as are the two references to flight beginning and ending the poem. At the beginning, the poet laments the loss of 'the path of flight / To follow for a life-time through white air', a flight that follows a path and has a definite purpose; at the end, the poet's 'writing' supplies more hurriedly panicky 'wings away'. Again, the poem confirms Spender's isolation yet has value by virtue of its sensitivity to what it calls 'men's buried lives'.

By contrast, 'The Pylons' (*SP33*; included in *CPS(1)*, *SPS*, and *CPS(2)*) is buoyed up by commitment to 'the quick perspective of the future'. 'Quick', there, refers to the accelerated pace of life, embodied in the electricity-conducting wires. But the word also recovers a largely archaic sense, 'living, alive' (*Concise Oxford Dictionary*, 7th edn, 3). That this sense is revived in a line which celebrates the 'perspective of the future' is, in its concealed way, an act of lexical wit. It alerts the reader to the struggle between past and future which the poem dilineates. Seeming to take the side of the future, Spender's language has that faintly parodic, disengaged quality evident in 'The Funeral'. The two poems are coupled by Spender who speaks of 'an obligation to "own up" to those poems, like *The Pylons* and *The Funeral*, which, when they were written, provided a particular label for some of the poetry of the 'Thirties: an embarrassment to my friends' luggage more even than to my own' (*CPS(1)*, p. 13). Though his tone here is difficult to gauge, Spender appears to accept the common view of the poems as propagandist, but the poems themselves will not sustain this view. 'The Pylons', like 'The Funeral', mourns even as it mocks:

> The valley with its gilt and evening look
> And the green chestnut
> Of customary root
> Are mocked dry like the parched bed of a brook.

A favourite Yeatsian symbol and value are sent packing in the second and third lines of this stanza. It is unsurprising that Spender was critical of Yeats's 'aristocratic faith' (*DE*, p. 129) as exemplified by 'A Prayer for my Daughter' from which he quotes lines 'mocked' by 'The Pylons': 'How but in custom and in ceremony / Are innocence and beauty born? / Ceremony's a name for the rich horn / And custom for the spreading laurel tree'.[3] Yet 'The Pylons' looks quizzically not merely at Yeatsian conservatism but also at Utopian confidence.

A. Kingsley Weatherhead argues that 'the poet unwittingly captures our sympathy for the traditionally poetic';[4] but it is hard to believe that Spender was writing 'unwittingly' when he causes us to think about the word 'secret'. 'The secret of these hills was stone, and cottages / Of that stone made', the poem begins; in the second stanza, after 'they have built the concrete / That trails black wire', these new structures – pylons – are said, notoriously, to be 'Bare like nude, giant girls that have no secret'. The end of secrecy represented by these 'nude, giant girls' is given only an ambiguous welcome by Spender's language; 'that have no secret' has the sound both of a step forward (the 'girls' no longer need to maintain the pretences that generate secrets) and of a loss (they lack the withheld possibilities that 'secrecy' invites speculation about). The calmly objective tone, the reader begins to realize, serves a double purpose: if the poem is read as advocating a new order founded on, and represented by, technological progress, it allows Spender to write as though from a perspective above and beyond 'individual grief'; if the poem is read more sceptically, it allows the poet room for manoeuvre. 'This', he can claim, 'is how life will be, or how "they" have decreed it will be.' Common to both readings is the sense that Spender is trying on a rhetorical guise. The effect is that the poem is most unsettling when apparently most assured. This unsettled feel comes, in part, from the off-rhymes and is apparent when, in the final stanza, Spender seeks to marry old and new:

> This dwarfs our emerald country by its trek
> So tall with prophecy:
> Dreaming of cities
> Where often clouds shall lean their swan-white neck.

The language holds in suspension opposite impulses. 'This' is shorthand for 'the foregoing vision of the future', but the curtness chops down to size what the word stands for even as it makes the word sound authoritative; 'dwarfs' is less superior a verb than it may seem because height has already been associated with the unfetchingly 'nude, giant girls'; 'our emerald country' identifies the poet, however ironically, with other inhabitants of a country whose beauty is suggested by 'emerald'. And the last two lines, with their reconciliatory movement, rob progressivism of its energy. Progressivism now participates in 'Dreaming'; although the cities it dreams of will presumably be so many skyscrapered Manhattans, they will be attended by 'clouds' whose 'swan-like neck' is a curious final note for this poem to sound. And Spender's use of 'often' is hopeful rather than strident. For a work often cited as proving political commitment can ruin a poem's health, 'The Pylons' emerges, on inspection, as markedly fluid in its tones and suggestions.

The critical issue of intention – however much outlawed by various theorists – remains: did Spender mean 'The Pylons' to be read as a poem which, for all its manifest commitment to a vision of the future, is aware of the cost to be paid for achievement of that vision? Whatever the answer (almost certainly 'Yes' in our view), the text's poising of opposites deserves attention. Even at his most programmatic, Spender's language can be seen assessing the cost of commitment. In doing so, it deserves praise for the quality of awareness sustained. An example is supplied by 'Not palaces, an era's crown', the final poem in *Poems*, 1933 and 1934 (included in *CPS(1)* and, under the title 'Not Palaces', in *SPS* and *CPS(2)*). The poem takes the form of valediction and imperative. It bids farewell to past cultural achievements and purely aesthetic delight, and it commands itself 'To will this

Time's change'. Yet in 'stamping the words with emphasis' Spender, for the last time in this self-conscious collection, provokes the reader and himself to recognize what his words are doing. And what they are doing is 'stamping' on impulses which will not, the poem's sub-text suggests, be stamped out:

> Eye, gazelle, delicate wanderer,
> Drinker of horizon's fluid line;
> Ear that suspends on a chord
> The spirit drinking timelessness;
> Touch, love, all senses;
> Leave your gardens, your singing feasts,
> Your dreams of suns circling before our sun,
> Of heaven after our world.
> Instead, watch images of flashing brass
> That strike the outward sense, the polished will
> Flag of our purpose which the wind engraves.

The movement of the verse is admirably controlled, reinforcing, yet tugging against, the command to trust in the 'polished will'. And the omission of definite articles seems appropriate not mannered, lending 'Eye', 'Ear' and the rest the status of quasi-personifications,

Revealingly, Spender's lyrical talents are fully aroused as the poet admonishes them to serve a 'purpose'. One word stamped with emphasis is 'drinking': 'Drink from here energy and only energy', the poet has already enjoined, yet – more bewitchingly – the eye is 'Drinker of horizon's fluid line', while the ear, listening to music, allows access to 'The spirit drinking timelessness'. 'Drinking', which involves consumption, a taking inside of what lies outside, attaches itself here more naturally to the aesthetic than the politicized; when the poet says 'Drink from here energy and only energy' the imperative and the 'only' limit the activity of his verse, sound restrictive. In fact, aesthetic 'drinking' is set against politicized 'watching' of 'images of flashing brass / That strike the outward sense'. These lines commit Spender to a course at odds with his real talents, which involve inward transformation of experience rather than subjection to 'the outward sense'.

The reader witnesses in this poem a moment when the writer confronts the hiding-places of his power and seeks to turn them into portals through which something else can emerge. As he spells out the 'programme' which, for this poem, that 'something else' involves, Spender merely sloganizes: 'No man / Shall hunger: Man shall spend equally. / Our goal which we compel: Man shall be man'. Unlike Shelley in *Prometheus Unbound*, Act 3, who devotes much linguistic energy to imagining a Utopia in which 'Man shall be man', Spender lets the will do the work of the imagination. And yet the poem would be the poorer for concentrating solely on the 'horizon's fluid line'. The reader is compelled by Spender's own compulsion to write about the 'goal which we compel', to confront the aesthetic with the moral. As the present study's discussion of Spender's work has been concerned to establish, the poetry admits, and at its best dramatizes, warring impulses.

4

Spender's main achievement as a poet in the thirties lies in the shorter poems collected in *Poems*, 1933 and 1934, and *The Still Centre*. But during the decade he produced two longer poetic works, *Vienna* and *Trial of a Judge*, which are interesting for the light they shed on his persistent concern with seemingly incompatible realms of experience and ways of representing them. Spender has described *Vienna* as a poem in which a number of criss-crossing tensions are expressed: 'It was my duty', he writes, 'to express the complexity of an ambivalent situation. For our individualistic civilization to be reborn within the order of a new world, people must be complex as individuals, simple as social forces' (*WWW*, p. 191). *Vienna* was written to express indignation at the crushing of Austrian socialists in 1934; it was also, Spender asserts, 'concerned with a love relationship' (*WWW*, p. 192). This concern is scarcely apparent, but it is the case that Spender strives to bring political and private spheres into connection. The writing is elliptical and unsettlingly jumpy in its movement between voices, and the reader misses the reassuring presence of a stable consciousness (however self-questioning) which gives coherence to both editions of *Poems*. At the same time it avoids the merely journalistic, conveying a stark sense of the difficulty of response to political crisis.

In the first section, 'Arrival at the City', Spender emphasizes inwardness, the poetry taking the form of a monologue; it describes the impact on the speaker of coming to Vienna where he is staying at a pension. The writing cuts between the satirical and the meditative, between mockery of the proprietor of the pension who represents the 'live dead' and earnest trust in the 'live ones', 'Those who, going to work early, behold the world's / Utter margin where all is stone and iron, / And wrong'. There is much to admire in the poetry: the withholding, for instance of 'And wrong' in the lines just quoted, the brooding over what is 'real' ('His real life a fading light his real death a light growing'). But the dominant impression is of a mind moving incoherently between extremes of doubt and hope: does Spender mean the reader, for example, to see the lovers 'Writing a new world with their figure 2' as representatives of the better world he hopes for, or as escapees from 'the whole world'? The poetry foreshadows failures in *The Still Centre* by giving itself too much rope; the result is over-elaboration coupled with loss of the structural shapeliness evident in *Poems*.

In 'Parade of the Executive', the second section, Spender imitates the layering of voices used so well by Eliot in *Coriolan*. Eliot's finesse and economy are sacrificed by Spender whose verse possesses satirical bite and imaginative energy, but seems not to know when to stop. To be fair to Spender, the difference is sometimes less one of poetic quality than of the purposes each poet is asking his language to serve. 'Triumphal March', the first poem of *Coriolan*, begins with the lines: 'Stone, bronze, stone, steel, stone, oakleaves, horses' heels / Over the paving', lines whose power is bound up with their perfect cadencing and refusal of comment (leading to a possible duplicity of tone); in 'Parade of the Executive' Spender's parallel to these lines works less secretly: 'Faces of our men beneath steel helmets / Should echo one face, stone face of a palace'. Repetition supports the notion that the soldiers' faces 'echo' the 'face' of power. However, the following lines about the unemployed point up, by contrast, the fineness of the writing in, say, 'Moving through the silent crowd':

> Dispersed like idle points of a vague star:
> Huddled on benches, nude at bathing places,
> And made invisible by crucifying suns
> Day after day, again with grief afire at night,
> They do not watch what we show.

'Crucifying suns' and 'grief afire at night' overstate, undoing
the quieter implications (of alienation from the dominant culture) conveyed by the second and last lines.

In the first of the Six Odes in *The Orators* Auden imagines a
'Beggar' who asks (in relation to 'the state of East Europe'):
'Have you heard of someone swifter than Syrian horses? / . . . Is
he seeking brilliant / Athens and us?'. This enigmatic, menacing
'he' is, arguably, Auden's rebuke to the yearning for a leader
which is strong in thirties poetry; it is a yearning with unstable
political implications. In Eliot's *Coriolan*, the hero stands aloof
from the crowd and statistics: in part he is the product of
romantic proto-fascist fantasy that recognizes itself as such:
'There he is now, look: / There is no interrogation in his eyes /
Or in the hands, quiet over the horse's neck' ('Triumphal
March'); in part he embodies, as does his counterpart in
Shakespeare's *Coriolanus*, a movingly expressed wish for an
escape from the world of power: 'The small creatures chirp
thinly through the dust, through the night. / O mother / What
shall I cry?' ('Difficulties of a Statesman'). The second section of
Vienna also ends by imagining a figure of power, in this case a
stranger who might, the poetry hopes, offer help and advice. But
the advice, 'Shoot!', is the least convincing voice adopted by the
poem; any poetic authority that *Vienna* has derives from its
presentation of dividedness and uncertainty.

Spender offers affecting pathos in the third section, 'The
Death of Heroes', which recounts, among other things, the
heroic careers of two workers, Weissel and Wallisch. Yet there is
more to hold the reader's interest in the final section, 'Analysis
and Statement'. Difficult as this section is, it returns the poem to
the personal and subjective; five voices confess their feelings and
weaknesses. *Vienna* may lack ultimate coherence, finishing with
a vague gesture of revolutionary hope. But there are many
salvageable moments when Spender obliquely describes the
problems of dealing with political crisis. Chief of these is the
obsessive feeling that people are 'complex as individuals',
however 'simple as social forces'. An example from the last
section occurs when the fourth voice says:

> Yet sometimes I wish that I were loud and angry
> Without this human mind like a doomed sky
> That loves, as it must enclose, all.

The lines convey a great deal about Spender: the longing for undivided being (the desire to be 'loud and angry'), the view of 'love' as a compulsion, the sense both of the mind's all-encompassing importance and inhibiting complexities.

Such complexities are at the heart of *Trial of a Judge*, a poetic drama whose style – by turns tortuously abstract and figuratively clotted – makes the play a vehicle for psychological and moral self-scrutiny. Spender lacks the uncluttered yet searching power of Eliot's choruses in *Murder in the Cathedral* (1935). But he achieves a power of his own in his presentation of 'a liberal's nightmare . . . a world mastered by fascism, from which history has been abolished' (Hynes, p. 304). The satirical gift that flickers in *Vienna* again shows to advantage, though 'satirical' does not do justice to the sombreness of Spender's perceptions: the grasp, for example, of the way anti-semitism functions in the minds of the Black Prisoners (the Fascists) at the start of Act IV ('Point Three – *The Jews are whatever we think they are: they are just bad dreams in our own minds*'). The Reds (Communists) and Blacks represent extremes between which the liberal Judge is caught. In Act V the Judge tells the Fiancée (of a murdered Jewish Communist) that should her side win, 'all will be the same; only / Those who are now oppressed will be the oppressors, / The oppressors the oppressed'. The language looks simple, even obvious; in context, however, it has considerable force. For *Trial of a Judge* is obsessed by the fear that all perspectives lead into cul-de-sacs: the clearer the speaker's vision, the darker the outlook.

The best poetry of the drama, such as the Judge's long speech from Act IV beginning 'I speak from the centre of a stage', presents an unsparing picture of liberalism's defeat by force. At the start of this speech the Judge denies the role of tragic hero (implicitly granted him by the play's subtitle: 'a tragic statement in five acts'): he is an actor not in 'a tragedy but a farce' in which he is 'the spiritual unsmiling clown / Defeated by the brutal swearing giant / Whose law is power'. Yet the act is impressive not only for the Judge's refusal of tragic glamour but also for his residual sense of the significance of his defeat. Combining reasoned argument and impassioned clarity, Spender succeeds in persuading the listener that the Judge is entitled to refer by the end of a later speech to his 'tragic error' and to lament 'the spirit of Europe destroyed with my defeat'. There is a nagging, wearied intelligence at work in the lines that makes the reference to 'Europe' seem hard-earned rather than grandiose.

Again, the conclusion shows how, at its finest, *Trial of a Judge* fuses the imaginative and the analytical. The meaning of the Judge's career is searchingly debated, the Judge now affirming an awareness of tragedy which is denied by the Fiancée and the Third Red. Voicing his creator's obsession with the 'real', the Judge asks 'what is madness / Except one's sense of final reality / Which has become an exile from his world / And from his time?' The Fiancée retorts 'you are not that mad and glittering snowman / Which you imagine', puncturing his individualism; rather, she says – and her words have application to many soul-searching thinkers and writers of the decade – 'being too honest for one time, you lacked strength / To be born into another'. The Third Red takes up the attack on the Judge in a speech beginning 'Your tragedy / Is not a Beethoven symphony'; the Judge is not as important as, duped by liberal delusions, he supposes himself to be. In words which sound like covert self-address on Spender's part, the Third Red asserts:

> There are no weak and meek whom you must pity
> Merging in them your own identity.

Does the reader believe the Third Red's analysis? Or does Spender simply catch the incisive tones of Marxist critique, allowing them their say without giving them the final word? What can be affirmed is that Spender has found a way of making intensely dramatic poetry out of deeply felt inner quarrels. Act V of the play achieves what in the last section of *Vienna* he was groping towards: a dramatic rendering of inner struggle and of the possible meanings or lack of meaning of that struggle.

5

The Still Centre groups together some of Spender's best poems of the thirties: it contains many of his poems about the Spanish Civil War (largely collected in Part Three but also occurring elsewhere in the volume), which are discussed in Chapter 8; it also includes such fine pieces as 'Polar Exploration', 'An Elementary School Class Room in a Slum', 'The Uncreating

Chaos', 'Hoelderlin's Old Age', 'In the Street', 'A Footnote (*From Marx's Chapter on The Working Day*)', 'Darkness and Light' and 'Two Kisses'. In all these poems Spender explores the self and history with a sombre, lacerating eloquence new in his work. And yet the collection suffers as well as benefits from the urgency with which it wishes to get to grips with the poet's deepest preoccupations. There is an intermittent tendency to strive too hard for exhaustive treatment of theme.

An example is 'Exiles from their Land, History their Domicile' (included in *CPS(1)* and, under the title 'The Exiles', in *CPS(2)*), an interesting poem which Spender has repeatedly revised without ever perfecting. In his Introduction to *Collected Poems 1928–1953* Spender describes the poem as 'still malleable', feeling that in its earlier version he did not satisfactorily express the poem's central 'idea'. Yet this 'idea', that there are people 'who have, after their deaths, obtained for their lives a symbolic significance which certainly passed unnoticed when they were living' (*CPS(1)*, p. 14), is clear enough. What goes wrong with the writing is the relegation of the poet's consciousness to the margins of the poem. Spender does appear at the end, but his appearance is long overdue. And locally affecting as his prayer is – 'And let my words restore / Their printed, laurelled, victoried message' – the poem seems to stumble on the notion of poetry's efficacy at the last moment. For the most part it has addressed itself, rather cumbersomely, to the theme of divided being. The theme is tortuously restated rather than explored: we 'endure / Perpetual winter, waiting / Spring', but theirs are 'just and summer skies'; we are the 'molten metal' which they were 'before death cast / Their wills into those signatory moulds'; we search for signs of 'Their similarity / To our own wandering present uncertainty'. The metaphors offer themselves as original, but merely decorate a paraphrasable idea; the use of 'we' and 'our' seems presumptuous. Whereas the first line of 'I think continually of those who were truly great', a poem on much the same subject, makes inward what follows, the opening of 'Exiles from their Land, History their Domicile' sounds a raspingly bombastic note:

> History has tongues
> Has angels has guns – has saved has praised –
> Today proclaims
> Achievements of her exiles long returned . . .

The Still Centre, then, is a collection beaten into shape by, and sometimes buckling under, pressures that are internal and external. 'Exiles from their Land, History their Domicile' is the work of a poet who, having written one or two collections, now knows his central themes almost too well, who, finding it increasingly hard to be surprised by his own feelings, resorts to stylistic over-emphasis. The external pressures, and their influences on his poetry, are defined by Spender in his Foreword:

> I think that there is a certain pressure of external events on poets today, making them tend to write about what is outside their own limited experience. The violence of the times we are living in, the necessity of sweeping and general and immediate action, tend to dwarf the experience of the individual, and to make his immediate environment and occupations perhaps something that he is even ashamed of. For this reason, in my most recent poems, I have deliberately turned back to a kind of writing which is more personal, and I have included within my subjects weakness and fantasy and illusion.
>
> (*SC*, pp. 10–11)

This is clear-sighted and, in its own way, courageous; yet the reader wonders whether the last sentence bodes well for the poems it describes. 'Deliberately' is a tell-tale word, suggesting a programmatic impulse, one borne out by the texture of Spender's writing in the last section. 'The Human Situation', for example, seeks to accept the poet for what he is, inner divisions and all; to embrace the condition of 'him who is always right' or of 'those who won the ideologic victories' would be impossible for Spender, would be

> Death to me and my way of perceiving
> As much as if I became a stone;
> Here I am forced on to my knees,
> On to my real and own and only being
> As into the fortress of my final weakness.

This compares well with the confused rhapsodizing of 'Exiles from their Land, History their Domicile'. Yet, though the writing is intelligent, it has little to offer the reader's imagination. The second line's use of 'stone' only weakens the resonance of the Yeatsian image in 'Easter 1916' ('Too long a sacrifice / Can make a stone of the heart') which it recycles. And the suggestion in 'fortress' that confession of 'weakness' is in fact a form of defence might, if developed, have made for a more interesting poem. But Spender is too concerned to state a position and take a stand (against taking stands) for such nuances to get the attention they deserve (and received in *Poems*).

The poem, like the paragraph quoted from the Foreword, marks a reaction against the imperative 'to make some choice outside the private entanglements of our personal life'; in the same passage Spender writes of the need 'to understand that objective life moving down on us like a glacier, but which, after all, is essentially not a glacier, is an historic process, the life of people like ourselves, and therefore our "proper study"' (*DE*, p. 223). Yet *The Still Centre* is most impressive when rehearsing, without simplifying, the disparate impulses described in the Foreword and in the passage referred to from *The Destructive Element*. The best poems admit both 'private entanglements' and the wish to 'make some choice'; they yearn for a Popean sweep ('The proper study of Mankind is Man')[5] yet demystify their workings much as the image of the glacier is demystified in *The Destructive Element*.

In 'Polar Exploration' (included in *CPS(1)*, *SPS* and *CPS(2)*), the collection's first poem, Spender takes as his subject the search for some bleak absolute of the spirit, but he enfolds abstract significance within convincingly rendered description: 'Our single purpose was to walk through snow / With faces swung to their prodigious North / Like compass iron'. The collection's pursuit of 'single purpose' is unremitting; it is also unsuccessful, though the account of the pursuit in this piece is highly successful – mainly because Spender's matter-of-fact tone authenticates the rigours and boredom of the imagined journey: 'Hate Culver's loud breathing, despise Freeman's / Fidget for washing: love only the dogs / That whine for scraps, and scratch'. By the end of 'Polar Exploration' the speaker is left asking:

> Is the North,
> Over there, a tangible, real madness,
> A glittering simpleton, one without towns,
> Only with bears and fish, a staring eye,
> A new and singular sex?

The writing flinches from a state it is fascinated by: a state where 'madness' is at least 'tangible' and 'real', where complications of gender have been resolved into 'A new and singular sex'; yet a state which is compared to a 'simpleton', and lies beyond humanity. The passage and the poem wring from the common thirties theme of quest a strange and rigorous eloquence.

Equally intent on crossing the barriers between inner and outer is the unpromisingly titled 'The Uncreating Chaos' (included in *CPS(1)* and *CPS(2)*). This work takes the form of a sequence (with four short parts), a form which Spender does not use at all in *Poems* (where the average length of the poems is much briefer). The sequence is a form which allows for sudden transitions, and the poem depends for its impact on the reader's grasp of the relationship between its parts. Throughout, Spender mixes the sardonically obscure with the transparently vulnerable; 'the uncreating chaos' is Spender's phrase for the welter of confusion which – in a quizzical version of the Romantic trope of the imagination marrying nature – 'descends / And claims you in marriage'. The poet suggests that his motives for remaining open to such 'chaos' are not as pure as they might be. The opening lines, with their overblown rhetoric ('your guts on skewers of pity'), are meant to be read as overblown, Spender mocking his emotions as self-indulgent. 'You were only anxious that all these passions should last', he remarks, and the poem turns into a judgement on his emotional life as a poet so far. Audenesque irony is conscripted by the poem, the poet's inner voice made to say, 'Whatever happens, I shall never be alone, / I shall always have an affair, a railway fare, or a revolution'. There is a different, more broodingly inward, kind of penetrativeness in the first section's concluding image of the 'you' staring 'in on yourself as though on a desolate room'. That image of an original emptiness which demands to be filled by 'uncreating chaos' haunts not just the poem but the collection as well.

The second section switches from 'you' to 'I', from irony to confession; it moves from a sense of consciousness altering all – 'In thoughts where pity is the same as cruelty, / Your life and mine seem water' – to a recognition of a world of 'facts' beyond the self. This world, Spender suggests, has little meaning to those involved in it but even less to the poet/onlooker who, in a moment of severe self-scrutiny, concludes the section with the famous Rilkean phrase, 'Alter your life' (from 'Archaic Torso of Apollo').[6] The effect is harrowing and redeems some laboured, though always investigative, lines.

The third section moves back from the life in need of alteration to the realm of 'History', a realm dominated by violence and catastrophe: 'A corporal's fiery tongue wags above burning parliament' gives substance to the section's account of 'visions of a faltering will / Inventing violent patterns', and the reader is reminded by the last line, 'Thoughts in a dying minister's brain', that Spender sees the 'real' as the product of 'thoughts', whether those of a liberal poet or of a crazed dictator or of a 'dying minister'. The insight would have more force if the wording were not so leadenly indebted to the end of Eliot's poem 'Gerontion', 'Thoughts of a dry brain in a dry season'. The final section, however, lifts the poem; short-lined, lyrical, full of yearning yet wryly clear-sighted, it is one of the finest things Spender wrote in the thirties: 'Shall I never reach / The field guarded by stones / Precious in the stone mountains . . . ?' The switch back to 'I' works well, and the symbolic imagery is unstrained, the more effective for contrasting so strongly with the turbid, agitated diction of the preceding sections. Even better is the section's (and the poem's) end. Where section two concluded with a phrase from Rilke, section four finishes with a glance towards the German Romantic poet, Hölderlin:

> Meanwhile, where nothing's pious
> And life no longer willed,
> Nor the human will conscious,
> Holy is lucidity
> And the mind that dare explain.

In 'The Half of Life' Hölderlin refers to 'heilignüchterne Wasser', or 'holy lucid water',[7] a phrase which, fusing 'precision and passion',[8] brings together dialectical opposites in his thinking. The allusion contributes to the power of Spender's lines which hinge on the turn (signalled by 'Meanwhile') from the symbolic imagining of what might be to the unadorned statement of what is. Spender chooses his words carefully as he puts his trust in 'lucidity' and the explaining 'mind' against the passively unwilled and the unconsciously willed; there are many statements of what the poet feels his position is in *The Still*

Centre, but the quietly desperate nobility attained here is unmatched in the volume. Spender's sense that 'lucidity' is 'holy' has more impact for his exploration of the obscure and murky in experience. In the last stanza of 'The Separation', Spender includes the phrase which gives his collection its title, as he imagines himself and his beloved 'Shuttered by dark at the still centre / Of the world's circular terror'. But though the geometrical imagery invites thematic unravelling, the reader would do better to ponder the end of 'The Uncreating Chaos' if he or she wishes to arrive at the volume's 'still centre'.

6

This chapter concludes with brief readings of two poems from *The Still Centre* that illustrate different aspects of Spender's achievement in a flawed but impressive volume. 'An Elementary School Class Room in a Slum' (included, under the title 'An Elementary School Classroom in a Slum', in *CPS(1)*, *SPS* and *CPS(2)*) takes up with new confidence the challenge of expressing pity for the underprivileged without being sentimental or condescending. Gone is the heavily emphasized self-reproach that characterizes Spender's treatment of similar themes in *Poems*. Here complicity in unfairness is admitted more quietly, by the sense that 'Shakespeare is wicked', as the third stanza sardonically puts it, if the cultural advantages he represents are denied the children; by the awareness, unadvertised, that the poet is employing a medium – language – from which the children are effectively excluded; their future is described as 'Far far from rivers, capes, and stars of words'. The last two words give bite to what had seemed sentimental lament for the children's remoteness from nature; the grammar makes the reader see 'rivers' and 'capes', as well as 'stars', as symbolic.

This avoidance of false sentiment is delicately sustained at the famous, but obscure, close. The poet imagines a Blake-like fantasy of release in which the children would be able 'to let their tongues / Run naked into books, the white and green leaves open / The history theirs whose language is the sun'. That the syntax of the last line and a half defeats total clarification is a flaw, though not a crippling one given the mood of quickened excitement (the lines begin 'Unless' and know they are fantasizing). The use of natural imagery may seem to deny the children's full humanity. However, to say that 'their language is the sun' – in the context of a poem where the natural has served symbolic functions – is less to see the children in a primitivist light than to affirm an innate potential whose release is lyrically imagined.

The poem is most memorable, however, for its sharp-eyed appraisal of the classroom, its children and their possibilities (or lack of them). Spender's metaphoric resources help here, as when he describes a child 'reciting a father's gnarled disease, / His lesson from his desk'. The metaphor of inherited disease as a recited lesson is both apt and suggestive. Again, the half-line, 'On sour cream walls, donations', gets a lot said in a few words; 'donations', picked out, implies the unthinking contempt behind charity. The poem is less sure when overtly expressing passionate feelings on behalf of the children. These feelings may betray Spender into caricaturing the children's existences, and there is an off-the-peg feel about the fourth stanza's imagery; 'the slag heap' and 'spectacles of steel / With mended glass' signal a move away from particular observation (of the kind offered in the opening stanza) towards well-intentioned generalization. Yet Spender avoids, even as he seems about to succumb to, hectoring rhetoric; this has to do with the fact that the poet includes himself in the list of those who, it is implied, must act if anything is to be done about those whose 'future's painted with a fog' (Spender addresses 'governor, teacher, inspector, *visitor*' (emphasis added)). For all the optimism of its close, the poem has the same sense of the vulnerability of innocence in 'a tragic, ignorant age' as 'A Footnote (*From Marx's Chapter on The Working Day*)' (included, under the title 'A Footnote (From Marx's Chapter, *The Working Day*)', in *CPS(1)* and *SPS* and, under the title 'A Footnote: from Marx's chapter in *Das Capital*, "The Working Day"', in *CPS(2)*): a piece where visionary outrage at the desecration of 'holiness' (in this case the 'stripped and holy mothers' made to work in mines) is eloquently expressed.

Personal where 'An Elementary School Class Room' is social, 'Darkness and Light' (included, under the title 'Dark and Light', in *CPS(1)*) represents Spender's most explicit attempt to define his identity as a poet. And yet the poem's imagery of 'centre' and 'circumference' calls into question any division between the 'personal' and the 'social'; both the core of self and the outreach of its concerns, it is implied, are interrelated: 'Centre and circumference are both my weakness'. Spender is saying that the circumferential interests of his poetry (its obsession with history) cannot be divorced from its central concern with self: this may result in 'weakness' in that his poetry, however social its concern, never frees itself from the personal. At the same time this 'weakness', and here the strong assertion is boast as well as confession, is also a strength.

Cast in the form of 'a loose sestina',[9] 'Darkness and Light' is obsessive, turned in on itself, intent on precise definition, intent on avoiding trite formulations. The poem takes an abstract theme, but offers an exploration of its theme, not just a statement of it. The theme is the poet's attempt to bring into relation sides of himself which he recognizes as opposite: he wishes, for example, to 'break out of the chaos of my darkness / Into a lucid day', yet he wishes 'equally, to avoid that lucid day / And to preserve my darkness'. For all its care, the phrasing seems oppressed by the inconsistent demands it records; the reader listens to someone who is both at the end of his tether and stubbornly hopeful that he will find a way out of his impasse by describing it as clearly as possible. And the listening is dramatically rewarding; rewarding, too, is the work Spender gets out of his seemingly conceptual language. At the beginning of the third stanza, Spender writes:

> To break out of my darkness towards the centre
> Illumines my own weakness, when I fail . . .

'Illumines' underlines the fact that such a failure may be, in its own way, a success in that it sheds light on the poet's 'weakness'; 'weakness', the lines imply, may be necessary for this poet's creativity. The suggestion is supple, and is supported by the end of the fourth stanza:

> My will behind my weakness silhouettes
> My territories of fear, with a great sun.

The image that ghosts the abstractions here returns to and develops the implications of 'illumines'; the phrase 'My territories of fear' is strongly possessive; such 'territories' may themselves be feared but they are also not to be ceded without imaginative loss. As it 'reconciles and separates / In lucid day the chaos of my darkness', the ending may risk the patness which the rest of the poem keeps at bay. But the opening of the final stanza affirms the impulse to 'grow towards' which characterizes Spender's best poetry, making it frequently dissatisfied yet often satisfying:

> I grow towards the acceptance of that sun
> Which hews the day from night.

6
Auden (3)
'A change of heart'

Stephen Spender once claimed to find 'a dualistic idea running through all [Auden's] work which encloses it like the sides of a box. This idea is Symptom and Cure'.[1] Certainly Auden's major poems of the thirties often seek both to diagnose and suggest ways of healing psychological and political ills. The 'dualistic idea' noted by Spender is evident from the start of Auden's career. So 'Sir, no man's enemy, forgiving all' (written in 1929) seeks release from 'the intolerable neural itch' and asks that the pseudo-Hopkinsesque 'Sir' it addresses should 'look shining at / New styles of architecture, a change of heart'.

Whether it does so authentically is another matter. Significantly Auden later rejected the poem as 'dishonest' on the grounds that 'I have never liked modern architecture' (Foreword to *CSPA*, p. 15). Though this may seem cavalierly puritanical, it is possible to see why the poem might have caused Auden unease – which is not to say that there is any obligation to share his poor opinion of it. What later Auden may have found difficult to stomach is the way his poem thrives on swaggering oddnesses of register. Those 'New styles of architecture' jar in a fashion characteristic of early Auden. By contrast with the preceding line's 'Harrow the house of the dead', where the religious allusion has a surprising gravity, the phrase sounds lightly modish, even frivolous. Again, the final off-rhyme both underscores and scrutinizes the wished-for 'change', an unsettling effect that accompanies many of Auden's expressions of desire for personal and social transformation in his thirties poems. In its parody of a mode (in this case prayer), its startling mix of

145

tones and its disconcerting force, the poem is typical of Auden's early work. But even when the poetry assumes a seemingly more decorous, responsible voice in following years, it still retains a welcome capacity to surprise as well as a good deal of subliminal tension.

1

'What do you think about England, this country of ours where nobody is well?' This question from *The Orators* is one which Auden poses, at least by implication, in nearly all his thirties work. As so often, the writing's impact stems from not knowing how fully Auden identifies with the voice he creates – and, also, from not knowing where Auden stands in relation to his reader. Poet and reader are, and are not, in the same boat: 'this country of ours' has a coercive togetherness before 'where nobody is well' springs the trap. If 'nobody is well' then the speaker is also 'sick'; yet to know you are unwell gives you authority over those who do not. Auden is able to tap his reader's feelings of guilt, to sound as though he were excavating buried sources of shame and anxiety; to sound, too, as though he were compensating for vulnerable feelings of his own with a tone of harsh authority. The poet is both an aloof judge and a secret sharer.

'If we really want to live, we'd better start at once to try': this somewhat flatly didactic codicil to 'Get there if you can and see the land you once were proud to own', a poem with the air of a rollicking psycho-socio-political last testament, does not choose to specify what 'trying' might involve. But often for pre-1940 Auden 'the word is love', as he would put it in 'August for the people and their favourite islands'. However, the word frequently vexes its own assurance. A second glance at the concluding section of 'It was Easter as I walked in the public gardens' will serve to recall early Auden's dealings with 'love'. The opening, 'It is time for the destruction of error', has an engagingly immodest self-confidence, a stylistic bravura which thrives on instabilities of tone that mirror and induce instabilities of feeling. From 'the destruction of error' to the imagining of what the end of the previous section calls 'the new conditions' is the move the poem seems intent on making; but, unpredictably, it switches from what 'destruction of error' might entail to sinister atmospherics:

> In sanatoriums they laugh less and less,
> Less certain of cure . . .

> The falling leaves know it, the children,
> At play on the fuming alkali-tip
> Or by the flooded football ground, know it . . .

The first example's repeated use of 'less' neatly captures the waning of certainty and hope; the second sacrifices argument in favour of assertion and attention-hugging detail. Having said 'yes' to the alkali-tip, the reader is ready to say 'yes' to the last paragraph's big pronouncements about the relation between 'love' and 'death'.

What Auden means by these two words is hard to gloss. Both have the ring, at one level, of blind instinctual drives, at another of potentially redemptive energies. They serve as nodes round which the poem's potently obscure feelings can cluster: the desire to get rid of 'the old gang', the longing for wholeness, the knowledge of isolation, the connection between this longing and knowledge, and the issue of choice. Economy of detail and sharply focused, riddling imagery are all-important; as Chapter 1 was concerned to demonstrate, Auden's poetry eschews the straightforwardly rational, despite its intellectual air. When he says that love needs more than 'the abrupt self-confident farewell, / The heel on the finishing blade of grass', he conjures up an instant of emotional drama that is tense, withheld and memorable. 'Finishing' works almost as a transferred epithet and ripples with suggestions: a relationship might be 'finishing'; the gesture might be made by one who, like the line itself, has poise or 'finish', though his finished manners will not save him from the fate of a class that is 'finished'. The difficulty of imagining the better, death-generated 'love' that lies the other side of such incisively sketched vignettes is briefly, and tellingly, allowed for.

But if the final lines gleefully depict the fate of upper-class types – 'The hard bitch and the riding-master, / Stiff underground', where the posthumous 'stiffness' jokes grimly at the expense of their bearing while alive – the writing then employs an image which leaves the gleeful or satirical behind: 'deep in clear lake / The lolling bridegroom, beautiful, there'. Is the bridegroom 'a periphrasis for the dead Christ' (Fuller, p. 43)? Fuller may be right; the poem does, after all, begin at Easter and end in the spring. Yet, as he himself half-concedes, and Chapter 1 has already suggested, the imagery's 'marvellously convincing' quality cannot be separated from its 'obscure' nature (Fuller, p. 43). Auden has gone deeper than parts of the poem would lead the reader to guess; an unexpected image travels into areas that are archetypal, strange, yet gnomically contemporary.

2

Written just under four years after 'It was Easter as I walked in the public gardens', 'Out on the lawn I lie in bed' (later titled 'A Summer Night') appears to dispense with the earlier poem's ellipses and obscurities. For free-ranging blank verse, Auden substitutes a tightly ordered, rhyming stanza; for love as instinct the poem offers a vision of love as agape. 'Out on the lawn I lie in bed' seems to go with the current of the reader's expectations rather than against them, as Auden's early work does; it might even be criticized as being less challenging for doing so. Seamus Heaney articulates a benign form of this criticism when he quotes the opening lines of 'Out on the lawn I lie in bed' in support of his assertion that 'The usual poem keeps faith with the way we talk at the table, even more with the way we have heard other poems talk to us before.'[2]

Certainly the poem is musical and initially invites the reader to be lulled by the music: 'Out on the lawn I lie in bed, / Vega conspicuous overhead / In the windless nights of June'. But any security into which we are lulled is false, and here Auden's use of traditional form reveals its subversive cunning. Heaney may be right to say that 'A poem floats adjacent to, parallel to, the historical moment',[3] but he fails to see that 'Out on the lawn I lie in bed' sets its poise, craft and elegance against a 'historical moment' recognized as being chaotic, dangerous and brutal. Moreover, Auden *is* defeating his contemporary readers' expectation: for a poet to alter his style can delight but it can also unsettle.[4] The use of 'we' in this poem is an index of Auden's changed mode of address; the pronoun does not hector in a self-incriminating way; rather, it urbanely extends itself from the group whose intimacy is celebrated at the poem's outset (where Auden is 'Equal with colleagues in a ring') to absorb quite

casually the – middle-class – reader. At any rate such a reader
finds it difficult to escape the indictment wittily made by this
stanza (subsequently omitted along with the two following):

> The creepered wall stands up to hide
> The gathering multitudes outside
>   Whose glances hunger worsens;
> Concealing from their wretchedness
> Our metaphysical distress,
>   Our kindness to ten persons.

By this stage in the poem Auden has faced up to the privileges
which allow 'Our freedom in this English house, / Our picnics in
the sun'; indeed, his irony (evident in the pinprick of 'Our
kindness to ten persons') is in danger of negating the real, if
vulnerable, validity of the well-being with which the poem
began. Yet, in fact, it is the interplay of irony and uncomplacent
self-acceptance that gives life to the poem and keeps Auden from
imitating himself. Poems like 'It was Easter as I walked in the
public gardens' shift excitingly between the psychological and
the political. But melodrama and mannerism are the risks that
lie in wait for, even if they do not ensnare, writing so boldly
uninterested in understatement as 'This is the dragon's day, the
devourer's'. By contrast, 'Out on the lawn I lie in bed' has a
soberer grasp on the historical; in it the personal may be
intimately related to the political but the two spheres do not – as
in earlier poems – bewilderingly swap places or share the same
poetic space. 'The tyrannies of love' which 'we' 'endure' direct
attention to other forms of tyranny and endurance without
wholly belittling the 'love' subsidized by an unfair political
system. To its credit sloganizing is avoided by the poem, which
states quietly rather than harangues. For instance, the
'creepered wall' in the stanza quoted above clearly serves as an
image of social exclusion. Yet it does so with an absence of
showiness that points up the difference between Auden's style
here and in, say, 'Consider this and in our time' with its
flamboyant use of such (admittedly enigmatic) details as the
'cigarette-end smouldering on a border'.

'Consider' is a product of the imagination galvanized into
frenetic excitement by the prospect of disaster: the political is felt
along the nerve-ends; the dominant tone is premonitory. 'Out on

the lawn I lie in bed' is written when premonitions are beginning to prove all too justified, and insists on a historical world beyond the enclosures of class and poem. This insistence is, however, conveyed through a series of smoothly uninsistent transitions, of which the most crucial is this stanza (the seventh) following the account of the moon looking down on 'Those I love':

> She climbs the European sky;
> Churches and power stations lie
>   Alike among earth's fixtures:
> Into the galleries she peers,
> And blankly as an orphan stares
>   Upon the marvellous pictures.

The first line's adjective widens the poem's scope: 'European' in 1933 is a politically loaded word. But Auden does not bang a verbal drum; instead, he is content to let implications look after themselves. The blankness and indifference of the moon's stare hint at that existential desperation which is one of Auden's strongest notes (it is heard again at the end of 'Spain', 'We are left alone with our day'). The 'galleries' full of 'marvellous pictures' upon which the moon stares like an 'orphan' (later changed to 'butcher') have a chill, comfortless effect. 'Marvellous' takes on a polite hollowness – not that Auden denies that the pictures are 'marvellous' but that he denies that they (or the culture they stand for) can alleviate the lot of anyone who is or will become an 'orphan'. If that way of putting it seems melodramatic, it needs to be re-emphasized that Auden successfully avoids melodrama, relying on his reader's awareness of the political gravity of a year in which Hitler had come to power in Germany.[5]

From now on the poem is troubled by the insufficiency of the happiness it began by celebrating: happiness which begins to seem dependent on an aversion of the eyes from history. The poet and his friends are described as 'gentle', the word recovering its social associations, and though they 'do not care to know, / Where Poland draws her Eastern bow, / What violence is done', the last line rebukes that indifference along with the decorum on which Auden seemed intent. That said, the poem does not abjure its decorum; Auden may concede his complicity in injustice, but he refuses to turn hysterically against himself and

his friends. Instead, the conclusion tries to feel its way by means
of painstaking allegory towards some reconciliation between the
unfair present and a largely hoped-for, partly feared, revolutionary future:

> Soon through the dykes of our content
> The crumpling flood will force a rent,
>   And, taller than a tree,
> Hold sudden death before our eyes
> Whose river-dreams long hid the size
>   And vigours of the sea.
>
> But when the waters make retreat
> And through the black mud first the wheat
>   In shy green stalks appears;
> When stranded monsters gasping lie,
> And sounds of riveting terrify
>   Their whorled unsubtle ears:
>
> May this for which we dread to lose
> Our privacy, need no excuse
>   But to that strength belong;
> As through a child's rash happy cries
> The drowned voices of his parents rise
>   In unlamenting song.

These stanzas attain a dignity which is a touch artificial, and yet
their impact depends on our recognition of the part played by
artifice. That is to say, Auden's Utopian imaginings and hopes
admit the degree of manipulation which governs their expression, conceding that they exist, as yet, within the confines of a
highly formalized speech. While the conceit of revolution as a
flood betrays contrivance, contrivance hits upon trouvailles that
illustrate an underlying conceptual vigour. So at the end of the
first stanza Auden nimbly evokes a condition which a Marxist
might call false consciousness: the revolutionary sea's size has
been eclipsed by 'river-dreams', a phrase which uncrudely
suggests liberal humanist hopes or fantasies of a personal or
political nature. Sympathy joins indictment in the treatment of
the old order's 'stranded monsters' – 'sounds of riveting terrify /
Their whorled unsubtle ears'. 'Whorled' implies an intricacy

which may not be subtle, but prepares us for the following lines
with their prayer-like plea that something of the present may
survive into the future 'strength'. The poem is unsure about
defining what that 'something' is, calling it 'this' rather than
'love', the word one expects and a word which pervades Auden's
poems of the decade. As Mendelson observes, 'To use the same
name [love] for the power he would later call agape would
amount to a desecration' (Mendelson, p. 171).

The reticence here differs from the reticence of an earlier poem
like 'From the very first coming down'; where that poem signals
its reticence, referring to the country god's stone smile 'That
never was more reticent, / Always afraid to say more than it
meant', 'Out on the lawn I lie in bed' does not. A major reason
for the later poem's strength is the alliance between this lack of
underscoring and the measured control evident in, say, 'un-
lamenting', with its hint that the impulse to lament the passing
of an old order is being disciplined, not disregarded; will the new
way of things come about and, if so, will it be desirable? The
poem wants to answer 'yes' to both questions, but its inability to
do so with complete confidence gives it pathos. So the last stanza
is more anxious diminuendo than climax as it prays that what is
now called 'it' will 'All unpredicted . . . calm / The pulse of
nervous nations'. But if Stan Smith is right to assert that 'The last
impression is of an unresolved contradiction' (Smith, p. 84), the
contradiction and lack of resolution are acknowledged by the
poem, part of its 'unpredicted' alertness to its own procedures.

3

If Auden's better thirties poems visualize malaise vigorously but
imagine cures tentatively, the most poignant verge on a near-
tragic sense of knotted contradictions. The fine sestina, 'Hearing
of harvests rotting in the valleys', intertwines hope and wretchedness in such a way that hope seems an aspect of wretchedness,
a fantasy of escape from present ills. Only in the last lines does
the implicit moral make itself explicit and even then it does so
longingly rather than surely, the final sentence beginning ellipti-
cally, 'Ah, water / Would gush' – that is, 'would gush' were 'the
sorrow' to 'melt' – and ending with a mention of the 'dream' it
advocates shunning: 'And we rebuild our cities, not dream of

islands'. Throughout the poem, Auden's quite masterly skill at subordinating description to allegorical nuance is apparent.

In this and other poems Auden's control does not simplify; his finest lyrics of the period suggest a careful reading of Yeats,[6] but achieve an idiosyncratic and rewarding balance between the musical and the intellectual. The trimeters, basically iambic in stress, of 'May with its light behaving' (1934) please the ear while the words exercise the mind. The poem begins as a celebration of spring and the renewal – emotional and erotic – that accompanies it. But even in this first stanza, consciously Yeatsian epithet ('the swan-delighting river')[7] must compete with the unYeatsian undercutting hinted at by the 'careless picnics': 'careless' evokes a positive freedom from care but also a negative indifference to what should be cared about. The next stanza shows Auden's capacity to deepen the terms of a poem's enquiry without sermonizing. From the actual scene inhabited, however glancingly, by the first stanza, he moves back to consider how, historically speaking, 'we' came to be here. The authority of Auden's 'we' is ultimately neo-classical in that it supposes the existence of shared assumptions and categories; the pathos of his 'we' derives from the sense it gives of concealing a more vulnerable 'I'. We have left behind the 'vague woods', a location which retains its specified vagueness, but, in context, draws to itself notions of innocence, childhood, fairy-tale 'Forests where children meet / And the white angel-vampires flit'. Auden's much-used definite article sharpens the focus of that last-quoted line; indeed, it is remarkable how much presence his essentially non-concrete language can generate: 'white' earns its place here, for instance. Is it the 'white' of innocence or of eeriness? Is it applicable to 'angel' or to 'vampire? Even as the questions are asked, the answer – that 'white' contains all these implications at once – proposes itself. Adroitly multi-layered in its workings, the stanza summons up an original state of psychic, moral and cultural existence, known only when it has gone.

The poem is now ready to make its central turn. Picking up the second stanza's concluding line, 'The dangerous apple taken', the third stanza begins, 'The real world lies before us'. Auden's Miltonic concern with the fall from innocence shows in his glance towards the end of *Paradise Lost*: expelled from Eden, Adam and Eve find 'The world was all before them'.[8] The mood darkens, however, as the lyric stresses Freudian entrapment rather than Miltonic freedom: natural instinct is tainted at its roots by perverse drives, 'The common wish for death'; happiness is elusive, 'The dying master sinks tormented / In the admirers' ring'; goodness is no earthly weapon, 'The unjust walk the earth'. The stanza marshals its observations with poise yet latent distress; the sharp phrasing is kept from glibness by the skilful rhyme scheme, the first line (as in all four stanzas) being left unrhymed while the remaining lines slant away from true rhymes.

The last stanza is the most difficult, for all its air of following on naturally ('And love that makes impatient'), and yet it brings the poem to a troubling, balanced, ambiguous close:

> And love that makes impatient
> The tortoise and the roe, and lays
> The blonde beside the dark,
> Urges upon our blood,
> Before the evil and the good
> How insufficient is
> The endearment and the look.

In that concluding recognition, 'insufficient' works because it contains within itself a longing to know what will suffice; 'endearment' falls with a distancing, ironic ring, love being reduced to instinct divorced from morality. The poem has come full circle from its opening celebration of instinct. Yet it is 'love' which urges the recognition of its own insufficiency, doing so 'Before the evil and the good'. Because of this line's grammatical ambiguity (it looks both before and after), 'Before' might imply love's primacy over as well as – the more evident construction – love's insufficiency in the face of 'the evil and the good'. 'Love' is at once the incarnation of instinct and the source of instruction, a dual role which allows Auden to suggest the mingling of unconscious drives and the possibility of conscious control in human beings. If the poem ends in a tangle, it does so clear-sightedly.

Written in late 1934, the poem 'Easily, my dear, you move, easily your head' (later titled 'A Bride in the 30's') addresses the same knot of ideas and feelings: 'love' is again an amoral drive and yet 'except at our proposal, / Will do no trick at his disposal', the bouncing rhyme at odds with the serious theme in a way that is typical of the poem. But the poem is more tonally and thematically expansive than 'May with its light behaving'. Its urbane control has something in common with 'Out on the lawn I lie in bed', and like that poem its second stanza introduces the idea of 'luck'. In 'Out on the lawn I lie in bed', the poet declares, 'Lucky, this point in time and space / Is chosen as my working place', where 'chosen' discreetly brings into play the contrapuntal idea of choice. In 'Easily, my dear, you move, easily your head' Auden writes, 'And in the policed unlucky city / Lucky his [that, is Love's] bed'. Even the rhyming of 'bed' here (sustaining the series of 'ed' rhymes) preserves the even 'easiness' of the poem's mood. However, that 'easiness' is already troubled; Love seems less a valued absolute than a dangerously irresponsible impulse; the speaker is 'led' by his attraction to the poem's 'you' (male, regardless of the subsequent title's misleading 'Bride') despite the (political) sombreness of 'the sixteen skies of Europe / And the Danube flood'. The 'sixteen skies' have that almost whimsical particularity which makes Auden's tone playful as well as 'sombre'.

This mixed tone, kept up through the poem, accounts for its capacity to unsettle. There is the innocence-cum-ignorance of Love caught in the quasi-Byronic couplet: 'He from these lands of terrifying mottoes / Makes worlds as innocent as Beatrix Potter's'. What might be 'terrifying' becomes terrifyingly 'innocent'. There is, too, the unexpected switch from stanza four to five; having established Love's role in the private sphere – its ability to induce self-absorbed happiness – Auden suggests that Love also works in the public sphere. Here the poem is fascinatingly elusive, making a tricky link between the private 'dance' of stanza four and 'such a music from our time' of the following stanza; Love leads both to self-engrossment and to an increased openness to projected collective desires and fears. As often with Auden, however, paraphrase irons out what in the poem comes across as a wayward, floating sense that the private and the public share in one another's life. So far as the summoned images are those that 'vanity cannot dispel nor bless' they have the capacity to shock (because they show how evil political fantasy and personal love, at root, are produced in comparable ways):

Ten thousand of the desperate marching by
Five feet, six feet, seven feet high:

> Hitler and Mussolini in their wooing poses
> Churchill acknowledging the voters' greeting
> Roosevelt at the microphone, Van der Lubbe laughing
>   And our first meeting.

Frustrated or misdirected eros leads to the adoration of fascist dictators described by Auden as 'wooing' their followers (the line about 'Churchill acknowledging the voters' greeting' is in ambiguous contrast: 'acknowledging' sounds neutral in comparison with the more loaded 'wooing', even as Churchill as a public figure exists by virtue of the projected desires of 'voters'). The nightmarish, nursery rhyme-like second line suggests how 'the desperate' appear both to those who fear them and to their own hysterically aggrandized selves. But, as the expressively terse last line brings out, the same force is at work in the poet's current relationship. It, too, has been made possible by the elimination of possibilities owing to neurosis and conditioning: 'Certain it became while we were still incomplete / There were certain prizes for which we would never compete': 'still incomplete' carries the dispiriting implication that 'completion' will involve the rigidifying of personality. And yet this Freudian determinism is offset by the poem's determination to believe in choice: the last five stanzas grow more urgent and direct while keeping on the right side of the line that separates pointing out from preaching: 'You stand now before me, flesh and bone / These ghosts would like to make their own. / Are they your choices?' 'Ghosts' are those forces present in the 'you''s development – which he is free to embrace (the seductively easier route) or to resist. The poem maintains its lightness of touch in further coolly provocative questions – 'Shall idleness ring then your eyes like the pest?' – before it concludes with one of Auden's typically crystallizing last stanzas:

> Wind shakes the tree; the mountains darken;
> And the heart repeats though we would not hearken:
> 'Yours is the choice, to whom the gods awarded
> The language of learning and the language of love,
> Crooked to move as a moneybug or a cancer
>   Or straight as a dove.'

The heart's reasoning comes across in the form of a voice we cannot afford not to listen to – or so the writing persuades us.

That 'though we would not hearken' is a fine touch, defending itself against the inattention which warnings tend to induce, and, so 'would' also implies, have induced in the past. 'Learning' and 'love' have need of one another; instinct must not be allowed to drive out the crucial idea of human freedom, choice. To put it like this, however, ignores two important aspects of the poetry: its crisply undidactic intensity and its half-desperate attempt to hang on to the clear-cut distinction between categories of 'crooked' and 'straight'. 'Crooked' was used by Auden to mean 'homosexual' and, as Mendelson points out, 'Auden's metaphors complicate the issue by bringing in his own sexuality' (Mendelson, p. 225). A poem that switches throughout between the playfully dawdling and the gravely existential ends on the brink of tragic starkness. Yet it glimpses out of the corner of its eye the possibility that right choice may not be so straightforward as the exigencies of the time make it seem proper to suppose.

4

'As I walked out one evening' (composed in November 1937) confronts this possibility head-on. The poem's scintillating re-working of traditional forms – ballad, nursery rhyme – allows Auden to convey his meanings more figuratively and less ana-lytically than is sometimes the case. As in other ballads of the period (notably 'Victor', written in June 1937), complications of eros are etched with a caricaturing, yet penetrating, vigour. In 'As I walked out one evening', romantic love's self-absorption is expressed through comic hyperbole ('I'll love you till the ocean / Is folded and hung up to dry') that sparks off counter-hyperbole of a more menacing kind:

> Into many a green valley
> Drifts the appalling snow;
> Time breaks the threaded dances
> And the diver's brilliant bow.

The fate of the 'green valley' recalls the opening metaphor for the 'crowds', described as 'fields of harvest wheat', and actual-izes the threat (of the wheat being cut down) which lurks within it. But here Auden offers a free-standing series of images for

Time's ravages, a concern at least as old as Shakespeare's sonnets, yet made new by the writing. The syntactical lead-up to, and positioning of, 'Drifts' is expressive of the undermining drift of time; 'appalling' blends colloquial outrage with latent metaphor (of the snow as a pall). The application of the same verb, 'breaks', to 'threaded dances' and bow-like diver illustrates the grim wit with which Auden brings his topos to life: dancing and diving may differ as activities, but each is endowed by Auden with a perfection which must break. Subsequent imagery exploits Freudian suggestions of neurosis and frustration in lines such as 'The desert sighs in the bed', but the poem claws its way out of hopelessness as it reconciles itself to imperfection:

> O look, look in the mirror,
>   O look in your distress;
> Life remains a blessing
>   Although you cannot bless.
>
> O stand, stand at the window
>   As the tears scald and start;
> You shall love your crooked neighbour
>   With your crooked heart.

Once more Auden assigns responsibility for saying something that matters a great deal to him to an external voice – in this case the voice of the clocks. It is a simple technical device that guards him against preachifying and puts a potential 'message' inside quotation-marks; here, though, a bleak salvation glimmers as the 'you' is admonished first to 'look' at himself, not narcissistically but honestly, then to 'stand at the window' and learn to look beyond himself. But this act of looking presupposes a love of others based on self-knowledge, 'crooked' – whatever its private meaning for Auden – taking on a deeper resonance than 'homosexual'. The writing is economical, deft and touching; it is significant that Auden does not end the poem here, with something close to a moral, but concludes with an image suggestive of life's inexplicable nature: 'The clocks had ceased their chiming / And the deep river ran on'.

'And the deep river ran on': the poet may have sorted out in his own mind certain problems concerning love, but apprehension of 'Life' involves more than intelligent or even wise formulae. Such a recognition lies behind 'Musée des Beaux Arts' (composed at the end of 1938). The poem may begin with an axiom: 'About suffering they were never wrong, / The Old Masters'. But the conversational tone regrets the inevitability of 'suffering' as much as it praises the rightness of the 'Old Masters': from here to 'poetry makes nothing happen' ('In Memory of W. B. Yeats') is a short step.

Towards the end of the decade, in fact, Auden makes the artist's vocation a central subject; poems such as 'Rimbaud', 'Voltaire at Ferney' and 'Matthew Arnold' are saved from being so many skilfully versified pocket biographies by the latent, but real, pressure brought to bear by Auden's own self-concern. When he writes of Arnold, for instance, that 'His gift knew what he was – a dark disordered city', Auden more than glances at his own sense of his 'gift'; Auden may have felt that, unlike Yeats but like Arnold, he had 'thrust his gift in prison' by making it serve his generation's politicizing ambitions. Such a view over-simplifies Auden's always troubled relations with public poetry, but this poem certainly looks forward to 'In Memory of W. B. Yeats', written around the same time; it anticipates the Yeats elegy's more explicit sense that the artist may occasionally glimpse the workings of, but is unlikely to be in a position to alter, history. His obligation is to his 'gift', which is itself a 'way of happening' that rivals and balances the happenings of history.

'In Memory of W. B. Yeats' shows Auden resisting the temptation to view poetry itself as the source of 'Cure', to use Spender's term. Yet 'way of happening' keeps in play the idea that poetry, though it 'makes nothing happen', is intricately related to the world of 'happenings', and the poem, like other poems of the period, is vitalized by Auden's quarrels with himself. Stan Smith has brought out the elegy's concern with 'alternative ideas of language' (Smith, p. 24), and certainly Auden the proto-deconstructionist is in evidence, showing the dead poet's loss of control over his poems ('he became his admirers') and our dependence on rather than mastery of language (worshipped by Time which 'forgives / Everyone by whom it [language] lives').[9] None the less, the poem does not take an extreme deconstructionist position. Ideas may indeed be composed of words, language may be a medium through which we achieve only brief glimpses of purpose, art may be 'a product of history, not a cause' ('The Public v. the Late Mr. William

Butler Yeats' (*EA*, p. 393)). Yet the poem manipulates its different styles to mount a rearguard action against the political quietism, emotional defeatism and intellectual scepticism by which it is tempted. Its first section includes low-key moments that outwit the conventions of elegy and surprise us into a fresh sense of loss: 'A few thousand will think of this day / As one thinks of a day when one did something slightly unusual'. Readers transmit and rework the text; that, if you like, is poetry's 'way of happening'. As Yeats becomes his admirers, his words 'modified in the guts of the living', the second section's conclusion is foreshadowed: poetry 'survives', writes Auden, the repeated verb sandwiching the 'executives' it mockingly rhymes with; 'it survives, / A way of happening, a mouth'. 'Mouth' is odd, as Smith points out, though whether 'the shock of its concretion' (Smith, p. 25) demystifies the humanist belief that poetry is controlled by the 'voice' of a 'subject' is arguable. The oddness serves, rather, to point up the seemingly minimal, but real, claim Auden is making for poetry, much as the opening section's anticipation of this line – 'The mercury sank in the mouth of the dying day' – humanizes its weather report, turning the 'dying day' into a terminally ill patient; indeed, the use of 'mouth' in the second section offsets the pessimistic effect of its use in the first.

Auden implies the importance of poetry's survival even as he interrogates its capacity to alter history. The third section's trochaic sonorities come close to reversing the earlier idea that 'poetry makes nothing happen' as Yeats is invoked to 'Sing of human unsuccess / In a rapture of distress'. Yet the paradoxes here make it plain that Auden does not see a close reading of Yeats's poems as a solution to the 'nightmare of the dark'. Moreover, Yeats, like Claudel and Kipling, has 'views' at odds with the poet's and cannot be hitched to any art-as-propaganda wagon. But he can, the poet prays, 'persuade us to rejoice', a way of putting it that lays as much stress on the reader as the poet; it is up to the reader, Auden implies, to see aesthetic excellence as a value in itself; the one humanist belief the poem clings to is that such perception of aesthetic excellence will, however indirectly, prove beneficial to the perceiver: 'In the deserts of the heart / Let the healing fountain start'. In this sense poetry does make nothing happen: the nothing that is 'no thing' but something inward, imaginative and spiritual. The poem is impressive for its shifts of style and for its double sense of poetry as marginal yet necessary.

In both these respects 'In Memory of W. B. Yeats' anticipates 'September 1, 1939', a poem whose importance has recently been exhaustively and vigorously re-emphasized by Joseph Brodsky.[10] Brodsky offers many scintillating perceptions, but his sensing of 'a voice shot through with the lucidity of despair over everyone's complicity'[11] is especially valuable. For this is a poem which articulates a dependence on and the possible inadequacy of 'a voice': 'All I have is a voice / To undo the folded lie', Auden says, his own voice at once assertive and deprecating. 'September 1, 1939' sets lucidity against near-despair, technical craft against historical chaos, poetry against rhetoric, wisdom against the ineffectuality of wisdom, 'an affirming flame' against 'negation', prayer against fear. Auden later disowned the poem, seeing the line 'We must love one another or die' as 'a damned lie' that proved the 'whole poem ... was infected with an incurable dishonesty and must be scrapped' (quoted in Mendelson, p. 326). But again, later Auden misreads his earlier work by applying to it an inappropriate literalism: in context the offending line makes good and moving sense, reinforcing the point that the State is a totalitarian fiction while the isolated self is a 'romantic lie' (see the same stanza), and offering a moral necessity (love) to complement the physical necessity (food) that unites 'citizen' and 'police'. What impresses about the poem is the way the concern with speech, its uses and uselessness – which dominates lines like 'Exiled Thucydides knew / All that a speech can say / About Democracy' and shows in the poet's ear for idiom (as when the 'commuters' of stanza seven are made to say 'I *will* be true to the wife, / I'll concentrate more on my work') – is related to the poet's vocation and present practice. Impressive, too, as both Brodsky and Smith have expertly brought out, are the poem's 'shifts of tone and register' (Smith, p. 25). Throughout, Auden shifts between confidence and insecurity, between sounding as though he is in a position to analyse why 'the clever hopes ... / Of a low dishonest decade' have come to nothing and implicitly conceding his involvement in the general refusal to 'see where we are, / Lost in a haunted wood'. Even there, 'haunted wood' offers its bleak perception the consolation of a poetic phrase, and, in doing so, allows us to witness the fascinating struggle the poem enacts between the exposure of lying speech and the struggle towards truthful speech. In turn, this is mirrored by the gap between knowledge and action. 'The elderly rubbish' spoken by dictators was known about, and recorded by, Thucydides; it does not save us from having to suffer it and its consequences again.

These movements of feeling are sensitively caught by Auden's tightrope-walking, irregularly iambic trimeters and by his control of diction. So, the last stanza begins by reformulating the grimly compassionate awareness of 'Our world' which pervades the poem: it lies vulnerably 'Defenceless under the night' and yet it *lies* – incapable, it seems, of truth – 'in stupor'. Auden might seem to distance himself from this covert indictment, claiming a perceptiveness denied to others. Yet, deftly outwitting this objection, he sustains, while never blowing the cover of, the stanza's hidden image of a man watching a city at night and noticing 'points of light' – which Auden describes as 'Ironic'. The word reverberates, defining the wisdom attained by the 'Just' posited by Auden as exchanging messages. 'Ironic' turns such wisdom into something intermittent, far from highfalutin and in keeping with the possible futility of correct perception which stanza three, in particular, has considered. At the same time, the lines also imply the importance of belief in the existence of 'the Just', a necessary fiction preserving the poet from solipsism or despair. They show him putting into practice his assertion that 'We must love one another or die' since one way of loving others is to believe them capable of justice.

The poem then turns back to the poet who, without claiming to be among 'the Just', declares his common humanity with them, 'composed like them / Of Eros and of dust, / Beleaguered by the same / Negation and despair'. 'Composed' may point to the fact that Auden's utterance is part of a poetic composition (see Smith, p. 30), but it attests as well to the difficult balance, the composure, achieved by the poem. The result is that the last line's longing for 'an affirming flame' flowers believably out of the poem. The poem does not end with a patched-up affirmation, but with something rather different: a wish to affirm, sustained in the face of what has been unearthed by the poem about human frailty. In keeping with this resolving stroke – that still leaves, and knows it leaves, many troubling issues unresolved – Auden concludes with a true rhyme ('flame' picking up 'same'), even as the earlier off-rhyme with 'them' still lingers, vexingly, in the reader's ear. If, then, the poem partly works to uncover 'the illusoriness of the unitary subject' (Smith, p. 25), it also makes us aware of the poet's capacity to mediate through words the workings of a particular consciousness that is intent on seeing 'where we are'.

Though his versatility is remarkable and gives the lie to most generalizations, it seems fair to say that in his poetry of the late thirties Auden does not broadcast inner tensions, offering his reader a deceptively smooth verbal surface. This is the case in 'Dover' (written in August 1937), a poem where the obsessions with love (or lovelessness) and history overlap. 'Dover' is neither obscurely prophetic in the manner of early Auden nor is it lyrically complex in the manner of middle thirties Auden. Rather, it has a documentary air which plays down both the author's personal involvement (apparent in the later version of the last line which changes from 'Some of these people are happy' to 'Not all of us are unhappy') and the poem's beautifully unforced, wider implications. Uncensoriously the poem captures the self-engrossment of individuals passing through this port, a 'frontier' (Fuller, p. 113), yes, but much less histrionically so than in the early poems. 'Each one prays in the dusk for himself', yet each is part of a network of connections which he hardly controls but which control him: 'all this show / Has, somewhere inland, a vague and dirty root'; 'The soldier guards the traveller who pays for the soldier'; planes fly 'On the edge of that air that makes England of minor importance'; all are part 'of a cooling star, / With half its history done'. The tone – balanced, reserved, unobtrusively watchful, alerted to history as to a rumour in 'the new European air' – is perfectly sustained, and the ending leaves the reader wondering what significance, if any, accrues, or will accrue, to private happiness (or unhappiness). 'Dover' plays an oblique variation on the theme set down with slapdash airiness in the rumbustious 'Letter to Lord Byron':

> It is a commonplace that's hardly worth
>   A poet's while to make profound or terse,
> That now the sun does not go round the earth,
>   That man's no centre of the universe . . .

5

Yet the Auden of the middle thirties at any rate is far from content with merely asserting that our real condition is marginalization. As poems in his collection *Look, Stranger!* (1936) continually seek to show, awareness that history does not correspond to egotistical desire or 'interest', to use a word often employed by Auden, might 'Make action urgent and its nature clear'. This line belongs to a poem, 'August for the people and its favourite islands', in which Auden tries to come clean about his and Isherwood's earlier arrogance in thinking they could stand apart from their society and adopt 'the spies' career'. The irony and precision of Isherwood's novels (such as *Mr Norris Changes Trains* (1935), which grew out of his experiences in Berlin) prompt Auden's praise in the poem for his friend's 'strict and adult pen'. Yet the resolve to confront more honestly 'this hour of crisis and dismay' falters; Auden still seems more than half in love with the role-playing and rhetoric he is intent on abjuring, and the poem dissipates its momentum in verbal decoration of 'every flabby fancy', to use its own phrase. But it concludes with an image that threatens more fascinatingly to undo Auden's insistence on choice and action: 'all sway forward on the dangerous flood / Of history, that never sleeps or dies, / And, held one moment, burns the hand'. Those final words surprise after the image of the 'flood', but the metaphors are mixed to good effect. Partly this is because 'I smoke into the night' a few lines earlier insinuates the idea of burning into the poem; partly because the mixed image suggests the hopelessness of trying to visualize holding the 'flood / Of history'. In the act of giving up the image of the flood, conceding that it is a dead metaphor (as it is not in 'Out on the lawn I lie in bed'), Auden makes us look at it afresh. What governs the 'flood / Of history' the lines do not say – but there must be doubt as to whether, here, Auden feels it is under the sway of human wills. To seek to hold it burns the hand: 'held' might imply 'held back' in which case Auden's view of history is determinist (a strong implication of the natural image – history is going its own way) or it might suggest 'held in the mind', as though the effort to comprehend its workings was too much for one consciousness. Either way, the image makes a thematically and autobiographically interesting poem into one whose emotional dynamics arrest. It is a poem in which 'the word is love' yet which itself offers (conscious) instances of 'all Love's wondering eloquence debased / To a collector's slang' – as when Auden writes, 'Surely one fearless kiss would cure / The million fevers', lines which suggest that 'love', as understood and used by Auden and Isherwood, may prove an inadequate response to 'history'.

The title-poem of *Look, Stranger!* operates with discreeter lyrical tact. The 'stranger' of this poem differs from the 'stranger' of 'The Watershed', who, 'frustrate and vexed', is admonished to 'Go home'. In this poem the stranger, true to a volume obsessed by the 'look', is told to look 'at this island now', and, initially, the poem seems hopeful that this look might hold steadily and wholly the island's natural beauty and its history. However, the dominant tense is conditional; like Seamus Heaney in 'From the Canton of Expectation' Auden may yearn

> to know there is one among us who never swerved
> from all his instincts told him was right action,
> who stood his ground in the indicative,
> whose boat will lift when the cloudburst happens. [12]

But his stranger does not stand his ground in the indicative; rather, he is instructed or pleaded with by the poet to 'Stand stable here / And silent be, / That through the channels of the ear / May wander like a river / The swaying sound of the sea'. In the act of imagining a fusion between the 'stable' onlooker and the 'swaying sound of the sea', the writing lulls the reader into supposing that what is desired is taking place. Certainly the prayer-like wish is entertained with a lyric delicacy that is austere, musical and supple; interlacing sounds that do not quite chime ('Stand' / 'sil*ent*' / '*chann*els' / '*wand*er' / 'sound', for instance) do much to convey the longing for union between subject and object; so, too, does the delaying of the first stanza's last line (which in ordinary speech would swap places with the penultimate line). In voicing longing, then – as Stan Smith has brought out – the poem admits the possibility of lack. [13]

But the relationship between speaker and addressee is more reticent and oblique than Smith allows. For Smith the gap between the two is the site of a 'primary estrangement' (Smith, p. 73) and anticipates the way 'a unitary world of experience breaks down into proliferating dualities' (Smith, p. 74) throughout the poem. Yet the wording of Auden's opening – 'Look, stranger, at this island now / The leaping light for your delight discovers' – does not necessarily imply the speaker's 'estrangement' from 'delight' or suggest that the 'stranger', because sealed off from language and its divisions, is closer to 'delight'. It might, rather, imply the speaker's initial apprehension of 'delight' which he desires that the 'stranger' should also be alerted to. There is, too, a strong sense that the address is self-address, that the speaker – known to the reader only as a disembodied voice – is addressing himself. 'Dualities' do exist (the light is 'leaping' but the stranger is asked to 'Stand stable', the stanza begins with a 'Look' but ends with a 'sound'); yet they *may* compose a unity. The poem reaps the positive benefits as well as the negative aspects of its conditional mood ('May wander like a river'); Smith's deconstructionist bias leads to an *a priori* scepticism which is more cut and dried than the poem warrants.

'The poem bears the same sort of relationship to Arnold's "Dover Beach" as a postcard does to a letter' (Fuller, p. 107): Fuller's suggestive sentence does not point out how ruthlessly Auden's postcard edits Arnold's letter or, indeed, his own earlier concern with frontiers, barriers and 'old systems which await / The last transgression of the sea' (*Paid on Both Sides*). Where Arnold allegorizes – the Channel's ebb and flow suggests thoughts about 'The Sea of Faith' withdrawing down the 'naked shingles of the world'[14] – Auden eschews abstraction and allows his images to speak for themselves: 'And the shingle scrambles after the suck- / ing surf', he writes in the second stanza, 'and the gull lodges / A moment on its sheer side'. Shingle, surf and gull: each is 'sheer', primarily itself and not another thing, even if the break in 'suck- / ing' enacts the interdependence between shingle and surf which replaces what in earlier poems by Auden might have been an emphasis on separateness. Again, however, the stanza's off-rhymes, lack of a main verb and use of paradox ('the small field's ending pause') play round disquiet, seeming to arouse it, succeeding in allaying it – for 'A moment'.

It is typical of this richly understated poem that 'A moment' rather than, say, 'History' – absent for once – should catch the eye. Yet History is a powerful absence, as the final stanza makes clear: 'Far off like floating seeds the ships / Diverge on urgent voluntary errands'. The lines compact the 'diverging' impulses out of which the poem wrests its momentary balance. To the eye

the ships seem 'like floating seeds', but the simile (with its –
mainly – hopeful hint of future germination) asserts a likeness
between the natural and the man-made that the next line
cancels. The ships are engaged in 'voluntary errands', errands
decided upon by human choice: 'voluntary' has the same high
profile at the end of 'Fish in the unruffled lakes', a love poem
written the following March (1936), where the poet gives thanks
that the poem's 'you'

> who have
> All gifts that to the swan
> Impulsive Nature gave,
> The majesty and pride,
> Last night should add
> Your voluntary love.

Both uses of the adjective show Auden's capacity to intellectualize a lyric form which, in 'Fish in the unruffled lakes' especially,
is rooted, as already suggested, in a close study of Yeats. But
whereas 'voluntary' in the later lyric picks out and underwrites
its point (that love given voluntarily is of all gifts the most
valuable), in 'Look, stranger, at this island now' the word's
suggestions shimmer more fleetingly. As many words in the
poem do, it calls up its opposite, 'involuntary', looking ahead to
a time, perhaps not so very 'Far off', when 'coercion'[15] might be
the order of the day, merchant ships giving way to destroyers.
The internal rhyme of 'Diverge' and 'urgent' also contributes to
the plaiting of effects: 'Diverge' contains the notion of freedom to
diverge, to go one's own way; at the same time it intimates
divergence from a course, possibly the course the poet wishes to
see history take; in this second sense the divergence might be
caused by 'urgent' pressures that will threaten the harmony of
the 'moment' celebrated by the poem. Such notions find their
way into the verse glancingly and lightly, and the poem ends on
a more buoyant note, suggesting that 'the full view' might 'move
in memory as now these clouds do, / That pass the harbour
mirror / And all the summer through the water saunter'. The
'full view', of course, half-glimpses the need to take into account
unpleasant realities temporarily out of sight, and its life in
consciousness is both assured and suspended, much as the clutch
of '-er' rhymes at once settles and rocks the mood. Though the

poem ends positively, it is recognizably the product of a writer who a year later will write: 'For Europe is absent. This is an island and therefore / Unreal' ('Journey to Iceland'). The end of 'Look, stranger, at this island now' describes a desired oneness ('Indeed *may* enter' (emphasis added)) between mind and 'view', and the final comparison ('as now these clouds do') illustrates the tact with which the poem suggests the workings of desire: the clouds may saunter through the water 'all the summer', but 'all' and 'summer' quietly diverge, the first word suggesting some grasped totality, the second introducing the idea of seasonal change as well as the further idea that the experience of oneness may prove only passing.

The metaphorical implications of seasonal change (and the possibility of escape from it) lie close to the heart of Shelley's 'Ode to the West Wind', one of the great political lyrics in the language, and it may well be that Auden's vehement rejection of Shelley in the thirties sprang from his 'recognition of the dangerous degree of sympathy which in fact he held for Shelley's purposes and style' (Mendelson, p. 201). The surreal urgencies of 'Now the leaves are falling fast' owe more to Blake than Shelley, but the poem's conclusion crosses an image of Utopian hope with in-built anti-Utopian analysis:

> Cold, impossible, ahead
> Lifts the mountain's lovely head
> Whose white waterfall could bless
> Travellers in their last distress.

Is the mountain an image born out of despair, or does it represent the possibility that the 'impossible' might be realized? The poem balances the two suggestions in its final rhyme.

In doing so it points towards a major strength – the sustaining, consciously or unconsciously, of contradictions – possessed by Auden's poems about history and love, Symptom and Cure, in the thirties. This strength can negotiate riskily with muddle, especially when Auden is astride some hortatory hobby-horse. 'O Love, the interest itself in thoughtless Heaven' (written in 1932), the bravura programme piece which serves as the Prologue to *Look, Stranger!*, is an example. Its didactic intention is manifest, yet it is preserved from woodenness by three things: the diction's quirky particularity that works zestfully against the grain of the poem's professed desire for greater simplicity; the novel significance it gives to 'Love', the seemingly dulled abstraction which takes centre-stage in the poem; and the startling break it makes at the end from wry presentation of what we know to breathtaking imagining of what we do not; 'at this very moment', writes Auden,

> Some possible dream, long coiled in the ammonite's
>   slumber
> Is uncurling, prepared to lay on our talk and
>   kindness
> Its military silence, its surgeon's idea of pain;
>
> And out of the Future into actual History,
> As when Merlin, tamer of horses, and his lords to
>   whom
> Stonehenge was still a thought, the Pillars passed
>
> And into the undared ocean swung north their prow,
> Drives through the night and star-concealing dawn
> For the virgin roadsteads of our hearts an
>   unwavering keel.

These lines get better as they unwind, leaving behind the bourgeois-baiting of the covert sneer at 'our talk and kindness' for the remarkable shock of the close where the envisaged entrance into 'actual History' is brought home by the delayed main verb, 'Drives'; the writing itself drives an unwavering keel for our hearts, its designs on the reader an arresting blend of the aggressive and the tender even as its idiom compacts the mythic and the Utopian.

The poem puts its trust in a quasi-religious fiction, 'Love', a providential power that will, the poet hopes, do for human beings what they have failed to do for themselves. In this Prologue to a volume obsessed by imaginings of change, Auden's style and voice are more than half in love with the messianic. In one of his greatest poems, 'Lay your sleeping head, my love', however, from the other end of the decade, Auden seems to turn his attention from history and Utopia to the fastidiously depicted foul rag-and-bone shop of the heart: 'seems to turn' because the poem is as shaped by what it excludes as by what it contains.

The poem may generalize ('Soul and body have no bounds'), but its grasp of what 'love' involves for the poet personally is unflinching. And what it involves – conveyed in rhythms that are gravely ravishing – is isolation, guilt or at any rate acceptance of the speaker's own faithlessness, and sensitivity to the perishable in experience.

The poem is pervaded by tensions, tugs and oppositions that strive towards, but cannot finally or completely attain, reconciliation. For instance, the trochaic tetrameters refuse to trip off the tongue easily. Instead, they keep a serious, contemplative yet lyrical pace:

> Time and fevers burn away
> Individual beauty from
> Thoughtful children, and the grave
> Proves the child ephemeral.

These lines communicate their sombre truisms as though they were freshly discovered truths, achieving a dignity that is the result of varied pauses, surprising polysyllables and the way the sentence is played across the line-endings.

Throughout, the speaker's vision is consistently double; his active, troubled, wakeful consciousness is stirred by the passive, sleeping 'you'. The poem's mode of lonely soliloquy qualifies the likelihood of reciprocal affection. So the intimate 'your sleeping head' modulates into the detached 'the living creature'. On the other hand, the scrupulously ethical gives way to an assertion of subjective value: 'Mortal, guilty, but to me / The entirely beautiful'. As those lines demonstrate, the poem's affirmative suggestions must contend with others that are more disquieting: for instance, does 'to me' undercut or validate?

Similarly, the second stanza both brings into play and puts into question the idea of a profitable movement between eros and agape, sense and intellect: the vision sent by Venus of supernatural sympathy is ambiguously 'Grave'; the 'hermit's sensual ecstasy', woken by 'an abstract insight', veers uncomfortably close to sublimation in reverse. Above all, the personal is, for once in Auden's thirties poems, given pride of place yet, as in a love poem by Donne, put into the context of a 'mortal world' that is largely indifferent to the claims of the personal. Auden concludes by praying that the 'you' will 'Find the mortal world enough'. But the implication is stark, even bitter; the lover must come to terms with 'the mortal world' since it is the only world there is. And, the most touching of all the poem's controlled quarrels with itself, its final prayer concedes that the speaker can do nothing to help the 'you', except to hope that 'the involuntary powers' and 'every human love' will intervene on his behalf. If the prayer is heartfelt, the forces it invokes have the air of having been pulled out of a conjuror's hat; they half concede their solely verbal existence. Among the great love poems of the decade, 'Lay your sleeping head, my love' denies the possibility of love lasting and denies, too, its power to avert fear and threat. The poem may seem composed in the margins of Auden's historical concerns. But it earns its central place in Auden's poems of the decade by virtue of the skill with which it steadfastly affirms, even as it allows for the precariousness of, the unique, individual, particular and ephemeral:

> Every farthing of the cost,
> All the dreaded cards foretell,
> Shall be paid, but from this night
> Not a whisper, not a thought,
> Not a kiss nor look be lost.

Even here Auden's wording belies his tone; he begins in the indicative ('Shall be paid'), but he ends close to the wish-fulfilling realm of the subjunctive; the elliptical 'be lost' (meaning 'shall be lost') momentarily resembles an elliptical form of the construction 'Let not [these things] be lost'. On either reading, Auden can be seen as warding off the worry that whisper, thought, kiss and look will 'be lost'.

6

Although Auden's sonnet sequence *In Time of War* was written for a particular occasion, the journey he made with Isherwood in 1938 to China during the Sino-Japanese war (the sequence comprises the final section of their book *Journey to a War*), it is Auden's most obviously generalized and conceptual poetry of the decade.[16] Self-evidently written to a preconceived plan, it is about choice and necessity, and wants to assert responsibility in freedom, that the future is ours to shape. In his Introduction to *The Oxford Book of Light Verse*, published in the same year in which he composed the sequence, Auden wrote:

> Virtues which were once nursed unconsciously by the forces of nature must now be recovered and fostered by a deliberate effort of the will and the intelligence. In the future, societies will not grow of themselves. They will either be made consciously or decay. A democracy in which each citizen is as fully conscious and capable of making a rational choice, as in the past has been possible only for the wealthier few, is the only kind of society which in the future is likely to survive for long.   (*EA*, p. 368)

In Time of War makes one aware not only of the 'deliberate effort of the will and the intelligence' behind its composition, but also of the impulse against which that effort was being made. Auden's view of evolution was fleshed out in another essay, *I Believe*, also contemporaneous with the sonnet sequence: 'each stage of moral freedom [is] superseded by a new one'. Mankind's increasing consciousness demands of us that we take our lives more and more into our own hands. This leads to Auden's relativist view of morality, that goodness can only be defined in relation to man's 'constantly changing' environment with its 'fresh series of choices'; hence his '*fairly* optimistic' belief that 'No society is absolutely good; but some are better than others' (*EA*, pp. 372, 375).

This evolutionary view of history informs the plan of *In Time of War*. The contemporary state of world crisis, as evinced by the Sino-Japanese war, is seen in mythic and temporal perspective, from the Creation, 'the years' (I), to 'the glorious balls of the future' (XXVII). The sequence traces mankind's growing consciousness up to the present time, when 'rational choice', as opposed to a determinist view of history, is the only way forward. As each epoch passes into the next, it proves inadequate to mankind's growing consciousness. The impression of a collective consciousness evolving through the ages is disorientatingly conveyed by the indeterminate subject of the sonnets, in the first twelve usually 'he', sometimes 'they', until in sonnet XIV the 'we' of Auden and our present epoch enters: 'Yes, we are going to suffer, now'. The present represents a crisis of opportunity, when 'we have the misfortune or the good luck to be living in one of the great critical historical periods', where 'we do have to choose, every one of us' (*I Believe*, *EA*, p. 379).

The sonnet form, with its potentiality for argumentation, would seem to support such a plan. Aphorisms and statements abound. Yet this is more than a propositional poetry. Its coherence is frequently only an air. Arguments change direction in the spaces between propositions; statements are set at right angles to one another. The poetry compels not for any demonstration of Auden's ideas, but for the humanity evinced in coming to terms with them. Indeed, the clarity of the essays cited above may well have emerged out of the troubled, compassionate intelligence at work beneath the surface composure of the poetry. For all their formal poise, the sonnets possess an inner tension between a simple but powerful yearning for 'the Good Place' (XIII), and the irreducible knowledge that 'life is evil now' (XVI). Like the dancers of sonnet XXII, the sonnets have their 'simple ... dream wishes', and would 'employ / The elementary language of the heart, / And speak to muscles of the need for joy'; and like the dancers also, the sonnets would 'speak directly to our lost condition' – as happens at the opening of the last sonnet, where mankind is found 'wandering lost'. But sonnet XXII turns on itself roundly in the sestet, and shows up the dangers of such compulsions. The sonnets are a compelling demonstration of what Auden had earlier hit on as 'the convolutions of your simple wish' (from 'Consider this and in our time').

The poetry knows that its optimistic strain, its need for joy, goes against the grain of 'admonitory' history (Fuller, p. 126): 'History opposes its grief to our buoyant song', begins the sestet of the pivotal sonnet XIII. This line is not merely a lament for the artist's social displacement: the potential to compose that song is an index of the Good Place. As Auden wrote in his Introduction to *The Oxford Book of Light Verse*, only in the ideal society, in a 'democracy in which each citizen is ... fully conscious and capable of making a rational choice', 'will it be possible for the poet, without sacrificing any of his subtleties of sensibility or his integrity, to write poetry which is simple, clear, and gay' (*EA*, p. 368). Subtleties of sensibility and integrity abound in the sonnets, but only intermittently is the poetry simple and clear. Even as sonnet XIII goes on to lament the absence of the Good Place, it demonstrates a subtle integrity: 'The Good Place has not been; our star has warmed to birth / A race of promise that has never proved its worth'. Even here the implication that there is worth to be proven betrays a *'fairly* optimistic' inclination.

Neither is the 'buoyant song' in the first quatrain of sonnet XIII simple and clear, despite appearances. The quatrain wants to praise the instinctive, unconscious life out of and beyond which, so the sequence has been arguing, we have evolved into rational consciousness. But the buoyancy sounds as though it is being sent up somewhat. 'Certainly praise' wavers between the defiantly celebratory and the ironically stand-offish. 'Let the song mount again and again' sounds possibly inflated, especially when heard in relation to the rest of the quatrain. The metaphors for the instinctive life, 'life as it blossoms out in a jar or a face' and 'the vegetable patience' sound flickeringly insouciant. There is a throwaway air in the manner with which the poem manages to rescue something from history: 'Some people have been happy; there have been great men'. The second quatrain implicitly contrasts understanding with the instinctive and unreflective: 'But hear the morning's injured weeping, and know why: / Cities and men have fallen'. The defiantly declarative 'and know why' gives way to what sounds like an ironic knowingness: 'still, all princes must / Employ the Fairly-Noble unifying Lie'. By the end of the sonnet instinct and intellect are in uncomfortable equilibrium: 'and prodigious, but wrong / This passive flower-like people who for so long / In the Eighteen Provinces have constructed the earth'. The organic metaphor has taken on a dismissive air with the phrase 'flower-like', and 'vegetable patience' has degenerated into 'passivity'. At the same time the active intelligence does not get unequivocal endorsement either: 'constructing the earth' sounds like an abuse of our natural habitat. 'Earth', with its 'mountains', is a recurrent motif in the sequence for our environment, our arena of action. It is supremely indifferent; that, however, does not relieve us of responsibility. As the conclusion of the next sonnet says:

> The mountains cannot judge us when we lie:
> We dwell upon the earth; the earth obeys
> The intelligent and evil till they die.

Here despair and hope cancel each other out. The indifferent earth, those unjudging mountains, will remain to preside after death. But the all-important issue is still how we order our dwelling upon the earth. 'Dwell' mingles a sense of transient lingering with a quiet reverence for this habitat of ours.

That Auden felt strongly poetry's temptation to stand aside from the 'deliberate effort of the will and the intelligence' is underlined by sonnet IV. This is a fairly straightforward illustration of the argument, outlined in *I Believe*, that

> each stage of moral freedom [is] superseded by a new one. For example, we frequently admire the 'goodness' of illiterate peasants as compared with the 'badness' of many townees. But this is a romantic confusion. The goodness we admire in the former is a natural, not a moral, goodness. Once, the life of the peasant represented the highest use of the powers of man, the farthest limit of his freedom of action. This is no longer true. (*EA*, p. 372)

The first quatrain of sonnet IV delineates the 'unprogressive life' (Fuller, p. 126) of the peasant, who allows himself to be limited by his natural environment: 'He stayed: and was imprisoned in possession', so that 'the mountains chose the mother of his children'. By contrast, in the second quatrain the townees 'pursued their rapid and unnatural course'. But the peasant's closeness to nature turns the all-providing earth into an image of conformity: 'But took his colour from the earth, / And grew in likeness to his sheep and cattle'. Significantly, the 'romantic confusion' which sees the peasant as a Noble Savage has poetic as well as political implications: 'The poet wept and saw in him the truth, / And the oppressor held him up as an example'. (This conjures up reactionary agrarian political movements of the time.) Throughout the sequence one can sense the poet having to guard against the reactionary romanticism implicit in his yearning for the Good Place, even as he endeavours to keep his optimism intact.

The optimism is in danger of teetering over into wishful thinking, but at the same time the poetry acknowledges such thinking as a fundamental motive, a fact of our psyche, and of the poetry, to be neither gainsaid nor applauded. The poetry participates in dreaming and also sends it up: as the last sonnet says, 'how we dream of a part / In the glorious balls of the future'. That sonnet states and demonstrates the tug in the sequence between responsibility and opportunity. It not only cites but also breathes life into Engels's dictum that 'freedom is the knowledge of necessity'. The first line, 'Wandering lost upon the mountains of our choice', is not as straightforward as its assured rhetoric suggests. Those mountains enigmatically blend constraint and liberation: either, this is what we have chosen (and we must take the consequences); or, this is our opportunity for choice. The line bewitchingly mingles elegy with expectancy, yearning with compulsion, regret with anticipation:

> Again and again we sigh for an ancient South,
> For the warm nude ages of instinctive poise,
> For the taste of joy in the innocent mouth.

'Again and again' implicitly acknowledges the futility of yearning. The poetry's Keatsian relish knows it is trapped in the prisonhouse of desire for a lost Eden, as it acknowledges when it later picks up on the word 'nude': 'we / Were never nude and calm like a great door'. This simile draws attention to itself, conjuring up exits and entrances with a hint of Audenish horseplay. Compulsion shadow-boxes with aimlessness:

> each intricate maze
> Has a plan, and the disciplined movements of the heart
> Can follow for ever and ever its harmless ways.

The phrase 'each intricate maze' lovingly acknowledges everyone's right to a dream plan, including that of the writer of these sonnets, while 'harmless ways' flirts with futility. Yet even as the phrase 'for ever and ever' mocks those private 'disciplined' emotional webs, its echo of the Lord's Prayer casts a holiness over the heart's affections which cannot be gainsaid whatever the unplannable course of history. (The word 'plan' itself follows a fascinatingly 'intricate maze' through the course of the sonnet sequence.) The last line, 'A mountain people dwelling among mountains', is a conclusion to the sequence that leaves everything to be played again, where still 'we do have to choose, every one of us'. The sonority of that line is both plangent and plaintive. We live in our proper habitat. 'Lost' in the first line has given way to 'dwelling' in the last, but the change signifies no more than a change of attitude, an acquiescence in our state of wandering. The poem begins with a head for heights – we are 'lost *upon* the mountains' – and ends accustomed to them: 'dwelling *among* mountains'. Again, the word 'dwelling' conveys a sense of impermanence as well as of customariness.

History seems like an irredeemable narrative; but each moment opens up a vista of choices. Only the desire to abnegate responsibility puts history beyond reach. If we are fatalistic, then indeed our destiny will be determined. This is what happens to the Japanese pilots of sonnet XV with their 'obedience for a master' (from 'To ask the hard question is simple'). Oxymoronically to 'choose a fate' is not to be fated; it is to be fatalistic. We can choose 'to turn away from freedom' in our acts of obedience, but the ensuing compulsion is of our own making. The 'now' of the Sino-Japanese war – the word is prominent at the start of XIV and the end of XVI – impinges with stark actuality: 'Here war is simple like a monument' begins sonnet XVI. Yet even the declarative formulae of XVI resist paraphrase. If we did not know it already, sonnet XXIV is to tell us that monuments are far from 'simple'. In XVI a tight-lipped ironic anger is audible in the deployment of simple statements. War's coercive impersonality comes across in the lines 'A telephone is speaking to a man; / Flags on a map assert that troops were sent', and in the sinisterly flat 'There is a plan'. Amidst this detached inhumanity the simple humanity of 'A boy brings milk in bowls' strikes home. In the second quatrain ironic anger deepens into pathos. The line 'For living men in terror of their lives' turns on itself bitterly. The caustically monosyllabic, repetitive, dead-pan thud of the line 'Who thirst at nine who were to thirst at noon' sounds as though it has despaired of remonstration; there is a hiccup in the 'plan', suffering occurs earlier than anticipated. 'And can be lost and are': in the space of six monosyllables the poet mimics the attitude of official command – we can afford to lose the men ('can be lost') – and then shatters it with the two words 'and are'.

But for all its outward bitterness, sonnet XVI conveys inner struggle. The scornful implication of the eighth line, that ideas cannot die soon enough, jolts the poet into the bold about-face at the start of the sestet, as if made newly aware of the imperative to choose, to recognize 'the justice of a cause' (Fuller, p. 126): 'But ideas can be true although men die'. The inelegance of this line, a result of the proximity of the two conjunctions, testifies to its faithfulness to the twists and turns of thought and feeling. If 'although' sounds awkward so soon after 'but', the transition that would seem to be signified by 'and' at the start of the next line is deceptive, for the ensuing statement, 'we can watch a thousand faces / Made active by one lie', contradicts the notion that 'ideas can be true': ideas can be false, too. Intransigent opposites meet. The emotional cul-de-sac is characteristic of the whole sequence. The 'passive flower-like people' of sonnet XIII are 'wrong', but as an alternative we are presented with these 'faces', an inhuman-seeming synecdoche, whose 'activity' is also wrong; it is not even true activity since it is in the passive voice; 'Made active by one lie'. The apparently detached 'And we can watch' is really a guilty collusion. All the poet can do to counter the asserting flags at the start is to point to maps that 'point'; all he can do is remonstrate: 'And maps can really point to places / Where life is evil now: / Nanking; Dachau'. Yet the insistence on irreducible fact transcends helplessness. That 'really' may teeter on the edge of clumsiness, but it is effective, as is the startled metrical dwindling of each tercet. The numbed naming must be enough; to attempt more would violate with language the unspeakable memories of the anonymous dead. Those two words are the poet's attempt to erect a 'monument' that is truly 'simple'; this is the obverse of 'The elementary language of the heart' (XXII).

The self-conscious nature of this poetry is never more acute than when it is trying to break out of the confines of self and envisage the collective ideal underlying the sequence, a 'Unity [which is] compatible with Freedom', in the words of Auden's 'Commentary' to the sonnet sequence. Sonnet XVII's admission that it is impossible to 'imagine [the] isolation' of the suffering comes as the result of the effort to do so, which produces the brilliant but self-preening line 'For who when healthy can become a foot?' – a line that does at least acknowledge that a foot is part of the body, that we are all parts of a larger whole. 'We stand elsewhere' denotes not only the perspective on us of those who suffer, but also, guiltily, our perspective on them. The ideal of unity encompasses time as well as space: as sonnet XX puts it, 'Time speaks a language they [the suffering Chinese] will never master', because they are part of time, one of the participants in history; by an act of communal sympathy 'we' can take on their predicament, and so their suffering becomes the world's: 'We live here. We lie in the Present's unopened / Sorrow; its limits are what we are' – which characteristically holds in tension necessity and choice, determinism and responsibility. But the poet is inclined to let his own mastery of language run away with him. One wonders how appropriate, in the sorrowing context, is the pun on 'present', the gift donated to the future (the pun recalls the first line of the first sonnet, 'the gifts were showered'). Whether later generations unwrap this gift will determine its place in history. History is in our hands, so to speak. And just how appropriate is the tone of the memorable apothegm, 'The prisoner ought never to pardon his cell'? The poet's inventiveness has continually to be kept in check in the interests of his graver purpose – how successfully, in this sonnet, can be judged by the concluding lines, which wonder, with a trace of scepticism, if there will be communion between present and future, so that whatever happens today, even defeat, may become meaningful:

> Can future ages ever escape so far,
> Yet feel derived from everything that happened,
> Even from us, that even this was well?

It has to be admitted that the sort of writing demonstrated by the above quotation has an uncomfortably willed air, the convolutions of its simple wish being responsible for the inertly convoluted abstractions. More telling are the many instances where the poetry relives the effort to feel, sometimes against the poet's seemingly better judgement, that 'this was well'. Such an instance is sonnet XXIII, which, through its deliberate act of remembering ('To-night in China let me think of one'), demonstrates the heartening power of the isolated 'great man' to speak to later generations, and to enable Auden to complete his sonnet with these mysteriously simple lines:

> And with the gratitude of the Completed
> He went out in the winter night to stroke
> That little tower like a great animal.

The way the rhythm of the last line barely keeps within the metrical norm is haunting, as is the opposition between the words 'little' and 'great'. In a dark and disunited time Rilke's poetry represents the ideal of unity. Unnamed in the sonnet, he becomes one of the representative anonymous, somehow the spokesman for all those nameless ones celebrated in the next sonnet ('No, not their names') for whom, such is the powerful implication, Auden too would wish to be spokesman.

Auden's way of celebrating the nameless in sonnet XXIV beguilingly reconciles the opposed impulses underlying the sequence. Our better selves are envisaged as finding an instinctual and unconscious relation with those who have not erected monuments to themselves in history, 'whose only memorial is their posterity' (Fuller, p. 127). They are associated with the ground of our being, the 'Earth' that 'grew them':

> they grew ripe and seeded;

> And the seeds clung to us; even our blood
> Was able to revive them; and they grew again;
> Happy their wish and mild to flower and flood.

This graceful reconciliation of choice and instinct works more by sleight of style than strength of argument. The instinctive seeds have a will of their own ('clung to us'), as does 'our blood' ('Was able to revive them'). Though the poem's imagery has the nameless ancestors unconsciously flowering in the blood of posterity, they are described in terms of conscious desire: 'Happy their *wish*'. The unfamiliar word order of the last line is undemonstratively alluring. The more usual order would be 'happy and mild their wish'; but in the line as it stands the suspicion of a syntactic parallel between 'wish' and 'mild' allows 'mild' to become, fleetingly but persuasively, emphatic: the seeds are 'mild that they should flower', their mildness will enable them to flower. Thus the line sinuously conveys the tug between the knowledge that 'we do have to choose, every one of us', and the desire that goodness should flower naturally, of its own accord.

7

MacNeice (2)
Autumn Journal:
'A monologue is the death of language'

1

Autumn Journal is distinguished by its voice. Unless this is appreciated the poem will not seem to rise above the level of very good journalism; indeed, too many readers have taken their cue from MacNeice himself when, ten years after composing it, he declared that 'after *Autumn Journal* I tired of journalism' (*SCM*, p. 161). The poem can be heard as confirming Auden's line 'All I have is a voice' (from 'September 1, 1939'), which is as much a defiant assertion in the face of public crisis as an admission of defeat; and when Auden wrote earlier in 1939 that 'poetry makes nothing happen' he also wrote that 'it survives, / A way of happening, a mouth'. Poetry is an event *sui generis* in the world, and *Autumn Journal* bears this out. Its way of happening, its weaving together of tones, moods and registers to convey a personality, is compelling. If its autumnal air sounds a retreat, it is a strategic one in the face of external events at the time of the Munich Agreement (September 1938; Neville Chamberlain found 'peace in our time' by offering the Sudetenlands of Czechoslavakia to Hitler), a regrouping of forces behind the lines to reassert the value of individual utterance in a world of, inevitably, mass emotion.

The voice for MacNeice is never isolated, a condition it could

181

approach in, for instance, Eliot's poetry: 'Still is the unspoken word, the Word unheard, / The Word without a word . . .' (from *Ash-Wednesday* V). As Chapter 3 showed, for MacNeice the language of poetry has its life in, and returns life to, the community. Eliot also knew that language is the voice of the people, that it is the function of the poet to 'purify the dialect of the tribe' (from *Four Quartets*, 'Little Gidding' II), but the tone of that statement betrays a very different attitude from Mac-Neice's to the cultural matrix of language. For Eliot contact is only to make withdrawal more possible, whereas for MacNeice it is to sharpen awareness of all that is other. However dubious Eliot's equation of language with the Logos, the Word, his emphasis is clear: 'the Word within / The world and for the world' denotes a temporary incarnation, for 'Against the Word the unstilled world still whirled' (from *Ash-Wednesday* V), which is a whirl of words from which the poet would extricate himself.

The urgency of *Autumn Journal*'s underlying impulse is explicit in section XXIII, where 'finding a voice' becomes a political imperative. The poet sees the eat-to-live/live-to-eat debate of section XXI being lived out in Civil-War Spain on the streets of Barcelona (centre of Republican resistance: see Chapter 8 for further discussion): in spite of starvation and homelessness, 'Here at least the soul has found its voice / Though not indeed by choice; / The cost was heavy'. But the poet of *Autumn Journal* is disarmingly honest enough to acknowledge that he has not earned the right to such a unified voice, that he has not had to pay the cost, and that he still has 'choice'. However guiltily, he must live and write according to his circumstances, as the ironic contrast with the previous section makes clear: spending Christmas in frivolous Paris on the way to agonized Spain, he assumes, with a crescendo of bagpipe-music verve, the voice of the cynic, no less cynical for being self-consciously so:

> How I enjoy this bout of cynical self-indulgence,
>   Of glittering and hard-boiled make-believe;
> The cynic is a creature of overstatements
>   But an overstatement is something to achieve.

This itself is a statement that tries not to overstate, but which gets close to doing so in its generalization about 'the cynic'. The tendency here to let the voice run away with itself demonstrates *Autumn Journal*'s characteristic self-awareness.

Section XV pays ironic tribute to the human voice:

> Let the aces run riot round Brooklands,
>   Let the tape-machines go drunk,
> Turn on the purple spotlight, pull out the Vox Humana,
>   Dig up somebody's body in a cloakroom trunk.
> Give us sensations and then again sensations . . .

The poet's tape-machine goes deliberately drunk in this section, taking on the bagpipe-music voice of mass hysteria and pulling out the *vox humana* stop (of what must be a cinema organ), a shared voice to be sure, but not one which 'the soul has found' but which, rather, has escaped the soul – until the hysteria spirals into a nightmare vision of a death-in-life procession of ghouls. The effort, renewed towards the end of the section, to escape such encounters with reality, all the more real for being imagined, is characteristically a vocal effort: the ghouls

>   are sure to go away if we take no notice;
>   Another round of drinks or make it twice.
> That was a good one, tell us another, don't stop talking,
>   Cap your stories, if
> You haven't any new ones tell the old ones,
>   Tell them as often as you like and perhaps those horrible
>   stiff
> People with blank faces that are yet familiar
>   Won't be there when you look again . . .

The scenario, terror suppressed by bar-talk insouciance, is familiar from 'Homage to Clichés'. It is a plausible way of hearing and attending to the whole of *Autumn Journal*: as an immensely winning demonstration of how not to 'stop talking', though all the time behind the talk lurks fear.

Yet fear coexists with more affirmative impulses in *Autumn Journal*; throughout, self is discovered in other: 'the eyes grow weary / With vision but it is vision builds the eye', and 'the ego cannot live / Without becoming other for the Other / Has got yourself to give' (XVII). Self has its being in the circumambient world, and by extension language is by nature multivocal:

> Why not admit that other people are always
>   Organic to the self, that a monologue
> Is the death of language and that a single lion
>   Is less himself, or alive, than a dog and another dog?
>   (XVII)

Verbal automatism, letting the voices of others compose the poet's own, is integral to MacNeice's poetic method. Chapter 3 argued that the tendency leads to variable results: to cerebral rambling in poems such as 'Train to Dublin' and 'Ode', to sympathetic satire in 'Christmas Shopping', to exhilarating despair in 'Bagpipe Music'. In *Autumn Journal* it is turned to fine account. Capturing the mood of the times means capturing thought and emotion in process. This gives the poetry a self-reflexive, even self-regarding quality, as it catches itself in the act of shifting tones. Spender indicates an essential feature of *Autumn Journal* when he writes of MacNeice's poetry generally that 'he seems *conscious* that [his] attitudes will soon be replaced by others' (Casebook, p. 49; emphasis added). In his essay 'Experiences with Images' MacNeice writes: 'The voice and mood, though they may pretend to be spontaneous, are yet in even the most "personal" of poets such as Catullus and Burns a *chosen* voice and mood, set defiantly in opposition to what they must still coexist with; there may be only one actor on the stage but the Opposition are on their toes in the wings – and crowding the auditorium; your lyric in fact is a monodrama' (*SCM*, p. 155). Though not what one would normally call a lyric, *Autumn Journal* is lyrical in this sense of a personal 'monodrama'. Frequently the opposition in the wings is brought centre stage: as MacNeice wrote to T. S. Eliot, the poem has 'a *dramatic* quality, as different parts of myself (e.g. the anarchist, the defeatist, the sensual man, the philosopher, the would-be good citizen) can be given their say in turn'. His 'various and conflicting / Selves' (XXIV) take on various and conflicting voices in this monodrama, as distinct from 'a monologue' that 'is the death of language'.

In his 'Note' at the head of *Autumn Journal* MacNeice defends 'over-statements and inconsistencies' by arguing that the nature of a journal is to be truthful to the flux of thought and experience: 'In a journal or a personal letter a man writes what he feels at the moment; to attempt scientific truthfulness would be – paradoxically – dishonest'. He is not 'attempting to offer . . . a final verdict or a balanced judgement. It is the nature of this poem to be neither final nor balanced'. He has 'certain beliefs' which he has however 'refused to abstract from their context' (*CPM*, p. 101). The voice of *Autumn Journal* makes one constantly aware of its context, the arena, personal or historical, in which it sounds. However much the poet wants 'To hit the target straight without circumlocution' (II), he knows this is a sort of death-wish, 'the death of language'. The poet is like the ironic spider of section II who, by 'spinning out his reams / Of colourless thread' and so, by punning implication, of words, suggests that life must go on, 'that to-morrow will outweigh / To-night, that Becoming is a match for Being'; likewise, the poet spins the web of his journal to keep despair at bay. 'Who am I – or I – to demand oblivion?' he asks; and 'history is reasserted' in the determination to carry on, 'to begin / The task begun so often' (II). The mingled defeatism and hope is characteristic. 'I must leave my bed and face the music. / As all the others do . . .' (II): frequently in *Autumn Journal* solipsistic despair gives way to a recognition of community. As section XXI discovers in arguing itself out of self-indulgent isolation, life is a continuum of new beginnings: 'But with life as collective creation / The rout is rallied, the battle begins again'. And implicit in the poet's recognition of life's continuum is the need to go on writing, his continual act of circumlocution. The whole of *Autumn Journal* can be heard as a series of new beginnings as the poet repeatedly performs a verbal act of pulling himself together, even as the poem captures the sense of an ending.

2

A journal is exactly the right medium for expressing MacNeice's sense of division. It can accommodate contradictions without sounding contradictory: faithful to the moment, to time passing, to capturing and holding the 'ephemeral' on 'tangent wings' (from 'An Eclogue for Christmas'), it can simultaneously evoke the doom-laden sense of time running out in the tense atmosphere of prewar Britain. Private anguish, occasioned by the recent collapse of MacNeice's marriage, mingles with public crisis: 'he was always a poet of private living, but in this poem he counterpoints private and public circumstances in a way that creates the mood of crisis as it must have been felt by men like himself' (Hynes, p. 368). Being a genuine journal, that is, where the present in the writing is the same as the time of writing, it is constantly ignorant of the outcome of the events and experiences it is living through; and, as is clear from the headnote, MacNeice was anxious not to violate its contingent quality by applying hindsight. A comparison with Tennyson's elegiac sequence *In Memoriam* is instructive: Tennyson's lyrics were written over many years, but were reorganized by the poet to convey the passage of three years, thus imparting to the progression of his emotions a curve and direction which they may not have originally possessed – although it is arguable that the reorganization clarifies rather than distorts, that the art involved in rearranging locates 'meaning' in the 'experience'. *In Memoriam* was composed in the form of a journal; *Autumn Journal* was written *as* a journal.

In the foreground of *Autumn Journal*, therefore, are the events through which the poet is living, for instance the felling of trees outside his window for an anti-aircraft emplacement (VII) or canvassing in the Oxford by-election of October 1938 (XIV; MacNeice's candidate, A. D. Lindsay, lost to Quintin Hogg, who defended the seat on the issue of the Munich Agreement), or his trip to Barcelona on the eve of the Republican defeat there (XXIII). But coexisting with the present of the poem is the constant backward look. Contemporary events take on personal and historical resonance in the poet's memories of his Irish upbringing (XVI), for example, or of his education at Marlborough and Oxford (XIII). And the journal is haunted throughout by the First World War: in the nightmare section XV he asks whether one of the ghosts that he vainly tries to dismiss isn't of 'someone at Gallipoli or in Flanders / Caught in the end-all mud?'; the end of VII draws a parallel between contemporary events and the outbreak of the First War. Throughout *Autumn Journal* the acute sense of present events plays off against a continual awareness of the past that is being unearthed, brought into the light of the present. The journal's coherence, its ability to contain all these materials without fragmenting into mere journalism, derives in part from the consciousness that is doing the experiencing and remembering.

But the poem creates the effect of moving beyond one person's consciousness: Edna Longley writes that 'the protagonist speaks as guilty Everyman', and of 'a personal and communal psychodrama' (Mac, pp. 73, 59). Like 'Christmas Shopping', *Autumn Journal* is poised between two world wars, looking back to past sins and omissions, personal and historical, individual and collective, to try to understand why the world and the poet are heading the way they are: 'Time is a country, the present moment / A spotlight roving round the scene' (XXIV).

For a journal the poem is deceptively coherent artistically, revealing to a marked degree the art that conceals art. A poem whose voice is many voices, whose present is a focus for the dishevelled selections of memory, whose details constantly settle into new patterns, which conveys what it feels like to be a particular individual at a particular time but also steps outside its time for implicit judgement, a moody poem that captures the public mood as well as the poet's, whose spotlight makes one as much aware of its centre as of its circumference, the viewing eye as much as the panoramic vision – such a poem needs, and discovers, unobtrusive but powerful forces of cohesion. Its formal patterning is one such force. The basic unit, a variously rhymed quatrain with irregular line lengths, permits fluidity but also makes for cohesion. It is the formal equivalent of 'the sea's / Tumultuous marble' (from 'Train to Dublin'). It gives shape to the poem while holding it open to the flux of experience. The poem's many variations on the quatrain demonstrate 'its potential for either closure or openness', in Longley's words (Mac, p. 109).

Another way the poem binds itself together is through the repetition of motifs. Events and details can take on symbolic weight through recurrence, but in such a way that the contingent seldom loses its particularity: the poet's procedures are attractively chancy. Thus his dog, in section I 'a symbol of the abandoned order', a jocose motif for private bad conscience given public resonance, is lost in VII to the accompaniment of the idly mock-hysterical 'This is the end of the old régime'. Elsewhere dog clichés – 'dead dog', 'lying doggo', 'a dog's life' – hover subliminally, taking on a life of their own: in section II the spider says 'Only there are always / Interlopers, dreams, / Who let no dead dog lie nor death be final', and a few lines later the poet braces himself to follow the example of those who 'Shake off sleep like a dog and hurry to desk or engine'. In XVII dogs get drawn with comic inappropriateness into the quasi-philosophical talk about community and communication: 'a single lion / Is less himself, or alive, than a dog and another dog'. Or there is the windscreen-wiper in section VII that shows MacNeice's ability to make a detail resonate, and which recurs in XIV on the poet's drive to Oxford, where it takes on a knowingly 'flashy' mood of futility

> The wheels whished in the wet, the flashy strings
>   Of neon lights unravelled, the windscreen-wiper
> Kept at its job like a tiger in a cage or a cricket that sings
>   All night through for nothing.

Even apparently slight motifs such as 'cushions' set up echoes. In section VIII they typify the private world of domestic happiness and security cushioning itself against the public world of 'mounting debit' and 'slump': 'Life was comfortable, life was fine / With two in a bed and patchwork cushions ...'. In XXIII they recur in the context of the poet's characteristic determination, engendered by events in Spain, to participate, to subjugate self to community, 'Not any longer act among the cushions / The dying Gaul'. The tensions conjured up by the cushion motif – the self-sufficiency of isolation versus head-in-the-sand defeatism – are familiar from 'Epilogue: For W. H. Auden', where 'Lonely comfort walls me in' with the delights of self-pity. Searchlights are another motif that suggests, without any feeling of deliberation, the collision of public and private; they scan the political horizon and probe the individual conscience: 'The guns will take the view / And searchlights probe the heavens for bacilli / With narrow wands of blue' (VII). Later, in Spain, individual and collective guilt merge in a bewitchingly attractive version of the searchlight image: 'The slender searchlights climb, / Our sins will find us out, even our sins of omission' (XXIII).

What is poetically important about MacNeice's motifs is that they are rooted in the everyday even as they focus the poem's larger concerns. So, imagery of water draws into itself opposites, reconciling but not negating them. In section XVII taking a bath becomes the jocular occasion for a long meditation on self and community, and an emblem for the desire for 'contact'. The bath denotes various pairs of opposites, fleetingly reconciled: it is filled 'with strata / Of cold water and hot'. Initially it conjures up feelings of sensuous togetherness:

> We lie in the bath between tiled walls and under
> > Ascending scrolls of steam
> And feel the ego merge as the pores open
> > And we lie in the bath and dream.

But loss of self turns into selfishness; the merging ego grows egocentric:

> And responsibility dies and the thighs are happy
> > And the body purrs like a cat
> But this lagoon grows cold, we have to leave it, stepping
> > On to a check rug on a cork mat.

It does not do to remain too long in the lagoon of self. In succeeding lines the water image enables the poet to interrelate the change/permanence and self/other opposites:

> And Plato was right to define the bodily pleasures
> > As the pouring water into a hungry sieve
> But wrong to ignore the rhythm which the intercrossing
> > Coloured waters permanently give.

'Permanently intercrossing waters' could stand as an epigraph for the whole poem, 'intercrossing' intriguingly at odds with 'permanently'. With mercurial logic, the poetry then moves from pleasure to desire, and more horseplay with the Ancients. Desire presupposes an object of desire:

> And Aristotle was right to posit the Alter Ego
> > But wrong to make it only a halfway house:
> Who could expect – or want – to be spiritually self-supporting,
> > Eternal self-abuse?

The poetry builds to a crescendo of praise for life as permanent flux, an endless merging, 'a sacramental feast' in which 'discontent is eternal'; it culminates in the line, 'Open the world wide, open the senses', which, with its Whitmanesque elation, may incline towards self-parody, although this characteristic

inclination soon gives way before what sounds like a more
genuine plea for contact, for escape from solipsism:

> try and confine your
> Self to yourself if you can.
> Nothing is self-sufficient, pleasure implies hunger
> But hunger implies hope:
> I cannot lie in this bath for ever, clouding
> The cooling water with rose geranium soap.

It is typical of the way MacNeice is content to allow contradictory impulses to emerge and coexist in his poem that these lines
should make the solipsistic 'lagoon [that] grows cold' sound
attractive: as a small poetic trouvaille, the 'rose geranium soap'
could not be resisted.

   Water imagery makes its first appearance in the journal with
the film star of section I who wants to live irresponsibly in the
present,

> As if to live were not
> Following the curve of a planet or controlled water
> But a leap in the dark, a tangent, a stray shot.
> It is this we learn after so many failures,
> The building of castles in sand, of queens in snow,
> That we cannot make any corner in life or in life's beauty,
> That no river is a river which does not flow.

In this casual manner the poet introduces the central duality
that water is to represent throughout the poem: control and flow,
fixity and movement. However much we may want to escape, to
give no thought for the morrow, we are all part of the river of
history. The argument is not quite that the independent life is
wrong-headed; rather, that however much we may suppose our
lives are separate we are part of the 'flow of history', a cliché
made vividly new in *Autumn Journal*. The river as history can
conjure up fearful horror:

> . . . all we foresee is rivers in spate sprouting
> With drowning hands
> And men like dead frogs floating till the rivers
> Lose themselves in the sands.

This, in section VII, is the poem's bleakest use of the river image, as history running away into a futureless future. In section XIV (the Oxford by-election) the poet, contending with public and personal indifference ('And what am I doing it for?'), with the individual and collective *laissez-faire* that is a constant refrain of *Autumn Journal* ('That Rome was not built in a day is no excuse / For *laissez-faire*, for bowing to the odds against us'), tries to confront those – including, by implication, himself – who would use the river-as-history image as an excuse for apathy:

> There are only too many who say 'What difference does it
> > make
> > One way or the other?
> To turn the stream of history will take
> > More than a by-election.'

Yet in the ensuing, nightmare section the river as history gets turned into just such an image of escape as the poet tries to dismiss the death-in-life devils summoned by his imagination out of a personal and collective past:

> You can't step into the same river twice so there can't be
> > Ghosts; thank God that rivers always flow.
> Sufficient to the moment is the moment;
> > Past and future merely don't make sense . . .

MacNeice's conversational, apparently casual, technique in these lines is itself impressively 'sufficient to the moment' of would-be escapism.

Elsewhere, the river has more positive implications, as when the transfiguring memory of the woman of section IV visits the poet with a sense of community and continuity. The line, 'Whose hair is twined in all my waterfalls', first associates water with a lost past and a powerfully nostalgic memory. Water is then associated with a future that takes him mercifully beyond memory: 'So that if now alone / I must pursue this life, it will not be only / A drag from numbered stone to numbered stone / But a ladder of angels, river turning tidal'. In this section MacNeice's expertly *ad hoc* way of handling the water imagery compellingly enacts the ebb and flow of emotion. That way is evident in section XXIII, where water imagery helpfully intervenes in a

passage that is in danger of lapsing into discursiveness, the poet
once again steeling himself to renewed effort:

> I have already had friends
>   Among things and hours and people
> But taking them one by one – odd hours and passing people;
>   Now I must make amends
> And try to correlate event with instinct
>   And me with you or you and you with all,
> No longer think of time as a waterfall
>   Abstracted from a river.

In trying to overcome the nostalgic backward look, represented
here, as in section IV, by the waterfall, the poet lights on another
of his water images, the river, as representing the passage out of,
and away from, the past. One would expect 'waterfall' and
'river' somehow to confirm one another, but MacNeice's provisional cast of mind, happy to seize on whatever comes to hand,
turns them into opposites to advance his argument. To 'think of
time as a waterfall' is to forget that each is part of the 'flow' of
history, that all our actions participate in a continuum. To
correlate 'me with you or you and you with all' is to be aware
that 'all' contains before and after (that, in the words of section
XXI, 'every wood is a wood of trees growing / And what has
been contributes to what is'). This meditation, occurring to the
poet in war-torn Barcelona, is part of the cumulative attempt to
realize individual and collective responsibility, to trace 'the roots
of will and conscience'. 'Here and now the new valkyries ride /
The Spanish constellations', but, such is the burden of section
XXIII, 'here and now' is rooted in then – a fact underlined by
the invocation of the mythic valkyries – and is responsible for the
hereafter. The present is the time for being called to account.

As the final section says, 'The future is the bride of what has
been'. And it is as future history that water appears in this
section, first as a Utopian dream of religio-political liberation,
'Where the waters of life are free of the ice-blockade of hunger',
and then in the concluding lines, which close the lullaby that
puts the past to rest in preparation for an uncertain dawn:

> If you have honour to spare, employ it on the living;
>   The dead are dead as Nineteen-Thirty-Eight.

> Sleep to the noise of running water
>   To-morrow to be crossed, however deep;
> This is no river of the dead or Lethe,
>   To-night we sleep
> On the banks of the Rubicon – the die is cast . . .

It is a quietly impressive stroke that the river one expects
MacNeice the classicist to allude to, Lethe, the mythical river of
forgetfulness, does not appear until the end of *Autumn Journal*,
and then only to be denied. The river here is still the river of
history, but now of time future as opposed to time past –
although in resisting the backward look these lines implicitly
acknowledge that the task of *Autumn Journal* has been to review
the past in order to cross the frontier into the future, appropriately conjured up by the Rubicon, suggestive not only of the
irrevocable but also of the threshold of war.

3

Sections of *Autumn Journal* interrelate artfully yet naturally, as
the rest of this chapter will show by referring to the first three
sections, and sections VII and VIII. The first two deceptively
but tellingly play off against each other. Although the first might
seem to be spoken by a slightly satirical 'public' voice and the
second by a more confessional 'private' voice, the two registers
intermingle. Section I might sound like implicit condemnation of
a society that is running down as it looks over its shoulder at a
past glory that was hollow; but sympathy mixes with the satire,
and any condemnation shades into an awareness of the deman-
dingly uncertain future in which we all have to participate: 'The
dying that brings forth / The harder life, revealing the trees'
girders, / The frost that kills the germs of *laissez-faire*'. Section II
is in the voice of an agonized Night Thoughts, but the poet's
desire for 'oblivion' recedes before a determination to pick
himself up and participate in the larger human endeavour, to
'build the falling castle; / Which has never fallen, thanks / . . . /
to the human animal's endless courage'.

Section I begins with satirical observation of a well-to-do
society. But the sneer audible in, for instance, 'the home is still a
sanctum under the pelmets, / All quiet on the Family Front' is

accompanied by an effort to understand causes. The military metaphor hovering behind 'Family Front' (Home Front) implies the failure of the older generation of 'retired generals and admirals' with their 'insulated lives', a failure repeating itself in the present; contemporary European chaos has its cause in the aftermath of the First World War. But these domestic complacencies anticipate section II's intimately and longingly evoked 'hive of home' from which the poet has become recently exiled. The tensions of his recent marriage break-up are also anticipated in the closing lines of section I, where the mingled feeling of defeat and renewal in his personal life seems to colour his reaction to the human comedy:

> And so to London and down the ever-moving
>   Stairs
> Where a warm wind blows the bodies of men together
>   And blows apart their complexes and cares.

Unexpectedly, but with breathtaking ease, these lines open themselves out to the human lot with unsolemn sympathy. 'Ever-moving' moves with anticipation into the next line, only to be brought up short by the unnerving monosyllable, 'Stairs'. After this the poised classical rhetoric of the last two lines comes as a release and a relief. Their complicated chiasmus surprises by offering balm. Where we were expecting the wind to blow the bodies apart, it blows them together; and their togetherness makes possible the dissolution of their 'complexes and cares'. Yet, because these complexes and cares appear right at the end of the section, they linger on in the reader's imagination.

At the start of *Autumn Journal* the sense of an 'ending' engulfs in satiric nostalgia the depiction of a stultified society:

> Close and slow, summer is ending in Hampshire,
>   Ebbing away down ramps of shaven lawn where close-
>   clipped yew
> Insulates the lives of retired generals and admirals
>   And the spyglasses hung in the hall and the prayer-books
>   ready in the pew
> And August going out to the tin trumpets of nasturtiums
>   And the sunflowers' Salvation Army blare of brass . . .

One image gently but mockingly gives rise to another: the last passing-out parade of the 'retired generals and admirals' turns their prized nasturtiums into 'tin trumpets' and their sunflowers into a 'blare of brass', the merging of the visual and the auditory capturing the 'insulated', befuddled senses of the geriatric generation that has let the present down. Yet nostalgia remains as a powerful auditory experience, and anticipates the drawing to a close of the poet's summer of marriage. As section VIII will reveal, the 'insulated' life he led with his wife has to be taken into account as part of the 'mounting debit'.

The sustained repetition of the undifferentiating connective 'and' right at the start of the poem sets a tone that allows the poet to observe while reserving judgement. It is a technique frequently used in *Autumn Journal*, sometimes to enable him to convey a rush of thought or perception as he tries to 'gather [his] mind up in [his] fist' (from 'Train to Dublin'), sometimes more evasively. Here, in section I, responses are flickeringly present but not pinned down. In the following lines the indiscriminate juxtapositions trivialize, and so are inclined to mock this life of moneyed 'ease':

> And bacon and eggs in a silver dish for breakfast
> > And all the inherited assets of bodily ease
> And all the inherited worries, rheumatism and taxes,
> > And whether Stella will marry and what to do with Dick
> And the branch of the family that lost their money in Hatry
> > And the passing of the *Morning Post* and of life's
> > > climacteric . . .

The next lines seem to take on, almost imperceptibly, the voice of the despised elders, in mocking mimicry:

> And the growth of vulgarity, cars that pass the gate-lodge
> > And crowds undressing on the beach
> And the hiking cockney lovers with thoughts directed
> > Neither to God nor Nation but each to each.

The effect of the mimicry, one might suppose, would be to elicit sympathy for the object of the elders' scorn, the 'vulgar' crowds, canoodling couples and the rest. But the poet eats his cake and has it too, for the crowds and lovers are leading lives as 'insulated' from the impending collapse as the generals and admirals. If the poet's sympathy moves out to the crowds and lovers, it is with a devil-may-care, bagpipe-music attitude, which he then voices more deliberately in his version of a thirties 'tired aubade and maudlin madrigal', with its jaunty music-hall clichés ('I loved her between the lines and against the clock, / Not until death / But till life did us part I loved her with paper money'), which nevertheless imply, unheeded by the 'jazz song' singer, a world of economic and spiritual bankruptcy.

At the start of section I, for the discredited elders 'close and slow, summer is ending'; at the start of section III, for the 'vulgar', who are the object of the elders' scorn, 'August is nearly over': the minute shift in register marks the sympathetically critical viewpoint. There is a wryly sympathetic note in the joke that 'a little / *Joie de vivre* . . . is contraband'. 'Whose stamina is enough to face the annual / Wait for the annual spree' may be critical, but the repetition of 'annual' brings out the drudgery from which the people would escape. That the poet is implicated in their escapism is hinted by the fact that their 'memories are stamped with specks of sunshine', a phrase which predicts the poet's radiant memories in section VIII, in which he accuses himself of having participated in escapist *joie de vivre*.

The poet's attempt to shun escapism in section III is hedged about by doubts and vacillations. Opening one's eyes to the realities of economic and social disintegration can result in a different sort of insulated escapism: simple-minded Utopianism. While trying to remove his own blinkers he knows that a new society can be 'travestied in slogans'; he knows the dangers of totalitarian solutions, that 'a better Kingdom' can only come from within and not by external imposition, that 'in time [it] may find its body in men's bodies, / Its law and order in their heart's accord'. But even as the voice contemplates the economic injustices that would be absent from the new order, it begins to take on an air of 'travesty' itself:

> Where skill will no longer languish nor energy be trammelled
>   To competition and graft,
> Exploited in subservience but not allegiance
>   To an utterly lost and daft
> System that gives a few at fancy prices
>   Their fancy lives

> While ninety-nine in the hundred who never attend the
> banquet
> Must wash the grease of ages off the knives.

The poetry sustains its to-and-fro Hamlet-like indecisiveness
(the phrase 'to sleep, to dreams perhaps' echoes Hamlet; see
Chapter 8 for further discussion of the Hamlet motif). Even the
words that whisperingly accuse the poet of being of the exploit-
ing class, words which one might suppose to belong to the voice
of reality, come from the mouth of a 'tempter', tempting him to
rest content in the *status quo*. The poet's answer, admitting and
chiding his élitism, begins to take on what will become one of the
familiar registers of *Autumn Journal*, a *vox humana* that perpetu-
ates itself in rambling self-address: 'And I answer / ... / That
freedom means the power to *order*, and that in *order* / To
preserve ...' (emphases added). In another context, in a poem
like 'Ode', such writing comes over as pointlessly rudderless, but
in *Autumn Journal* it possesses a saving self-awareness: 'Which
fears must be suppressed', the poet breaks in, and a few lines
later 'Which fantasies no doubt are due to my private history',
with an air of self-mockery in the arch latinate diction that
predicts the start of section XIII: 'Which things being so, as we
said when we studied / The classics'. The resolution that finally
emerges, a sort of prayer for action typical of many section
endings, encompasses previous doubts and hesitations even as it
attempts to transcend them. There is an affecting shift into a
more purposive frame of mind: the poetry wavers, doubts,
hesitates, then works itself up to a state of determination:

>   the worst of all
> Deceits is to murmur 'Lord, I am not worthy'
>   And, lying easy, turn your face to the wall.
> But may I cure that habit, look up and outwards
>   And may my feet follow my wider glance
> First no doubt to stumble, then to walk with the others
>   And in the end – with time and luck – to dance.

The hesitation in the concluding cadence produced by the
interpolated phrase 'with time and luck' skilfully captures the
stumble of doubt to be overcome.

If the poetry intermittently pulls itself together like this, coming down on the side of unreflective impulse, 'Of those who abjure the luxury of self-pity / And prefer to risk a movement without being sure / If movement would be better or worse in a hundred / Years or a thousand', it does so because *Autumn Journal* is a reflective poem by a writer aware of (and inclined to) the luxury of self-pity: 'Soon or late the delights of self-pity must pall' (XXIII). Not surprisingly, this lesson is brought home to the poet by his visit to Civil-War Spain, where he tries to master himself with renewed determination, 'For never to begin / Anything new because we know there is nothing / New, is an academic sophistry'. But sophistry is what the poet of *Autumn Journal* is good at, as he is well aware; and it is his way with his self-reflections that make the journal a winningly human document.

4

Sections VII and VIII are mirror-images of each other. In VII public events are the overt subject, but personal loneliness and loss are never, one senses, far away; in VIII personal memories are central, although the public dimension increasingly encroaches, culminating in the Munich Agreement. Section VII implicitly weighs unforced feelings of personal loss against the forced emotions, however well meant, of the political arena. It strikes a note familiar in *Autumn Journal*: fear of the future, and a frantic, bagpipe-music, attempt to stifle fear. From the start, the tone shifts agilely and the voice is not easy to pin down. In the opening lines carefreeness masks a sense of doom as the poetry tries to capture a mood of public hysteria. But is there not something dismissive in the hysterical staccato of the first three lines? 'Flights in the air, castles in the air' mocks the endeavours of politicians, but at the same time the voice sounds reckless. 'The autopsy of treaties' accuses politicians of a damagingly ineffectual backward look in their dissection of moribund treaties; but it also self-accusingly throws up the sponge. 'The end of *laissez faire*' is a sneer at do-nothing politicians with their incompetent economic policies; but it also sounds tinged with regret that the world is being compelled to brace itself; and too, in the light of the next section, the voice of conscience self-accusingly hints that the poet is now to pay for his former days of carefree oblivion. In the following lines suppressed hysteria belongs to the poet even as it is being sent up:

Think of a number, double it, treble it, square it,
　And sponge it out
And repeat *ad lib*. and mark the slate with crosses;
　There is no time to doubt
If the puzzle really has an answer. Hitler yells on the
　wireless . . .

Here satire blurs with sympathy as the voice finds itself participating in what it is inclined to ridicule. It is a strength of *Autumn Journal* that different attitudes and responses can coexist like this without any sense of incoherence or emotional inconsequence.

The feeling of being 'hounded by external events', in Spender's phrase (*WWW*, p. 137) is memorably represented by what is happening to Primrose Hill, the view from the poet's window. Section V has already anticipated the gun emplacement: 'The bloody frontier / Converges on our beds'. Section VII shows the frontier converging closer and closer. The sense of an ending merges with an atmosphere of preparation for a scarifying future:

　　　　　　　Hitler yells on the wireless,
　The night is damp and still
And I hear dull blows on wood outside my window;
　They are cutting down the trees on Primrose Hill.
The wood is white like the roast flesh of chicken,
　Each tree falling like a closing fan;
No more looking at the view from seats beneath the branches,
　Everything is going to plan;
They want the crest of this hill for anti-aircraft,
　The guns will take the view . . .

The modulation from the hysterical to the elegiac, from Hitler yelling to the closing fan, is artful and moving. The lines, 'I hear dull blows on wood outside my window; / They are cutting down the trees', mingle nostalgia with a sense of threat. This sense intensifies with 'the roast flesh of chicken', which is arresting, but also accurate as descriptive simile; indeed much of the arrest comes from the accuracy, and also from the edgy sound of the words 'white like'. Such artistry allows the poet to get away with the chilling associations – in the context of war preparations – of 'roast flesh'. Public catastrophe merges with private loss in the domestic associations of roast chicken, and in the mournful 'No more looking at the view from seats beneath the branches', so that 'Everything is going to plan' comes over with bitter, tight-lipped irony: the collapse of the poet's domestic life happens as unstoppably as the preparations for war. A similarly flip despair accompanies the business of the lost dog, which is a satiric side-show to the immense loss being enacted in the interval between one world war and the next: 'This is the end of the old régime' sounds, in the context, like self-deprecating play on the sense of loss. From one perspective the bitter jest reflects badly on the poet; from another it captures the quirkiness of human emotions.

The tendency for the poet's mood to find itself reflected in the mood of the times runs the risk of solipsism. But the tendency is part of his refusal to fudge his feelings; the result is that the reader trusts him more readily as a witness. That trust depends on the adroit handling of voice and register. The poet can betray bewilder-ment at his own responses, a saving suspicion of his emotions:

> . . . and [I] heard a taxi-driver
> Say 'It turns me up
> When I see these soldiers in lorries' – rumble of tumbrils
> Drums in the trees
> Breaking the eardrums of the ravished dryads –
> It turns me up; a coffee, please.

While the taxi-driver's lament is being echoed like this in the consciousness of the poet it could be turning into private elegy (for these are the trees where the poet used to sit 'looking at the view'). 'Rumble of tumbrils / Drums in the trees' mingles terror with a suspicion of elegiac sonority. The phrase 'ravished dryads' fleetingly distances poet from driver (for presumably the driver does not have a classical education, 'The privilege of learning a language / That is incontrovertibly dead' in the words of section XIII), thus reinforcing the impression that the poet is indulging his elegiac feelings. Does the echo of 'It turns me up' signify endorsement of the driver's mood, or slightly derisory mimicry? No answer is provided by 'a coffee, please', which sounds a momentary retreat, not only from the temptation to indulge in easy laments for the times, but also from his own inscrutable emotions. The poker-faced air is finely judged. The poet does not want to be caught wearing his heart on his sleeve, is the implication; but his very reluctance hints at depths of feeling that he dare not fathom.

The windscreen-wiper, like the searchlights that 'probe the heavens', captures a mood, but not just the mood of the times:

> And as I go out I see a windscreen-wiper
> In an empty car
> Wiping away like mad and I feel astounded
> That things have gone so far.

– so far in his domestic affairs, one may conjecture, as well as in the world of Realpolitik. The ensuing episode of the curtain material bears out the conjecture. The sudden apprehension of loneliness gives way to a sense of public danger, but it is a dutiful giving way which recognizes that selfishness is the motive and that hysteria governs actions, even as the poetry itself becomes more hysterically apocalyptic with the vision of 'rivers in spate sprouting / With drowning hands'. It is not quite right to say that the mood of this vision captures the public mood, although public hysteria is certainly audible in the poetry. The poet knows he is sounding hysterical even as he does so, which renders suspect his involvement in the mood. He mimics the voice of 'panic and self-deception', although the very use of that phrase shows a saving critical self-awareness. But he still finds himself acting and thinking in ways he despises, ways which he and like-minded contemporaries through the past decade had tried to analyse and so resist. Hence he cannot after all escape a representative role: by the section's conclusion he has earned the right, almost in spite of himself, to speak of 'we':

> And we who have been brought up to think of 'Gallant
> Belgium'
> As so much blague
> Are now preparing again to essay good through evil
> For the sake of Prague;
> And must, we suppose, become uncritical, vindictive,
> And must, in order to beat
> The enemy, model ourselves upon the enemy . . .

That laconic 'must, we suppose' signifies bewildered compliance in the way things are: conscience will be, as it has been before, knowingly violated. The fake public emotions in which the poet foretells he will participate, give way to the section's last line, 'We shall have fireworks here by this day week', whose inscrutability seems to denote the poet's attempt to disown involvement.

The note of bewildered compliance returns at the close of the next section, in the passage about the Munich Agreement, only now steeled with ironic anger ('Save my skin and damn my conscience'). But significantly this central event comes after nostalgic memories of early married life in Birmingham. Guilt connects these memories with events in the public arena: 'the autobiographical passages are more than that: they are also judgments of the past imposed by the disastrous present' (Hynes, p. 369). The poetry presents private memories as representative: 'But Life was comfortable, life was fine', not 'our life was . . .'; 'With two in a bed', that is, any couple, not just this particular two. But the past provides no easy explanation for present ills: memory can hinder as much as facilitate.

Like 'Epilogue: For W. H. Auden', section VIII ponders independence and responsibility. Today's Birmingham sunshine – 'Sun shines easy, sun shines gay' – throws into relief the poet's present loneliness and takes him back to the irresponsible sunshine of the early days of his marriage, to the collapse of the second Labour government in 1931, and to the onset of the Depression: 'And sun shone easy, sun shone hard'; 'the train ran down the line / Into the sun against the signal'; 'Sunlight dancing on the rubbish dump, / On the queues of men and the hungry chimneys'. The section then returns to the present, with an explicit contrast between past and present to mark the delusiveness of present sunshine, a bitterly stiff-upper-lip personal regret merging with and giving way to a sense of impending crisis:

> Just as in Nineteen-Thirty-One
>   Sun shines easy but I no longer
> Docket a place in the sun –
>   No wife, no ivory tower, no funk-hole.
> The night grows purple, the crisis hangs . . .

The poet would like his funk-hole, but, such is the feel of the passage, so would everyone else. 'Easy' has eased from carefreeness in the first line to irresponsibility here.

The section plays on the familiar theme of love versus the world. The theme preoccupied MacNeice, as it had Shakespeare, a fact acknowledged by the quotation from *Antony and Cleopatra* in 'The Sunlight on the Garden'; as it had Donne also, whose poem 'The Sunne Rising' invokes the sun in much the same spirit as section VIII of *Autumn Journal*. In Donne's poem, however, the sun symbolizes the outer world and all it contains, its commonwealths and kings, over against the lovers' world, whereas in *Autumn Journal* the sun negotiates between private and public worlds. Both poems contrast the lovers' bed with the outer world, but the consequences are different. In Donne's, the bed triumphs in its defiant engrossing and belittling of the world, which, 'contracted thus', acknowledges what has been triumphed over:

> Aske for those Kings whom thou saw'st yesterday,
> And thou shalt heare, All here in one bed lay.

> She'is all States, and all Princes, I,
>   Nothing else is.[2]

But in *Autumn Journal* the world triumphs, for the lovers' bed can only be defiant by refusing to acknowledge what it belittles:

> But Life was comfortable, life was fine
>   With two in a bed and patchwork cushions . . .
> There were lots of things undone
>   But nobody cared, for the days were early.
> Nobody niggled, nobody cared,
>   The soul was deaf to the mounting debit . . .

By the end of 'The Sunne Rising' love has transformed the world. The sun is at the service of love and is renewed by it: 'since thy duties bee / To warme the world, that's done in warming us. / Shine here to us, and thou art every where'. Whereas the play of Donne's trope highlights his serious purpose, the play of MacNeice's sun is trickier. Even section VIII's opening lines, with their syntactic levelling, their string of 'on' clauses, begin to sound suspect in their manner of conveying the sun's impartiality. 'Bug-house', 'pubs', 'chromium hubs', 'sleek macadam', signs of poverty and signs of riches, all viewed by the sun's carefree-cum-careless eye, are uttered at the same tonal level. Later the sun's symbolic indifference becomes more overt: 'We . . . took no notice / Of how the train ran down the line / Into the sun against the signal. / . . . / Sunlight dancing on the rubbish dump, / On the queues of men and the hungry chimneys'.

'And sun shone easy, sun shone hard': the sun's easy gaze turns into the hard gaze of humanity's indifference. 'And life went on – for us went on the same': though the first person plural is beginning to implicate more than the married couple, it becomes representative only of a guilty exclusivity, of 'we together'; and the couple's 'getaway' slides into the getaway of history:

> But roads ran easy, roads ran gay
>   Clear of the city and we together
> Could put on tweeds for a getaway
>   South or west to Clee or the Cotswolds;
> Forty to the gallon; into the green
>   Fields of the past of English history;
> Flies in the bonnet and dust on the screen
>   And no look back to the burning city.
> That was then and now is now,
>   Here again on a passing visit,
> Passing through but how
>   Memory blocks the passage.

These lines try to turn class guilt into more than the guilty conscience of one of the privileged. The movement of 'English history' between the wars has been governed by nostalgic yearning for a past cloaked in a falsifying haze; and the poet becomes guilty spokesman for such attitudes. He and his sort could get 'Clear of the city' with 'no look back' to its unemployed and its factory hooters, but that was merely taking flight from contemporary reality. *Autumn Journal* may want to open the conduits of memory to trace the source of individual and collective wrong, but memory can equally well 'block the passage'. History is how we remember it. 'That was then and now is now' is tonally elusive: the past is passed, the nostalgic impulse must be resisted; it is strangling the poet's and his country's future; it avoids the reality of the past, of 'the burning city', of the urban apocalypse which is emblematic of all wars, of flaming Troy for instance, or of London which is about to go up in 'fireworks' and which contrasts with an idyllic vision of English history ('the green / Fields of the past'). But the ironic undertow of 'That was then and now is now' is *plus ça change, plus c'est la même chose*: because the lessons of history have not been learnt, 'now' is about to repeat history's 'then'. What at first sounds like an ungainly tangle of 'past-passing-passage' turns out to be a compelling verbal equivalent of emotional cul-de-sac: our 'passage' out of the 'past' is blocked because we are only on a 'passing visit' which misses the reality of what it is 'passing through'.

In *Autumn Journal* love does not transform the world; how it fares is how the world fares. The way of love is the way of the world; the one is an index of the other. This is also the implication of 'The Sunlight on the Garden'. The private world is not, as it is in 'The Sunne Rising', so much a refuge from the outer world as a guilty reflection of it. The nostalgically delightful isolation of the married couple turns into a metaphor for the head-in-the-sand isolation of Everyman in an inward-looking outer world. On the political front this attitude culminates in the Munich Agreement: 'Save my skin and damn my conscience. / . . . / And here we are – just as before – safe in our skins'. 'Just as before' catches the ironic inflection in 'That was then and now is now'. In the last lines words are allowed to run away with the poet and the voice turns into an angry automaton:

> And stocks go up and wrecks
>   Are salved and politicians' reputations
> Go up like Jack-on-the-Beanstalk; only the Czechs
>   Go down and without fighting.

The bathos of 'down' after the two 'ups' is obvious, but none the less effective; indeed, *Autumn Journal*'s effectiveness is bound up with its subtly unobvious dealings with obviousness, with common experience and what lies to hand. It has all the attractions of a journal, yet patterns emerge that take it beyond the journalistic. Though open to the casual and the random, it conveys the sense of a unique convergence of events. Faithful to fluctuations of response and mood, it nevertheless captures an unprecedented moment in history.

8

Poetry of the Spanish Civil War 'See Spain and see the world'

1

'See Spain and see the world': the sentence is Rex Warner's and opens the last stanza of 'The Tourist Looks at Spain'. In *Poems for Spain* (1939), edited by Stephen Spender and John Lehmann, the poem concludes the section entitled 'The Map' (begun by Auden's 'Spain' to which Warner's panoramic quatrains appear to be indebted). Warner's poem inclines to didactic solemnity. But it makes clear the way many writers viewed the Civil War that broke out in Spain after Franco and his fellow-generals mounted their *putsch* against the Republican Government in July 1936. As Robin Skelton puts it: 'The Spanish Civil War was a symbol become reality; it embodied the class struggle, and also the struggle of the artists against the philistines (did not the Fascists murder Lorca? Was not Picasso on the side of the Government?)'.[1] Yet if the Civil War prompted writers to wear their ideological hearts on their sleeves, the best poetry in English to come out of it – much of which was composed by Auden, MacNeice and Spender – is often marked by inner divisions.

'The Tourist Looks at Spain' delivers its message by way of staple devices of thirties poetry: the authoritative voice, the half-gleeful warning that the 'normal' conceals a sinister unreality, the reliance on a diagnostic idiom patented by Auden. As a result Warner's poem has dated; its air of menace and suspense is not without power, but it is the power of well-marshalled rhetoric:

> Not the long hands that fingered the fearful mystery,
>   not the bland and soothing voices
> can bring us peace, nor the roar and rant of bullies
> declare decision or disguise the ferret's temper.
> (Quoted from *PFS*; text is also available in *PBSCWV*)

That last phrase illustrates the bathos into which thirties poetry can fall when intent on indictment. What wants to be Auden-esque quirkiness comes across as imitative. Warner's central point – both like and unlike Auden's in 'Spain' – is that to look at Spain is to realize that the struggle taking place prohibits the detachment of the tourist; the voice of those 'who speak in deeds' concludes:

> It is the aim that is right and the end is freedom.
>   In Spain the veil is torn.
> In Spain is Europe. England also is in Spain.
> There the sea recedes and there the mirror is no longer
>   blurred.

The penultimate line's equations are wooden, even if the last line's wording anticipates the title of Auden's meditation on art and life, 'The Sea and the Mirror' (1944). Certainly Warner's poem is of interest for its concern with the relationship between art and reality, between perception and action, between seeing clearly and saying clearly. The sentence, 'See Spain and see the world', draws to itself and puts in propagandist perspective earlier uses of 'see' in the poem: 'Was what we saw the thing, or do we see it now?'; 'What we saw dead was all the time alive, / and what we see is living. / It is over our own eyes that the mist holds'; 'we' are asked to 'See in the mirror' our culture's supposed accomplishments as 'trash and blots and blurs on the moving truth'.

But 'The Tourist Looks at Spain' is, at best, a waxwork replica of Auden's 'Spain' (title and text taken from *PBSCWV*, which prints the original published version (1937)) that serves to point up what gives life to Auden's controversial, self-rejected masterpiece. For instance, Warner sprinkles his poem with 'we', 'our' and 'us' to underscore complicity and solidarity. In doing so he borrows a feature of Auden's poetry in the thirties: in the third Ode at the end of *The Orators*, for example, Auden speaks with curt, unmawkish eloquence of 'The slight despair / At what we are'; in 'Brothers, who when the sirens roar', 'we' is used to ventriloquize a yearning for comradeship: 'If you would help us we could make / Our eyes to open, and awake / Shall find night day'. But in 'Spain' itself Auden is warier of the attractions of togetherness, even as the poem takes sides, a dimension of its subject being, in John Fuller's words, 'the defence of the Spanish Republic against a fascist military insurrection' (Fuller, p. 259). 'Our' and 'us' are used by the 'poor' who invoke a conception of history the poem seems to take pains to correct:

> 'Our day is our loss. O show us
> History the operator, the
> Organiser, Time the refreshing river.'

These lines will not yield easily to thematic pigeon-holing. For one thing, they are part of a passage (lines 25-44 in *PBSCWV*) that mingles the trenchant and the indeterminate. Auden appears to offer a series of exempla (poet, investigator, the poor), all illustrating the false expectation that some external force will intervene redemptively in history; yet at certain moments these exempla cease to be exempla and take on a life of their own. There is, for instance, no assurance that the 'poet''s invocation of his 'vision' is being exposed as an example of irrationalism; when he prays for 'the luck of the sailor' he voices a wish that must be known to most poets. 'Spain', too, surrenders to 'lucky' verbal chances while at the same time constructing its tripartite argument: 'Yesterday', 'To-day', 'To-morrow'. The poem's stanza form blends or, rather, offsets the will-driven with the wayward, its rhythms and diction seeming to combine the chosen and the stumbled upon. And the syntax of lines 25-44 refuses to clinch a didactic meaning; beginning with the words 'As the poet whispers', it leaves the reader unsure how to take 'As'. If it has the force of 'while', it would refer back to the preceding line's 'But to-day the struggle': possibly suggesting the obstinate persistence of private obsessions at a time of 'struggle', a persistence the poem's official voice condemns but the writing relishes. Or 'As' may seem to be opening an 'As . . . so' construction, yet the 'so' side never appears, giving way to a series of 'ands' (lines 29, 33, 37 and subsequently 45). On one reading the effect is of purposeful argument doing its best not to be sidetracked by human vagaries – on the next of human vagaries doing their best not to conform to purposeful argument. Similarly, in the lines quoted above, the opening assertion, seemingly simple, is fluid in its effect. It might mean 'the days in which we live are filled with evidences of our losses' – unlike (or like) the lives of those whose activities fill 'the sheets / Of the evening paper'. It might even suggest 'we shall have had our day – as "the poor" – when we have lost what makes us what we are now, our poverty'.

The intonations of speech can be stimulatingly hard to interpret in Auden as the last stanza of 'Letter to R. H. S. Crossman Esq.' indicates: 'Harden the heart as the might lessens' the stanza begins, drawing on the Anglo-Saxon poem *The Battle of Maldon*, with how much irony the verse refuses to say. Yet the stanza does concede that when history is *in extremis* the would-be liberal optimism which has piloted the poem's thinking may be supplanted by 'The anarchist's loony refusing cry': 'No choices are good. / And the word of fate can never be altered / Though it be spoken to our own destruction'.[2] The fatalism here transgresses the poet's earlier advice to himself, yet Auden is able, however briefly, to occupy the state of mind in which 'No choices are good': a state of mind relevant to that which makes itself felt at the end of 'Spain'. Among the deepest notes in Auden throughout his poetic career is this awareness of forces which will not be vanquished by an axiom, even if such awareness can be expressed axiomatically. As 'In Memory of Ernst Toller' (1939) has it, 'We are lived by powers we pretend to understand' (quoted from *WHACP*).

'Spain' tries to hold this quasi-Freudian recognition at bay since it threatens trust in the will. Yet when that trust is sabotaged by the prayer of the poor, Auden is less censorious than sympathetic; partly due to the line ending's hint of a let-down, the phrasing of 'History the operator, the / Organiser' is wry rather than grand. The sonority is calculatedly fake; in the guise of 'operator' or 'Organiser' History is imagined by the poor less as Hegelian *Geist* or impersonal destiny than wily politico – an essentially, if desperately, humorous perspective. Auden's tone just avoids the callous or condescending. Certainly it

eschews the earnest or ponderous. Astringent playfulness is the
effect; and if one of its targets is the persistence of human longing
for some *deus ex machina*, another is the poet's style of presenting
such longing. Throughout 'Spain' Auden seems to hear himself
in the act of utterance. When Valentine Cunningham rebukes
Auden's article 'Impressions of Valencia' (*New Statesman*, 30
January 1937) and, by implication, 'Spain' for 'a slick management of words that wilfully rebuffs any human connection with
what is being described' (*PBSCWV*, p. 69), he fails to see that
Auden's 'slickness' in both article and poem bears witness to his
acutely uneasy awareness that writing – about any subject –
involves the 'management of words'. By highlighting his own
such 'management' in 'Spain' Auden attains a difficult integrity,
giving self-indulgence the slip by a hair's-breadth. Here, the
contrast with Warner's 'The Tourist Looks at Spain' is marked:
a poem which, so far as it is alert to its own ways of talking,
registers them with self-approval.

2

Warner's poem describes the scales dropping from the eyes of
those he refers to as 'we' when the significance of what is
happening in Spain is borne home: 'What we saw dead was all
the time alive'. Auden's presents the Spanish conflict as an
externalization of 'our' thoughts and feelings:

> On that arid square, that fragment nipped off from hot
> Africa, soldered so crudely to inventive Europe;
>   On that tableland scored by rivers,
> Our thoughts have bodies; the menacing shapes of our fever
>
> Are precise and alive. For the fears which made us respond
> To the medicine ad. and the brochure of winter cruises
>   Have become invading battalions;
> And our faces, the institute-face, the chain-store, the ruin
>
> Are projecting their greed as the firing squad and the bomb.
> Madrid is the heart. Our moments of tenderness blossom
>   As the ambulance and the sandbag;
> Our hours of friendship into a people's army.

Robert Lowell praises Auden for 'constantly writing deeply on the big subjects, and yet keeping something wayward, eccentric, idiosyncratic, charming and his own'.[3] His point is shrewd and helps to account for the peculiar authority of 'Spain', whose readiness to admit the 'wayward' and 'eccentric' into its treatment of a 'big subject' is apparent in these stanzas. The lines begin by affecting a detachment that is denied in the act of being articulated. The sheer oddness (to the Audenesque eye) of the fact that Spain has become the battleground on which humanity's future is being decided is both allowed and exorcized in the account of the country as a 'fragment nipped off from hot / Africa'. Auden eschews the propagandist temptation to versify historical commonplaces, and elects not to display the awareness of Spain's previous struggle for liberation against Napoleon which informs Spender's introduction to *Poems for Spain*: 'The poets of the English Liberal tradition responded to Spain crushed by Napoleon', Spender writes, 'much as they do to contemporary Spain crushed by Fascism' (*PFS*, p. 9); he goes on to quote Wordsworth's sonnet, 'Indignation of a High-Minded Spaniard'. Rather, looking 'inventively' at the map, Auden anticipates the view of Spanish affairs as distant, inviting admiration for the fastidious precision of 'nipped' and 'soldered'; then, having lulled the reader, the poetry surprises him or her with its point (that events in Spain externalize 'our' inner states, the conflict between our 'good' and 'bad' impulses). The jump from the geographical to the psychological is prefigured by the account of Spain as 'that tableland scored by rivers', where suggestions of division are introduced by 'scored'.

In fact, it is less the writing's aloofness that gives cause for concern than the risk it takes of not allowing for the otherness of Spanish history and politics, of too quickly seeing Spanish events as mirroring the predicament of the writer's own culture. The poetry is not always able to hold the simplistic at bay. Even if the Civil War could be viewed in Keats's words about Peterloo as 'No contest between Whig and Tory – but between Right and Wrong' (quoted by Spender in *PFS*, p. 9), Auden's equations – between, say, Franco's 'battalions' and our neuroses – are as debatable as they are ingenious. The poet writes 'as if firing squads were the exclusive property of Franco's invading forces' (Mendelson, p. 318). Auden seeks to suggest both that conflict within 'us' is mirrored by the external conflict between Republicans and Fascists, and that the side 'we' are on is that of the

Republicans. The simultaneous effect of detachment and commitment is not without its muddling aspects. And yet such
muddles are closely related to Auden's readiness to embroil his
poem in difficulty: a major source of its vitality.

The passage under discussion shows how Auden uses 'our'
and 'us' to implicate himself and his reader in the Spanish Civil
War, yet to do so in a way that grapples with what being
implicated involves; 'disconcerted aloofness' (Cunningham,
p. 448) is only part of the poem's tonal range. If the scenario of
projection oversimplifies, it also subtilizes; the run-on between
the two last stanzas, for example, induces a muted jolt that gives
precision and life to 'the menacing shapes of our fever'. Auden
drastically cut these stanzas in the version of the poem printed in
Another Time (1940), an early sign of his unhappiness with
'Spain'. The idea of Spain as the focus of 'our' inner conflicts was
severely curbed; all that remains of the 1937 stanzas is the
modified line 'Our fever's menacing shapes are precise and
alive', where revision eliminates the expressive run-on from
stanza to stanza just described. In making the changes Auden
protects himself against the charges of simplifying and muddle.
But the poem's vulnerability to such charges at this stage is
inseparable from Auden's willingness to bring into play the
range of his feelings and thoughts about the Civil War: that it
could be seen as externalizing Western cultural contradictions,
that one of the sides was worthier of support than the other, and
that fighting on its behalf was praiseworthy yet would involve
bloodshed and violence (the last point only fully confronted at
the end of the poem). Elsewhere Auden's facility could get him
into trouble; here he triumphs over it. In the concluding lines,
'Madrid is the heart' uses its short-sentenced directness to
suggestive effect. The sentence may say that 'The heart of the
conflict is to be found in Madrid', but it implies, too, that the
heart's best impulses have taken shape in Madrid. Previously
'heart' was used in a way that aroused before deflating its
romantic associations; 'the life, if it answers at all, replies from
the heart', and, for a second, the writing attributes sincerity to
the words of the 'life'. But this implication is punctured by the
succeeding words, 'And the eyes and the lungs', which turn
'heart' into a physiological rather than emotional term. In
'Madrid is the heart', however, Auden allows full rein to the
feeling which was earlier choked back and prepares for the

moving, if partisan, lines which follow. That said, these lines are the more impressive for their restraint. The value of what is being celebrated is emphasized by the poetry's suggestion of its rarity: 'Our *moments* of tenderness', 'Our *hours* of friendship' (emphases added).

The reader approaches here, however, a problem at the centre of 'Spain', one to which Mendelson has drawn attention. He points out that the poem associates natural metaphors – as in 'Our moments of tenderness *blossom*' (emphasis added) – only with one side in the war (the Republican) and thus undercuts its seeming insistence on history as the sum of men's choices (see Mendelson, p. 319); more searchingly he argues that

> The two contradictory arguments in *Spain* gave Auden the insoluble problem of reconciling his image of the hours of love that blossom into a people's army with the violent acts that armies actually commit. "To-day the struggle," even among the people's army, is not a time for the good and the beautiful.
> (Mendelson, p. 320)

And he goes on to quote the lines made controversial by George Orwell's attack in *Inside the Whale*: 'To-day the deliberate increase in the chances of death, / The conscious acceptance of guilt in the necessary murder'. Orwell described the 'necessary murder' as a phrase that 'could only be written by a person to whom murder is at most a *word*' (quoted in Mendelson, p. 321). Auden himself later accounted for his choice of 'necessary' as his attempt to say that '*If* there is such a thing as a just war, then murder can be necessary for the sake of justice'.[4] Mendelson sees a secondary sense in 'necessary', however, reading it as meaning 'inevitably fixed and determined' and detecting in the interplay between 'conscious' and 'necessary' a 'paradox':

> The necessary murder is the harshest of the unchosen unconscious processes associated, in the metaphoric argument, with the people's army. The poet chooses to accept guilt in this murder, but the act itself is a necessary step taken by others towards History's inevitable fulfillment.
> (Mendelson, p. 322)

Mendelson describes this as 'contemptible' (Mendelson, p. 322), and it may indeed be the case that Auden saw the stanza in this light in the aftermath of the poem's initial publication (in *Another Time* 'the necessary murder' was revised to read 'the fact of murder'). Yet while Mendelson's reading is acute, it lays too great a burden on the imagery Auden uses about those who go to Spain. It supposes Auden wished to preserve a distinction between choice and instinct, whereas the writing is less existentially stark. Those who go to Spain both choose and act on instinct. This combination is a consequence of the double-take involved in gifting 'the life' with a voice that is only the voice of those it speaks to and through: 'I am whatever you do'; 'I am your choice, your decision. Yes, I am Spain'. Having insinuated that choice may not manifest itself to choosers as choice, Auden implies that the decision to go to Spain presents itself to many individual choosers as inevitable while still remaining choice.

However, in referring to the murders which war entails as 'necessary', Auden insists that the nature and effects of choice be brought out fully into the open. Paradoxically, 'necessary' points up what happens as a result of choice; it does not subscribe to a determinist view of history. Auden is, as he later claimed, pointing out a painful but unavoidable consequence of being 'unable to adopt the absolute pacifist position':[5] a consequence which holds true for all the participants in the War rather than merely or mainly the poet himself. Critically, the key question is that of Auden's elusive personal presence in the poem's closing movement. To see him as using the line 'The conscious acceptance of guilt in the necessary murder' to legitimize murders which others are committing on his behalf sells the impact of his words short. Auden is not accepting guilt yet refusing to engage with what his words mean. Rather, his generalization is the more potent for seeming to apply to the writer with particular force without forfeiting a wider relevance. Though the playing off against one another of 'conscious' and 'necessary' flaunts the writer's intelligence, the effect is grimly, rather than smugly, knowing – and typifies the troubled skill with which the poem switches tones and reconsiders positions. For the stanza in question follows and undercuts the Utopian account of 'To-morrow', which itself comes close to self-mockery in these lines:

> To-morrow for the young the poets exploding like bombs,
> The walks by the lake, the weeks of perfect communion;
>   To-morrow the bicycle races
> Through the suburbs on summer evenings.

The lines imagine the future as a return to what the Marxist would see (and, one feels, was meant to see) as bourgeois individualism: Auden's tone, hard to gauge precisely, flickers between the derisory and the affectionate, but if the lines have a satirical target, that target is less the complacent bourgeois than the Utopian revolutionary. Auden's self-ridiculed fantasy is of a world where the banal and the intense can co-exist freely. Certainly he does not put the money of his feelings on a revolutionary vision of the future. As Samuel Hynes points out (Hynes, pp. 259-60), Christopher Caudwell deplored the inability of 'bourgeois artists' to realize such a vision:

> They [bourgeois artists such as Auden, Spender and Day Lewis] know "something is to come" after this giant firework display of the Revolution, but they do not feel with the clarity of an artist the specific beauty of this new concrete living, for they are by definition cut off from the organisation which is to realise it . . .[6]

This crisply doctrinaire rebuke was delivered in *Illusion and Reality* (which Auden reviewed favourably, his review appearing in May 1937, the same month as 'Spain' was published). But Auden's seeming frivolity in the lines quoted above bears out his honesty; he does not lay claim to a revolutionary ardour he does not feel; if anything this endows the poem with a secret compassion for ordinariness. 'To-day' is the site of 'struggle', but for what? To be allowed to continue as, at our best yet also most characteristic, 'we' are is the poem's deepest, if not wholly spelled-out, reply.

To the degree that the poem is in a muddle about history, that muddle is remarkably aware of itself as muddle; and, furthermore, seems hard to avoid. Viewed before it reifies into event, history presents itself as the sum of present and future choices; viewed retrospectively, history is what has happened and nothing else. The poem sustains this dual view most famously in the final stanza, which Auden was later to disown:

> The stars are dead. The animals will not look.
> We are left alone with our day, and the time is short, and
>   History to the defeated
> May say Alas but cannot help nor pardon.

'To say this', Auden wrote about the last two lines, 'is to equate goodness with success. It would have been bad enough if I had ever held this wicked doctrine, but that I should have stated it simply because it sounded to me rhetorically effective is quite inexcusable' (Foreword to *CSPA*, p. 15). But Auden is too severe on his former self. Mendelson's attempts to explain the way in which Auden may have misread his lines as equating 'goodness with success' (see especially Mendelson, p. 320) demonstrate that the lines do no such thing. In fact, they owe their pathos to their sense that goodness and success may have little to do with one another; it is no consolation, the lines imply, to be 'good' if the cause you support is 'defeated'; nor can you expect to be 'pardoned' if you do wrong things in a 'bad' cause – or, indeed, wrong things in a 'good' cause. The 'defeated' could, then, be the Republicans who will find no 'help' forthcoming; they could be the Fascists who will not be 'pardoned'; 'pardoned' could also apply to the Republicans because of their embroilment in activities ('necessary murders') that will require, but not receive, 'pardon'. 'History' is viewed in realistically cheerless terms, and its inability to offer retrospective 'help' or 'pardon' is likely to have given offence to the later Christian Auden.

The writing is impressive because of the way it simultaneously personifies and demystifies 'History', Auden allowing for human intervention in the shaping of what happens. The poem's final use of 'we' is its most affecting; momentarily the poet speaks for the human race, out of his deepest sense of the human predicament. The lines mingle stoic acceptance with recognition of the need for urgency. 'Our day is our loss', the poor said earlier in the poem; 'We are left alone with our day' both recalls and holds at bay the earlier linking of 'our day' with 'loss', substituting for it a beleaguered loneliness that avoids posturing and has an emotional impact that transcends the 'rhetorically effective'.

Indeed, the stanza engages with the issue of 'rhetoric'. It abandons the quasi-propagandist formulae – 'To-morrow ...' and 'To-day ...' – which have governed the previous six stanzas. The stark statements which replace such formulae are themselves rhetorically effective yet able to convey awareness of what lies beyond rhetoric. This twofold sense is present at the end. Imagining 'History' as able to say 'Alas', Auden sustains the device of personifying an abstraction and endowing it with a voice (used earlier in relation to the 'life'); at the same time Auden does not surround 'Alas' with speech-marks. History's sorrowing is mute; indeed, the phrasing indicates to the reader what the poem has throughout suggested, that History has no existence independent of human beings. Its 'Alas' is projected, the retrospective human response of those who come after a great historical conflict and can do nothing to alter the plight of the 'defeated'. For all its swaggering air, 'History' in 'Spain' has, as Stan Smith argues, a kinship with the 'Muse of the unique / Historical fact, defending with silence / Some world of your beholding' (*WHACP*) addressed by the poet in the later 'Homage to Clio' (1955).[7]

The ending of 'Spain' urges the need for involvement, but it does so in terms that are elegiac before the event; even as they exhort, the lines mourn. Positively advertising itself as a public poem, 'Spain' teems with the artist's private awareness of complexity. Yet this troubled, even tragic dimension, which keeps the poem from lapsing into propaganda, emerges from and coexists with a quirky relish for human idiosyncrasy.

This relish makes 'Spain' a poem that enacts a debate between the particular and the general. Often, its synecdochal details are chosen less to indict or diagnose than to provoke thought by making the familiar strange. In other words, whereas an earlier poem disdainfully singles out 'The exhaustion of weaning, the liar's quinsy' (from 'Sir, no man's enemy, forgiving all'), 'Spain' takes a more tolerant view of civilization, even though the earlier poem holds a more optimistic view of the possibility of 'forgiveness'. 'Spain' catalogues past achievements with an urbanity that can be pinned down neither as diagnostic nor as chilly, though it implies the chilliness of viewing cultures from a great height:

> Yesterday the installation of dynamos and turbines,
> The construction of railways in the colonial desert;
> > Yesterday the classic lecture
> On the origin of Mankind. But to-day the struggle.

These lines do not say that what they describe is of no worth; rather, they isolate their details – each item caught as in a snapshot – in order to convey the awareness of history into which the poet has been shocked by the impact of 'the struggle'. And this awareness goes deeper than the apparent slickness of the writing might seem to warrant. What the poem's first line calls 'all the past' has led to the present: hence the evolutionary movement of the opening stanzas; 'the past' is what enables the struggle (history has reached a particular point only because of preceding events) and what is rendered strangely irrecoverable as a result of the struggle. The catalogue, then, glimpses, while holding at bay, a tourist-like view of history; it demonstrates the artist's mastery (millennia condensed into lines) even as it implies the necessary surrender of such mastery to the demands of the struggle. Auden's achievement is to absorb such implications and tensions into a poetic texture that remains controlled without being remote, clever but not smart-alecky, detached and yet involved. 'Spain' may lack the blend of ideological commitment and front-line courage which ensures that John Cornford's 'Full Moon at Tierz: Before the Storming of Huesca' will always be preferred by some readers. But it has its own rewards. Where Cornford versifies the Marxist dialectic, pinpointing the 'dialectic's point of change' (quoted from *PBSCWV*), Auden finally evades the imposition of a programmatic grid on history. Cornford sloganizes, 'Raise the red flag triumphantly / For Communism and for liberty', albeit movingly (the lines follow his personal confession of fear and his recognition that 'Freedom is an easily spoken word'); Auden meditates. Cornford speaks with unself-conscious intensity in his own voice; Auden's voice emerges the more compellingly for weaving in and out of other voices and inflections.

3

One major poetic voice of the thirties with which Auden's had briefly meshed (in *Letters from Iceland*) was that of Louis MacNeice. 'Down in Europe Seville fell, / Nations germinating hell' is how the third stanza of MacNeice's 'Epilogue: For W. H. Auden' begins.[8] The lines typify one aspect of MacNeice's poetic response to historical crisis: his ability to imply that immunity from what is happening in Europe is cowardly, deeply to be desired, improbable. At the same time MacNeice the nimble-fingered craftsman is in evidence, conjuring a flicker of a pun out of 'germinating' (with its glance at German involvement on the side of the Fascists), winning from the beat of his lines a trochaic drum roll that is both doom-laden and sprightly. MacNeice supported the Republican cause but knew about, and was able to address in his writing, the temptations (and responsibilities) of detachment; his declaration of support for the Republican side is unequivocal yet characteristically wry about the imperfections that taint most feelings:

> I support the Valencia Government in Spain. Normally I would only support a cause because I hoped to get something out of it. Here the reason is stronger; if this cause is lost, nobody with civilised values may be able to get anything out of anything.[9]

The sense here of being confronted by history with a challenge that cannot be evaded permeates the two sections from *Autumn Journal* that deal with Spain; the first, VI ('And I remember Spain'), describes a visit to Spain in the spring before the Civil War broke out; the second, XXIII ('The road ran downhill into Spain'), arises from a visit to Barcelona in December 1938, just before the city fell to Franco. The *Autumn Journal* sections correspond to two vivid chapters, XXXII and XXXV, in *The Strings Are False*, MacNeice's unfinished autobiography, first published in 1965, but given to E. R. Dodds for safe keeping in 1941. A briefer account of the visit to Barcelona, entitled 'Today in Barcelona', appeared in *The Spectator*, 20 January 1939. Of these writings 'Today in Barcelona' is the most straightforwardly partisan. The poet observes in the people 'the fear of sudden death which enhances the values of life' and asserts: 'I have never been anywhere where these values were so patent. It would be difficult to be a Hamlet in Barcelona.' (*PBSCWV*, p. 142.) With his self-concern and irresolute brooding, Hamlet has glimmered throughout *Autumn Journal* as the 'prototype of the artist/liberal facing the problem of constructive action in troubled times' (Longley, p. 82). *Autumn Journal*'s emotional rhythm derives, in fact, from our sense that MacNeice both is and is not Hamlet; at one moment he is every inch the solitary sceptic, at the next he is robustly asserting his solidarity with the crowd. In section XXIII MacNeice, as so often in the poem, wavers between identities. The courage he witnesses in the war-stricken city leads him to this rueful New Year's resolution:

> May God, if there is one, send
> As much courage again and greater vision
> And resolve the antinomies in which we live
> Where man must be either safe because he is negative
> Or free on the edge of a razor.

The writing does not show MacNeice at his best; his 'anti-nomies', as expressed here, do not carry the charge which gives force to Yeatsian antinomies in poems such as 'Sailing to Byzantium' (or such MacNeicean poems as 'Snow'); and one could apply to the above lines the poet's own description of late Yeats: 'His philosophy has become a philosophy of antinomies, a dialogue where himself does all the talking.'[10] MacNeice is thinking aloud and the pressure of his thinking is not great, as is betrayed by the wording of the last line which uses, but for once fails to revivify, a cliché. What both weakens and gives interest to the lines, however, is MacNeice's dutiful gesturing towards 'greater vision'; it is evident that, as a poet, he is more at home with problems than solutions. And as MacNeice moves from a wished-for solution to intensified consideration of the problem the poetry rallies; the evaluative issue this raises again in relation to *Autumn Journal* is whether the slacker passages can be defended, as Chapter 7 has implied they can, on the ground that they are surrounded by 'intonational quotation marks' (in Bakhtin's phrase). In this instance such a view would regard MacNeice as wanting the reader to see that he is going through the motions even as he goes through them. Certainly there are many moments in *Autumn Journal* where a switch of tone or perspective exposes MacNeice's only limited commitment to some previous utterance. The poem derives its life from the poet's foreground-ing of his inner debates, shrinkings, enthusiasms, cynicisms. None the less, such a procedure does have risks.

The poetry's ability to pick itself up is apparent in the ensuing lines. These quicken the poem's tempo as MacNeice turns away from praying in general terms to considering his own isolated condition. Barcelona in December 1938 contained, it seems, at least one Hamlet:

> I admit that for myself I cannot straiten
>   My broken rambling track
> Which reaches so irregularly back
>   To burning cities and rifled rose-bushes

> And cairns and lonely farms
>   Where no one lives, makes love or begets children,
> All my heredity and my upbringing
>   Having brought me only to the Present's arms . . .

The lines offer a version of autobiography by way of an image
that extends itself into brief allegory, always a device favoured
by MacNeice; life as a 'broken rambling track' is animated by
the rhythms which themselves reach 'irregularly back', intermittently sharpened by the irregular fall of the rhymes. Once again
the reader is reminded of the variety of poetic discourses in
Autumn Journal. This section has begun to leave behind the
journalistic, descriptive idiom of its opening; even there Mac-
Neice's sharp eye is linked to a figurative gift that widens the
implications of his theme:

> When I reached the town it was dark,
>   No lights in the streets but two and a half millions
> Of people in circulation
>   Condemned like the beasts in the ark
> With nothing but water around them:
>   Will there ever be a green tree or a rock that is dry?

The brisk simile stresses the people's entrapment and confinement, but the glance at the biblical story of Noah and the flood
complicates its effect. The allusion seems to express a flickering
hope that, even at this eleventh hour in the Republic's fortunes,
some reprieve might be forthcoming, just as the flood gave way
to God's covenant with Noah. Giving support to this reading is
MacNeice's reminder in the 'Note' at the head of *Autumn
Journal* that 'the section about Barcelona having been written
before the fall of Barcelona, I should consider it dishonest to
have qualified it retrospectively by my reactions to the later
event' (*CPM*, p. 101). At the same time the lines concede sadly
that miraculous interventions are unlikely, that the idea of a
providential deity overseeing history is merely a Sunday School
fable; the last line's question empathizes with yearning but
knows it is unlikely to receive an affirmative reply.

  In fact, this section draws a good deal of resonance from its
use of religious language. This use is common in MacNeice, the
son of a clergyman. In 'Experiences with Images' (1949) Mac-
Neice writes: 'My favourite reading at about the age of eight was
the Book of Revelation but, long before that, biblical imagery

had been engrained in me' (*SCM*, p. 159). But religious imagery is a provocative presence in a poem about a political struggle one of whose aims was to reduce the influence of religion (especially State Catholicism) in Spain. As Hugh Thomas observes, 'The onslaught on the church in Catalonia and Aragon astonished many of those who lived there. Few suspected that anti-clericalism was so strong'.[11] In section XXIII the writing makes the reader conscious of the spiritual dimension of the struggle. MacNeice lets religious phrases appear to drop from him casually: cultural clichés that take on renewed because secular-ized life. Without forgetting that 'There is no such thing as a snow-white cause' (*SAF*, p. 197), section XXIII suggests that Barcelona is a place of testing, where 'Our sins will find us out, even our sins of omission'. This abstraction emerges effortlessly out of the previous line, 'The slender searchlights climb'; the searchlights scrutinize 'us' as well as the sky, a moralizing of the image that does just enough to remind the reader that the speaker of the section is more than merely a curious, roving eye.

MacNeice visits the city in the aftermath of Christmas. 'So much for Christmas' he wrote disparagingly of his stay in Paris in the previous section, a detail which gives added point to the lines which conclude section XXII: 'Over there are pain and pride beyond the snow-lit / Sharp annunciation of the Pyrenees'. What has undergone a difficult birth beyond the Pyrenees is a new, secular society in which the 'soul has found its voice' in the face of a sky 'pregnant with ill-will'. The stoical endurance of the people displays an unposturing heroism, the more valued by MacNeice in section XXIII for being unsought ('not indeed by choice'). What he praises them for is their reaffirmation of 'human values', which have been 'purged in the fire', even though 'the golden calf / Of Catalan industry' has been, for various reasons, 'shattered'.[12]

These religious references insist on a humanist application; without detracting from the poetry's responsiveness to the surfaces of life, they show MacNeice's desire to explore the deeper significance of what is happening, and has happened, in Barcelona. Two further examples will reinforce the point. 'To-day in Barcelona' was content to list under 'impressions': '*The crowing of cocks*: most characteristic sound in Barcelona (as if you were to hear cocks in Picadilly)' (*PBSCWV*, p. 144). Interestingly, in this prose account MacNeice's religious allusions work merely at the level of the wryly comic: 'to give a man a cigarette is to give him the Kingdom of Heaven' (*PBSCWV*, p. 144). But section XXIII develops the potent associations of cock-crowing with Peter's denial of Christ:

> The cocks crow in Barcelona
>   Where clocks are few to strike the hour;
> Is it the heart's reveille or the sour
>   Reproach of Simon Peter?

The answer to the last question is 'Both'. The poetry is full of MacNeice's sense of guilt by association with those who have betrayed the people of Barcelona. The ways of, and motives for, betrayal are analysed in the section and in *The Strings Are False*. There is what the poem indicts as 'The original sin', the refusal to 'begin / Anything new because we know there is nothing / New'. Here the writing's inwardness with the cynicism it condemns helps. The wearied non-surprise of the repeated 'New' is especially eloquent. There is, too, the non-interventionist stance of the English, which MacNeice's prose condemns in terms drawn from the parable of the Good Samaritan: 'And I began to hate the English too who had passed by on the other side. Passed by under an umbrella. And then, very logically, I found myself hating myself' (*SAF*, p. 196). The umbrella's wryly updating touch coexists with a delayed triggering of self-hatred, the self-hatred which is an unshowy, taut presence in section XXIII. Edna Longley takes the arguable view that in the earlier section about Spain, VI, the poetry cannot hit home because in it MacNeice 'adopts the role of guilt-tripper' (Longley, p. 86). Yet section XXIII cannot be dismissed as an exercise in guilt-tripping, not because the poetry wears its earnestness on its sleeve, but because it surprises itself and its reader with volatile swings of awareness.

Yet if these swings bring the poet close to despair, doubt and self-hatred, they also expose to him the hypocrisy of loving 'defeat and sloth, / The tawdry halo of the idle martyr'. What his experience in Barcelona reveals to him is the difficult need to hope, to realize that it is open to him to interpret the crowing cocks as 'the heart's reveille'. Yet much of the writing's interest comes from the fact that any such conviction is fluid and provisional even as it is heartfelt. In the section's final lines

MacNeice seeks to convince, but cannot eradicate a sense that 'the cock crowing in Barcelona' is a profound enigma as well as bizarre oddity:

> Whereas these people contain truth, whatever
>   Their nominal façade.
> Listen: a whirr, a challenge, an aubade –
>   It is the cock crowing in Barcelona.

The first two lines sound like someone sounding off, flagellating his guilty conscience: not unlike the Hamlet of 'How all occasions do inform against me'. Yet the next two lines shift to the 'façade' of experience about which MacNeice is always so subtly generous. Their workings bring out that for this poet each moment is an interpretative, existential test; the sound heard is three things – 'a whirr, a challenge, an aubade': something meaningless, something intimidating, something full of promise. It is by allowing for the different aspects of his response to the cock-crow that MacNeice's determination to see it in hopeful terms carries real, if unstable, conviction.

Throughout section XXIII, in fact, MacNeice's openness to the fluid seesawing of response is evident; it is illustrated by the second example of religious language promised above. 'All my heredity and my upbringing', writes MacNeice, have

>   brought me only to the Present's arms –
> The arms not of a mistress but of a wrestler,
>   Of a God who straddles over the night sky;
> No wonder Jacob halted on his thigh –
>   The price of a drawn battle.

MacNeice alludes to Genesis 32: 24-32, the account of Jacob's wrestling with a man all night; the conflict having no resolution, the man 'touched the hollow of his thigh; and the hollow of Jacob's thigh was out of joint' (32: 25; Authorized Version). But the man praises Jacob, assures him of his future and blesses him. Though Jacob 'halted upon his thigh' (32: 31), he rejoices: 'I have seen God face to face, and my life is preserved' (32: 30). In MacNeice's version, the emphasis is on the cost of the conflict; obliquely comparing himself to Jacob, he has wrestled with the Present, yet the Present is likened not to a providential deity but to 'a God' whose threateningly looming presence is suggested by 'straddles'. The fluent yet 'halting' movement of the lines underscores the force of 'The price of a drawn battle'. To have got so far is made to sound an achievement, but the section is intent on moving beyond the isolated, divided self's 'drawn battle' with the Present. In lines that are crucial for the poem as a whole as well as for MacNeice's response to the Civil War, he exhorts himself to 'try to correlate event with instinct' and discover 'the roots of will and conscience'. 'Try', there, does much to breathe life into MacNeice's abstractions; but one is struck by the distance his meditation – sparked off by being in Barcelona – has taken him from events in Spain.

This is not to criticize the poem adversely, and indeed the conclusion returns to the specific historical struggle which has prompted the poet's reflections. But it is to suggest that what makes section XXIII of *Autumn Journal* fascinating is Mac-Neice's partial failure to heed the moral he drew from Franz Borkenau's *The Spanish Cockpit*: 'Borkenau's point', he writes, 'is that you must not see Spain through foreign glasses' (*SAF*, p. 180). He may have in mind this passage from Borkenau's preface: 'I began my studies under the common delusion that the Spanish revolution was simply an incident in the fight between Left and Right, Socialism and Fascism in the European sense of the word; I have been convinced by observation on the spot that this is not so'.[13] Certainly MacNeice's view of Spain, attentive as it is to the particularity of Spanish culture, focuses on the rebuke delivered to 'Our niggling equivocations' by 'the matter-of-fact faith and courage' shown by the people of Barcelona. The effect is both affecting and predictable – and, for all his strenuous attempts to escape it, enmeshes the poet even more firmly in the role of 'Hamlet in Barcelona'.

Curiously, section VI is more conscious of the various perspectives, mostly distorting, being a foreigner in another culture can generate. Throughout this section, MacNeice plays his former self's apolitical concerns against the awareness he implies he has now attained. 'And I remember Spain', the section's memorable opening, combines the sombre and the chatty: the poet as retrospective prophet and the reminiscing 'tripper' for whom 'the rain / Was worse than the surly or the worried or the haunted faces'. Again, the poet remembers how he and his friend (Anthony Blunt) 'glibly talked / Of how the Spaniards lack all sense of business'; the tone is at once self-critical and attuned to the kind of generalization people do make on vacation. By contrast with section XXIII, the poetry does not pause to brood or meditate, passing on (via another 'And') to the next stage of the journey: 'And Avila was cold'. The 'And's' do justice to the flow of impressions that make up the journey, that await yet resist categorization. As a result, MacNeice's glancing eye and sceptical mind suggest disquietingly without committing themselves wholly to judgement: for instance, he notices

> peeling posters from the last elections
> Promising bread or guns
>   Or an amnesty or another
> Order or else the old
>   Glory veneered and varnished
> As if veneer could hold
>   The rotten guts and crumbled bones together.

The 'peeling posters' come from the elections of 16 February 1936 won by the Popular Front. The Popular Front regained power from the right-wing coalition government which had been in charge from November 1933 to January 1936. The 'amnesty' probably refers to 'an amnesty for political prisoners' which Hugh Thomas calls 'one of the main proposals of the Popular Front programme'.[14] So far as the passage has political leanings, they are against the right-wing's adherence to 'the old / Glory veneered and varnished'. But the series of 'or's' reduce to a single catalogue the promises of right and left; MacNeice does not, the writing persuades us, tamper with his initial response, one element of which is a certain agnosticism towards all political programmes.[15] This honesty, accurate rather than guilt-tripping, means that when the section's *volta* comes it convinces:

> But only an inch behind
>   This map of olive and ilex, this painted hoarding,
> Careless of visitors the people's mind
>   Was tunnelling like a mole to day and danger.

This 'But' swerves against the current of 'And's' which have subtly prepared for it (as have two previous uses of 'But', neither of which has the fully blown oppositional ring of this one: 'But can what is corrupt be cured by laughter?'; 'But that, we thought to ourselves, was not our business'). 'Careless of visitors' allows for the carelessness of visitors; it recognizes that Spain is other than the 'map of olive and ilex' the deftly word-spinning poet on his travels can make of it. In a similar way the 'Cambridge don' who knows ' "There's going to be trouble shortly in this country" ' is engaged with such 'trouble' only at the level of detached comment; his analysis is offered, the poetry implies, from much the same motive as his ordering of 'anis', 'Glad to show off his mastery of the language'. MacNeice brings alive the fact that something new is taking place in Spain by evoking yet deflating the inevitably irrelevant responses of outsiders; if in the lines quoted above the 'people's mind' strikes a sloganizing note, the next line's simile and zeugma turn slogan into insight.

Here the otherness of Spain is uppermost; in the section's last lines it is the relevance of 'Spain' (the word used talismanically) that comes to the fore. MacNeice and Blunt leave,

> forgetting Spain, not realising
> That Spain would soon denote
>   Our grief, our aspirations;
> Not knowing that our blunt
>   Ideals would find their whetstone, that our spirit
> Would find its frontier on the Spanish front,
>   Its body in a rag-tag army.

With its balance between ignorance and awareness, this passage brings to a head the section's underlying conflicts of perspective; the claiming of 'Spain' for 'our blunt / Ideals' is not, because of what has preceded it, a sign of indifference to Spain's otherness, but rather a description of what, in fact, turned out to be the case. Even in these sombre lines MacNeice's wit flickers: in the play on 'frontier' and 'front', in the pathos of 'rag-tag army', the phrase ending the section on an unrhymed downbeat, even, perhaps, in the concealed reference to his friend's name and Marxist beliefs in 'blunt / Ideals'. The section ends finely, poised between acceptance of this 'bluntness' and anticipation of a possible sharpening of 'Ideals' on the 'whetstone' of the Spanish conflict. If the section, like the poem from which it comes, still arrests our attention, it does so because it engages the reader with a mind responsive to history in the making.

4

In a review of books on the Spanish Civil War Cyril Connolly refers to 'Mr Spender's not very martial muse'. Connolly makes his remark in passing while commenting on the decreased appetite for belligerent rhetoric observable in England a year after the Civil War had broken out; with perceptible relief he writes: 'we are experiencing a vicarious war-weariness at last'.[16] Connolly was playing his own variation on a theme eloquently developed by Spender the previous month in the *New Statesman*. In an article entitled 'Heroes in Spain' he sounds the passionately anti-heroic note which characterizes his poems: 'The final horror of war is the complete isolation of a man dying alone in a world whose reality is violence. The dead in wars are not heroes: they are freezing or rotting lumps of isolated insanity'. And he continues, '. . . to say that those who happen to be killed are heroes is a wicked attempt to identify the dead with the abstract ideas which have brought them to the front, thus adding prestige to those ideas, which are used to lead the living on to similar "heroic" deaths' (*PBSCWV*, p. 337). Reading this brings to mind Wilfred Owen's determination to quash sentimental heroics in poems such as 'Dulce et Decorum Est'. But for all their debt to Owen's example and practice, Spender's poems about the Spanish Civil War have a distinctive force and originality.

Certainly anti-war polemic forms an integral part of 'Two Armies'. As in Owen's 'Exposure',[17] Keats is a master ironically recalled only to be found irrelevant at the poem's start, with its glance at the famous opening line of *Hyperion*; whereas Saturn is stationed 'Deep in the shady sadness of a vale', Spender's poem eschews myth for the improbable, absurd factuality of battle: 'Deep in the winter plain, two armies / Dig their machinery, to destroy each other' (*SC*; included in *CPS(1)* and *CPS(2)*). From the beginning the poem refuses to take sides; the poet in Spender is more affected by what later in 'Two Armies' he calls 'a common suffering' than by what the reluctant Republican propagandist in him calls the 'terrible necessity' (*PBSCWV*, p. 338) of the war. The sense of the 'terrible' offsets the edge of laconic mockery in the phrase 'to destroy each other'; though Spender can write effusively, he is capable, more frequently than he is given credit for, of a tense control in his wording. Such control is clearly at work in the rest of the first stanza, shaping the unsentimental 'Men freeze and hunger' as well as the grimly jocose 'No one is given leave / On either side, except the dead, and wounded. / These have their leave'. The comma after 'dead' turns the following phrase into an after-thought that seeks to be scrupulously fair to the amount of 'leave' permitted; the effect is to increase the sense of claustrophobic entrapment. The writing couples an air of reportage with hints of the more tragic grasp of war's meaning (or lack of meaning) which will surface later; here, for instance, the reader pauses over 'violent peace' – Spender's oxymoronic phrase for the reprieve which 'new battalions' will bring is suggestive, too, of the 'violent peace' of death.

Samuel Hynes has argued that 'There is something missing from Spender's war poems, some authority for the right to pity; without that authority, which perhaps a poet must earn by sharing in suffering, pity becomes a patronising, distant attitude' (Hynes, p. 251). But this ignores the degree to which the problem he outlines is acknowledged by the workings of the poetry. A more helpful entry into the war poetry is offered by a subsequent remark of Hynes: 'His compassion is in the poems, but so is the distance' (Hynes, p. 251). This comment need not necessarily carry adverse implications. For instance, in 'Two Armies' the second stanza puts the urge to pity in contention with a throttling back of vicarious involvement; the style generalizes, yes, but induces sympathy by suggesting that the writer is caught between 'compassion' and 'distance':

> All have become so nervous and so cold
> That each man hates the cause and distant words
> Which brought him here, more terribly than bullets.

The unstuffily dignified rhythms stress the poetry's point but do so convincingly, the switch from 'All' to 'each man' allowing for individuality as well as collectivity. Spender's poem is, it transpires, not aiming at reportage of a real battle; rather, it offers – here in almost diagrammatic form – an imaginative analysis of the psychological stresses endured in any war. The weighty, even relentless way the poem advances step by step is relevant to this point. 'All have become so nervous . . .' in stanza two; 'From their numb harvest, all would flee . . .' in stanza three; 'Finally, they cease to hate' in stanza four. And yet the poem does not simply state the same point in various forms; along with the relentlessness goes a capacity to deepen and surprise. Indeed, the poem is moved by the gap between surface and depth, between what war makes of men and what men in their innermost hearts or sub-consciousnesses desire, between what the third stanza calls 'discipline' and 'wishing'. The third stanza brings into the poem the first fully articulated sense of an alternative perspective, a sense which following stanzas will develop and which turns a poem that wears its conscience on its sleeve into one that, doing so, gets close to a tragic vision:

> Yet when they sleep, the images of home
> Ride wishing horses of escape
> Which herd the plain in a mass unspoken poem.

These fine lines find a proper use for an image tried out in 'Who live under the shadow of a war' (where Spender is 'shot with thought / That halts the untamed horses of the blood'). Again the rhythms attune themselves persuasively to the theme; the shorter line's emphases lend support to the escapist longing. And in the final phrase Spender locates a function for the poem now being spoken, to evoke the 'mass' humanity of the soldiers. The fourth stanza falls into derivativeness as it pursues this aim; in the lines 'who can connect / The inexhaustible anger of the guns / With the dumb patience of these tormented animals?' only 'dumb' (with its implication of the need for a voice, the poet's) adds anything new to the loud echo of Owen's 'Anthem for Doomed Youth': 'What passing-bells for these who die as cattle? / — Only the monstrous anger of the guns'. But in the next stanza, as Geoffrey Thurley perceptively remarks, Spender 'achieves the classic serenity that marks off the merely good from the momentarily great' (Casebook, p. 160):

> Clean silence drops at night when a little walk
> Divides the sleeping armies, each
> Huddled in linen woven by remote hands.
> When the machines are stilled, a common suffering
> Whitens the air with breath and makes both one
> As though these enemies slept in each other's arms.

And yet it is a 'classic serenity' that finds room for a supple, even eroticizing compassion. The choice of words in this passage is apt and resonant. That the 'walk' is 'little' between the two armies aloofly belittles the reasons for their division. The third line's adjectives play richly against one another: 'Huddled' glancing at a wretchedness which those 'remote hands' cannot prevent, despite their probably far from remote involvement in the lives of those fighting. 'Linen' carries suggestions of burial cloths, subliminally preparing for the 'common suffering' of the next line. 'Common' brings to a tragic focus the poem's emphasis on the shared humanity of both armies, even as 'each' in the second and last lines reminds the reader of the separateness which the final line's 'As though' fictionalizes away. The passage memorably combines the tragic and the tender, allowing a sense of waste to negotiate with a sense of human potential. Only in sleep, however, does it seem 'As though these enemies slept in each other's arms'; and, daringly, the poem chooses not to end on this note but to withdraw to a remoter, chillier perspective, that of 'the lucid friend to aerial raiders, / The brilliant pilot moon' whose lucidity is that of uncomprehending coldness. The blankness of her stare is suggested by the verb 'regards' in the penultimate line:

> Where amber clouds scatter on no-man's-land
> She regards death and time throw up
> The furious words and minerals which kill life.

These lines set themselves against the previous stanza's release of compassion into the poem; the quasi-personifications 'death and time' justify their presence by being the object of the moon's gaze (rather than a lapse into rhetoric); it is 'as though' (to employ the previous stanza's construction) the moon had a glimpse of the abstractions controlling the soldiers' fate. The effect is, finally, to hold compassion within a starker, steady framework which may concede that the poet does not have the right to dwell exclusively on the simpler emotions of anger, solidarity or fellowship. But the poem's achievement lies in the way that its language glimpses what life is like both when central human values are excluded and when they are brought to mind. In this respect the final phrase 'which kill life' (later revised to 'which destroy') invests 'life' with a meaning that transcends merely living.

Indeed, Spender's poems about Spain elude being the poems of 'a tourist' less by MacNeice-like admissions of outsiderness than by their meditative intensity. And what they meditate on most intensely is the riddling relationship between life and death. The poet's 'love and pity' in 'The Coward' seek, possibly over-assertively, 'to bring [the coward's] ghost release' 'Lest every eye should look and see / The answer to its life as he' (*SC*; included in *CPS(1)* and *CPS(2)*). The restrained, ballad-like 'A Stopwatch and an Ordnance Map' describes a dead man 'From his living comrade split / By dividers of the bullet' (*SC*: included in *CPS(1)*, *SPS* and *CPS(2)*): there 'living' introduces a grief that is the stronger for being offset against cosmic indifference, and later 'the moon's timelessness' is followed by lines which bring into play a different kind of 'timelessness', experienced by one who 'lives on': 'But another who lives on / Wears within his heart for ever / The space split open by the bullet'.

'War Photograph' (*SC*; included, under the title 'In No Man's Land', in *CPS(1)*) contains a comparable sense of the individual's powerlessness in the face of larger forces: 'I am that numeral which the sun regards, / The flat and severed second on which time looks, / My corpse a photograph taken by fate'. But the ironies of powerlessness and annihilation rouse in the poem a strong if subdued counter-desire to assert uniqueness and significance; in the last line, though 'the years and fields forget' 'the whitened bones remember'. The impulse to remember fortifies the shamblingly distressed 'Fall of a City' (*SC*; included in *CPS(1)*) against defeat; the final stanza rises to a 'bitter' dignity as it affirms the value of those who in their lives fought for life:

> But somewhere some word presses
> On the high door of a skull, and in some corner
> Of an irrefrangible eye
> Some old man's memory jumps to a child
> – Spark from the days of energy.
> And the child hoards it like a bitter toy.

'Somewhere some word', 'some corner', 'Some old man's memory': Spender's uses of 'some' suggest that hope is being built on hopefulness; at the same time a sombre defiance stiffens the hope. The polysyllabic 'irrefrangible' reinforces the sense of defiance. The word means 'inviolable', but it draws to itself the meaning, 'indisputable', possessed by Spender's first choice, 'irrefragable' (used in the versions printed in the *New Statesman*, 6 August 1938, and *PFS*). The 'irrefrangible eye' may lack the haunting unliterariness of the eyes noted in the anonymous International Brigade poem, 'Eyes': 'The eyes of the wounded sodden in red / The eyes of the dying and those of the dead' (*PFS*). But it looks out of the poem at and beyond contemporary history with heartening, unfacile courage. The syntax makes the likely owner of the eye the old man, yet it may just as easily belong, one feels, to the poet bearing witness. Indeed, Spender's fussing over whether the second line should begin with 'On' or (as in *CPS(1)*) 'In' shows his concern with inner and outer; if the word presses 'On' the skull's high door it is probably spoken to the person; if it presses 'In' the skull's high door the wording suggests that the source of the pressure is within. Spender wants a suggestion of inner constancy and the suggestion of trans-mitted fervour which his last lines convey. The consequence is the most charged writing in an uneven poem; a poem that is full of references to mutilation, erasure, deletion and forgetfulness concludes with an image of hoarded remembrance. Elsewhere, as in the fine 'At Castellon' (*SC*), the poetry gives almost its last word to its awareness of the forces intent on deletion:

> The car moves on to suns and time
> Of safety for us and him.
> But behind us on the road
> The winged black roaring fates unload
>
> Cargoes of iron and of fire
> To delete with blood and ire
> The will of those who dared to move
> From the furrow, their life's groove.

The last line is redeemed from cliché by taking us back to the 'working man' of stanza four whose 'lines ploughed with ravage // Lift to a smile'. But here the 'groove' of the couplets is overrun only by the destructive energies of 'The winged black roaring fates'. Just as 'the names of heroes in the hall' in 'Fall of a City' are 'angrily deleted', so in this poem the Fascist planes seek to 'delete' the people's will. Spender makes his partisan point in a way that compels attention – partly through the writing's power, partly through his awareness of the difference between the 'safety' he is moving towards and the threatening danger which afflicts 'those who dared to move / From the furrow, their life's groove'.

Perhaps the clearest expression of Spender's obsession with the relationship between death and life in these poems occurs at the start of the sestet of 'Sonnet' (*SC*), a poem which starkly opposes history and the private life: 'Drowned in your life, I there encountered death / Which claimed you for a greater history'. Spender seems to say that love for the poem's 'you' (presumably involved in the fighting) has brought him face to face with the reality of death. Again, in 'Ultima Ratio Regum' (*SC*; included in *CPS(1)*, *SPS* and *CPS(2)*), which focuses on the death of a boy (the poem does not say for which side he fought), Spender writes:

> The world maintained its traditional wall
> Round the dead with their gold sunk deep as a well,
> Whilst his life, intangible as a Stock Exchange rumour, drifted
>   outside.

The pathos of the boy's death is sharpened by being put into bitterly ironic context. In the above lines 'the dead' half suggests the living dead who make up the world of high finance, whilst the significance of 'his life' is pointed up by 'intangible' and 'drifted' that carry suggestions of elusiveness transcending the mordant humour of the simile: mordant because implying the only terms in which the boy's life might be grasped by 'The world'. The poem has already offered different terms, the frankly erotic, for viewing the boy: 'He was a better target for a kiss'. As in 'Two Armies' confrontation with killing provokes Spender to a reassertion of the need for and impulse towards love; that the line in 'Ultima Ratio Regum' has about it an air of vulnerably unembarrassed tenderness makes it the more expressive of Spender's twin feelings of shock and helplessness.

Throughout – and this is a common feature of Spender's Spanish Civil War poems – 'Ultima Ratio Regum' foregrounds the difficulty of honest speech in a world where the dominant discourses lie. This is pointed up by the title, a motto inscribed on Louis XIV's cannons meaning 'force is the final argument of kings' (see Hynes, p. 250) but given an anti-capitalist twist in the poem's first lines: 'The guns spell money's ultimate reason / In letters of lead on the spring hillside'. Again, one wants to point to Spender's rhythmic art, the way feeling is both wrought up and held back by decasyllabic lines that avoid iambic regularity. The deadpan, brutal ironies here mimic the brutality they seek to expose; 'money's ultimate reason' is highly irrational even in its own terms as the poem brings out. Mockingly, sorrowfully, the poem employs as one of its idioms the narrowly utilitarian: 'Consider', the poem ends, 'One bullet in ten thousand kills a man. / Ask. Was so much expenditure justified / On the death of one so young and so silly / Lying under the olive trees, O world, O death?'. The abrupt imperatives and the ironized language of 'expenditure' do not have the final word, which is given to a different style; this style may move from irony to distress, but its Romantic timbre is consciously deployed; Spender's final apostrophes would seem an out-of-date throwback to Shelleyan lyricism, were it not for the fact that 'world' and 'death' have been given particularized, intertwining meanings in the poem: 'world' meaning 'the world in which we live with all its greed-inspired injustices', 'death' meaning both 'spiritual death' and what is doled out by 'Machine-gun anger'. 'Ultima Ratio Regum' is driven by indignation, but its ironies and interplay of idioms give it a more complicated and more satisfying impact than 'indignation' might suggest.

At a more conversational pitch the thematizing of language is at the centre of one of Spender's most impressive poems in the thirties, 'Thoughts During an Air Raid' (*SC*; included in *CPS(1)*, *SPS* and *CPS(2)*). In the version printed in *The Still Centre* Spender trains a cool mockery on his self-centred concern for his own skin, for his separate 'I':

> Of course, the entire effort is to put myself
> Outside the ordinary range
> Of what are called statistics. A hundred are killed
> In the outer suburbs. Well, well, I carry on.

The tonal flexibility of these lines is considerable and typical of the poem. A speaking voice that spans the wry and the sombre can be heard throughout: not only in such conversational tics as 'Of course' and 'Well, well', but also in the colloquial way the adjective 'entire' behaves. The matter-of-factly, yet sharply,

enjambed 'A hundred are killed / In the outer suburbs' –
throwing 'killed' into relief – illustrates the poem's point about
'statistics', that the word is a convenient fiction designed to let us
get on with our major concern, ourselves. 'Ourselves', however,
is never employed by Spender who in this version incriminates
'myself', but in *Collected Poems* (1955) refers to 'oneself'; this
later version makes witty fun of the upper-class mannerism of
referring to the self as 'one', a wit which, directed both at self and
others, strikes notes that go beyond, even as they include, the
funny:

> Yet supposing that a bomb should dive
> Its nose right through this bed, with one upon it?
> The thought's obscene. Still, there are many
> For whom one's loss would illustrate
> The 'impersonal' use indeed.
>
> *(CPS(1))*

The flinching from death in the jokey phrasing of 'with one
upon it' illustrates the 'impersonal' use, captures the obscenity of
the unthinkable thought and by enacting the difficulty of speaking appropriately about its subject involves the reader in the
poem's subject. The lines have the edge over the earlier version
of the passage, fine as that is, with its more straightforward
point-making: 'Still, there are many / To whom my death would
only be a name, / One figure in a column' *(SC)*. Paradoxically,
Spender's voice comes across more fully in the revised version
because he allows for the way his voice has been socialized,
'Englished', taught how to conceal personal concern behind the
use of 'one'. Valentine Cunningham, who mostly writes well
about Spender, fails to see this, making the poem's revision an
example of the damage caused by Spender's inability to 'resist
the temptation to rejig his past, and tinker with the admirably
personal presence he once sought to grant his poems' *(PBSCWV,*
p. 85). This fails to engage with the fact that Spender is acutely
aware of the function served by his revision's '"impersonal" use'
of language.

In fact, crucial as pronouns are to the workings of each
version, what gives both an 'admirably personal presence' is a
blank verse that impressively fuses the weighty and the colloquial. The reader hears Spender's voice in a line such as 'This

girdered bed which seems more like a hearse' (*SC*), changed
later to 'The girdered bed which seems so like a hearse'
(*CPS(1)*). In both cases the sensed likeness makes itself felt
through the hidden chime of 'girdered' and 'hearse'. The poetry's
rhythms enable it to suggest the attempted insouciance of the
speaker and the 'pressure' on him of what he wishes to 'ignore':
'I can ignore / The pressure of those names under my fingers /
Heavy and black as I rustle the paper' (*SC*); 'rustle' with its
intimations of lightness must contend with the 'heaviness' of the
casualty lists. Elsewhere, tones move from the ironically poker-
faced, 'The essential is / That all the "I"s should remain
separate' (*SC*), to the resonantly (or ironically) mysterious:

> Then horror is postponed
> For everyone until it settles on him
> And drags him to that incommunicable grief
> Which is all mystery or nothing.
>
> (*SC*)

That even in this first version Spender shifts from first to third
person at the poem's close drives a further nail into the coffin of
Cunningham's case. The poem shifts perspectives; the 'I' whose
feelings have been so accurately portrayed now becomes the
unknowable 'he' which 'horror' makes of us all; if the 'he' is
'unknowable' the grief he experiences is 'incommunicable'.
'Incommunicable' has a Wordsworthian impressiveness, recalling the speaker's surmise in 'The Affliction of Margaret' that her
son may have drowned and been doomed to 'keep / An
incommunicable sleep'.[18] However, Spender seems to attribute
'grief' more to the person who dies than to those who survive.
And the last two words of the poem suggest that the 'grief' may
be 'incommunicable' because there is nothing to communicate.
Conrad-like 'horror' may accompany acquaintance with 'mystery'; it may also – anti-climactically – herald the discovery of
'nothing'.

It should be said that Cunningham pinpoints the reason for
the achievement of Spender's war poems when he writes that
'Spender's poems about Spain simply register his feelings, his
fears, in a quite personal way, and often inhabit regions and
report incidents in which the war crops up only incidentally,
with a kind of inevitable naturalness' (*PBSCWV*, p. 82). The

poem he mentions in support of this assertion, 'Port Bou' (*SC*; included in *CPS(1)* and *CPS(2)*), is among the finest poems to emerge from the Spanish Civil War. Spender makes good use of the space he gives himself in this poem; unlike 'The Room Above the Square' (*SC*; included in *CPS(1)* and, under the title 'The Room above the Square', in *SPS* and *CPS(2)*), another impress-ive poem which came out of Spender's experience of the war, 'Port Bou' employs a discursively narrative style. 'The Room Above the Square' benefits from the need to compress; the result is a poetry that states for all its figurative richness: 'Torn like leaves through Europe is the peace / Which through me flowed'. This assertion draws to an emotional centre the poem's elements. 'Port Bou' also states, but its statements work in interestingly centrifugal ways – until at the end of the poem the 'I' can no longer evade the fear which has been held uneasily at bay. The speaker is left alone in the town while shooting practice starts:

> My circling arms rest on the newspaper,
> My mind seems paper where dust and ink fall,
> I tell myself the shooting is only for practice,
> And my body seems a cloth which the machine-gun stitches
> Like a sewing machine, neatly, with cotton from a reel;
> And the solitary, irregular, thin 'paffs' from the carbines
> Draw on long needles white threads through my navel.

When Spender revised these lines, he regrettably chose to spell out what is eloquently latent here; the revised version of this passage's fourth line begins 'But I am the coward of cowards' (quoted from *CPS(1)*). Not only does this overstate, it also sacrifices the elision of moods which the unforthcoming 'And' effects. The 'machine-gun' as 'sewing machine' picks up on the earlier account of it 'wrapped in a cloth – old mother in a shawl'. Typically, this earlier metaphor was floated briefly, then dropped, before being returned to and developed fully. The entire poem is characterized by obliquity and a seeming irrelevance that, in fact, is better construed as a fidelity to the workings of conscious-ness. The final lines achieve a mingled effect; the machine-gun's operations are compared to the domestic activity of stitching, but the only sense in which 'the war finds peace' in these lines is that they glimpse the peace of bizarrely imagined extinction: an extinction the more Spenderian for being imagined as not annihilating consciousness, and the more unsettling for the last line's brutal parody of the navel-cord that attaches child to mother. The writing – level-toned but candid, conversational but sardonically weighted, long-lined and adjectivally meticulous ('the disgraceful skirring dogs') – is not really like anything else in the period; in 'Port Bou' Spender's style and vision are equally his own.

The obliquity praised above is borne out by Spender's use of the apparently neutral adjective 'circling'. The 'circle' is an important image in other poems in *The Still Centre*, notably 'Darkness and Light'. In Spender's hands it can suggest reconciliation between the central self and the circumferential world; it can also imply the self's solipsistic inclination to put itself at the centre of experience; at the same time this inclination is seen (by most of Spender's Spanish poems) as necessary for the kind of truth-telling the poems set themselves. When, after the economically wry description of the village emptying, Spender says 'I am left alone on the bridge at the exact centre', the last phrase is suggestive; the 'exact centre' turns out to be the self face to face with its 'own individuality, [its] own isolation'. And the lines quoted above take the reader back to the start of the poem; 'my circling arms rest on a newspaper' near its beginning as well; the later line ('My circling arms rest on the newspaper') brings one round full circle, as though this were a Coleridgean conversational poem. But whereas Coleridge offers reconciliation and harmony, Spender articulates a sense of stasis and loss of grip on the relations between inner and outer. The poem opens, moreover, with an image of an imperfect circle, though in this imperfection resides the possibility of release:

> As a child holds a pet
> Arms clutching but with hands that do not join
> And the coiled animal watches the gap
> To outer freedom in animal air,
> So the earth-and-rock flesh arms of this harbour
> Embrace but do not enclose the sea
> Which, through a gap, vibrates to the open sea
> Where ships and dolphins swim and above is the sun.

These lines serve as description and as impressive symbolic prelude. No other poem of the Civil War expresses with such yearning obliquity the longing for 'freedom', which is here displaced completely from the human to the natural; the 'gap' in this confining circle offers hope, suggested by the resonant verb 'vibrates'. To allegorize in a way that the passage satisfyingly avoids, 'freedom' is as near and as far as that 'open sea / Where ships and dolphins swim and above is the sun'. And no sooner has the reader registered a flicker of disquiet at the painstaking way the image is set up than Spender involves him or her in his own poetic endeavours: 'I search for an image / And seeing an image I count out the coined words / To remember the childish headlands of this harbour'. The reflexiveness is more than candid admission; it prepares us for the true subject of the poem, the workings of a highly self-conscious consciousness which is finally disquieted by, rather than complacent about, the fact that the poet's 'mind seems paper where dust and ink fall'.

'To a Spanish Poet', the last poem in *The Still Centre*, is a less compelling if more earnestly direct attempt to address the question of the poet's role in troubled times. A feeling that the earlier version suffered from its own earnestness possibly provoked Spender's fascinating revisions of the poem's second half in both his *Collected Poems*, 1955 and 1985 (it is not included in *SPS*). In both he excises the poem's original conclusion; in the 1985 *Collected Poems* (where it is titled 'To Manuel Altolaguirre') he recycles pungent anecdote (from *WWW*, pp. 232-3). What he chose to cut is, none the less, one of the more ponderable thirties manifestos:

> Oh let the violent time
> Cut eyes into my limbs
> As the sky is pierced with stars that look upon
> The map of pain,
> For only when the terrible river
> Of grief and indignation
> Has poured through all my brain
> Can I make from lamentation
> A world of happiness,
> And another constellation,
> With your voice that still rejoices
> In the centre of its night,
> As, buried in this night,
> The stars burn with their brilliant light.

The lines may suffer from overstatement; they make too pro-grammatic that surrender to suffering which gives Spender's best poems their inwardness; it is hard, for instance, to defend '*all* my brain' (emphasis added). It should be noted, however, that what pours through the brain is emotion: 'grief and indignation'. Spender, as so often, is saying something more nuanced than may initially appear to be the case; he is not saying simply, 'I must be responsive to external events'; rather, he is saying, 'I must allow myself fully to be possessed by my feelings (and the feelings of others) about external events'.

Samuel Hynes points out that 'The similarity between this poem and Auden's elegy for Yeats [first published in *The New Republic*, 8 March 1939] is unavoidable', though he goes on to say 'It is not a matter of influence or imitation' (Hynes, p. 366) Spender, too, is elegizing a poet (Manuel Altolaguirre, some of whose poems about the Civil War Spender translated with his wife, Inez) as Auden is; just as Auden addresses Yeats – 'With your unconstraining voice / Still persuade us to rejoice' – so Spender calls on Altolaguirre's 'voice that still rejoices'. How-ever, Altolaguirre serves as an alter ego for Spender in a way Yeats does not for Auden; the Spanish poet's response to disaster – 'Every sensation except loneliness / Was drained out of your mind' – is recorded with a vividness (the impact of the intent rhythms and the word 'drained') that closes the gap between 'I' and 'you'. This impression is both reinforced and modified by the Pyrrhic victory that Spender imagines Altolaguirre's con-sciousness achieving over adversity: 'Only you remained whole / In frozen wonder, as though you stared / At your image in the broken mirror / Where it had always been silverly carried'. Here integrity ('you remained whole') vies with narcissism ('you stared / At your image') and narrowly wins the day; in the act of articulating this conflict and triumph, Spender credibly turns Altolaguirre into one of 'the truly great', a beckoning exemplar.

However, though Spender's poem may seem more private than Auden's, more intent on creating a compensatory imagina-tive 'world of happiness', the impact of his star imagery in the closing lines (quoted above) modifies any such impression. The first simile in these lines audaciously transforms the speaker into the 'sky ... pierced with stars' looking down on 'The map of pain': an image which implies distance from, even as it urges empathy with, suffering ('pain' is mapped out, the poet is 'looking'). 'The terrible river / Of grief and indignation' introduces a figurative diversion; but when the star imagery resumes (in the 'constellation' the poet will make), Spender admits his longing to create an autonomous world in poetry, a longing which is also, the poem recognizes, a near-tragic temptation to abjure the public and historical. The concluding lines imply that each poet creates his own world; Altolaguirre's voice 'still rejoices / In the centre of its night' as though every poetic world was an individual world, each possessing its own night. But the final reference to 'this night' makes a last-minute return to the 'world, which is the world / Of all of us, – the place where, in the end, / We find our happiness, or not at all!'[19] The last two lines strike a balance between the realization that all too often 'stars' are 'buried' and the hope-sustaining belief that they continue to 'burn with their brilliant light'. The passage and the poem wrestle with the clash between the individual and the historical; it is the distinction of Spender's finest poems about the Spanish Civil War that they never unwittingly cede primacy to either of those mutually troubling, mutually necessary terms.

Notes

Introduction

1. 'Introduction', to Helen Vendler, *The Music of What Happens: Poems, Poets, Critics* (Cambridge, Mass. and London, 1988), pp. 1–2, 2.
2. Louis MacNeice, *The Poetry of W. B. Yeats* (1941; rpt London, 1967), p. 194.
3. *The Poetry of W. B. Yeats*, p. 15.
4. See chapter of that title in Cleanth Brooks, *The Well Wrought Urn* (New York, 1947), pp. 176–96.
5. 'Criticism, History, and Critical Relativism' in *The Well Wrought Urn*, p. 198.
6. See *The Well Wrought Urn*, p. 198, where Brooks writes, 'how is a critic, who is plainly the product of his own day and time, hopelessly entangled in the twentieth century, to judge the poems of his own day – much less, the poems of the past – *sub specie aeternitatis!*'
7. Brooks, however, comes close to one of our own emphases when he compares poetry to drama on account of its 'dynamic nature'. 'The Heresy of Paraphrase', in *The Well Wrought Urn*, p. 187.
8. 'Literary Studies: A Reply', in F. R. Leavis, *Valuation in Criticism and Other Essays*, collected and ed. G. Singh (Cambridge, 1986), p. 208.
9. *The Well Wrought Urn*, p. 186.
10. 'Making, Knowing and Judging' in W. H. Auden, *The Dyer's Hand* (London, 1963), p. 50.

1. Auden (1) 'An altering speech'

1. This chapter discusses *Paid on Both Sides* as printed in 'Part I' of *EA*, and poems by Auden as printed in 'Part II: Poems 1927–1931' of *EA*. 'Part II' corresponds to the two published editions of *Poems* (London, 1930; second edn 1933, containing seven new poems to replace seven in the 1930 edition).
2. Stephen Spender, 'W. H. Auden and His Poetry' in *W. H. Auden: A Collection of Critical Essays*, Twentieth Century Views, ed. Monroe K. Spears (Englewood Cliffs, N.J., 1964), p. 30.

3. Seamus Heaney, *The Government of the Tongue: The 1986 T. S. Eliot Memorial Lectures and Other Critical Writings* (London and Boston, 1988), pp. 123, 117.

4. *The Government of the Tongue*, p. 116.

5. *Poems* (1930) contained two poems written before 'The Watershed' which were not included in *Poems* (1933): see *EA*, pp. xiii, 21–2.

6. *The Government of the Tongue*, p. 111.

7. 'Come, Words, Away', in Laura (Riding) Jackson, *The Poems of Laura Riding: A New Edition of the 1938 Collection* (Manchester, 1980). Subsequent quotations from Laura (Riding) Jackson's poetry are taken from this edition.

8. Preface to Laura Riding, *Selected Poems: In Five Sets* (London, 1970), pp. 15, 12.

2. Spender (1) 'The sense of falling light'

1. Randall Jarrell, *Kipling, Auden & Co.: Essays and Reviews 1935–1964* (1981; rpt Manchester, 1986), p. 239.

2. *Kipling, Auden & Co.*, p. 240.

3. 'Insensibility', *The Poems of Wilfred Owen*, ed. and intro. Jon Stallworthy (London, 1985). This edition is used for all quotations from Owen's poetry throughout the book.

4. *Oxford Poetry* 1930, ed. Stephen Spender and Bernard Spencer (Oxford, 1930).

5. Lionel Trilling, *Sincerity and Authenticity* (London, 1974), p. 11.

6. In Trilling's view, autobiography is sincerity's quintessential literary vehicle. See *Sincerity and Authenticity*, pp. 24–5.

7. Quoted in Cunningham, p. 34. Cunningham attributes the remark to Norman Cameron.

8. Quoted from T. S. Eliot, *Collected Poems 1909–1962* (London, 1963). This edition is used for all subsequent quotations from Eliot's poetry.

9. Interestingly Spender argues that Eliot 'never appeals to a material reality outside the mind' (*DE*, p. 144).

10. Appendix B, 'Two Statements on Poetry', in Bernard Spencer, *Collected Poems*, ed. with intro. Roger Bowen (Oxford, 1981), p. 131.

11. Quoted from Bernard Spencer, *Collected Poems*.

12. A. Kingsley Weatherhead, *Stephen Spender and the Thirties* (Lewisburg and London, 1975), p. 205.

13. H. B. Kulkarni, *Stephen Spender: Poet in Crisis* (Glasgow, London and Bombay, 1970), p. 83.

14. Quoted from Bernard Spencer, *Collected Poems*.

15. 'Sincerity and Poetry' in Donald Davie, *The Poet in the Imaginary Museum: Essays of Two Decades*, ed. Barry Alpert (Manchester, 1977), p. 146.

16. The poem's revised and truncated version, 'The Photograph' (*CPS(2)*), turns a study of memory's tangled workings into an emotionally simpler, verbally chaster, less absorbing poem about loss.

17. *Stephen Spender and the Thirties*, p. 215.

18. See the end of Douglas's 'Mersa': 'I see my feet like stones / underwater. The logical little fish / converge and nip the flesh / imagining I am one of the

dead'. Quoted from *Keith Douglas: Complete Poems*, ed. Desmond Graham (Oxford, 1978).

19. Lines 381, 384–5 and 460. Quotations from Shelley here and elsewhere are from *Shelley's Poetry and Prose*, eds Donald H. Reiman and Sharon B. Powers, Norton Critical Edition (New York and London, 1977).

20. *Kipling, Auden & Co.*, p. 239.

21. 'Stephen Spender: Journals and Poems' in *The Music of What Happens*, p. 167.

22. See 'The Windhover', line 11, and *Macbeth*, line 7. 27.

23. Stephen Spender, *Forward from Liberalism* (London, 1937), p. 26.

3. MacNeice (1) Turning the Music On

1. Michael Longley, 'The Neolithic Night: A Note on the Irishness of Louis MacNeice', in *Two Decades of Irish Writing*, ed. Douglas Dunn (Cheadle, 1975), p. 104.

2. Louis MacNeice, *The Poetry of W. B. Yeats*, p. 197.

3. Robyn Marsack, *The Cave of Making: The Poetry of Louis MacNeice* (1982; rpt Oxford, 1985), p. 14.

4. Auden (2) *The Orators:* 'They stole to force a hearing'

1. The text of *The Orators* used in this chapter, from *EA*, 'restores cuts and changes made to avoid libel, obscenity or discourtesy at the time of publication'.

2. The borrowings from *Poems* (1928) are pointed out by Fuller, pp. 56–8.

3. Borrowing pointed out by Fuller, p. 59.

4. Borrowing pointed out by Fuller, p. 58.

5. *The Government of the Tongue*, p. 114.

6. Auden himself acknowledged the influence of *Anabase*: see Mendelson, p. 96. Quotations are from St.-J. Perse, *Anabasis*, with a translation into English by T. S. Eliot (London, 1930).

7. The echoes mentioned in this paragraph are pointed out by Fuller, pp. 56–61 *passim*.

8. W. H. Auden, *The Enchafèd Flood* (New York, 1950), p. 111; and see Smith, p. 61.

9. According to Mendelson, *The Orators* was probably composed between Spring and November of 1931; 'Triumphal March' was first published, as a pamphlet, in October 1931: 'Difficulties of a Statesman' was first published in *Commerce*, Winter 1931/2.

10. Auden himself acknowledged the influence of Ludendorff's *The Coming War* (London, 1931): see Mendelson, p. 96. Ludendorff's book contains an apocalyptic account of forces that he believed were conspiring against Germany.

11. This account of *Coriolan* draws on Gareth Reeves, *T. S. Eliot: A Virgilian Poet* (London and Basingstoke, 1989), pp. 78–81.

12. Eliot's borrowing from *The Coming War* is pointed out in Grover Smith, *T. S. Eliot's Poetry and Plays: A Study in Sources and Meaning* (1956; 2nd ed. Chicago and London, 1974), pp. 162, 334.

13. Auden himself acknowledged Lawrence's influence: see Mendelson, p. 96.
14. John Blair, *The Poetic Art of W. H. Auden* (Princeton, N.J., 1965), pp. 78–81.
15. William Langland, *The Vision of William Concerning Piers the Plowman*, ed. Walter W. Skeat (1886; rpt Oxford, 1924), Vol. I., B-text, p. 2.
16. Karl Marx, *Zur Kritik der Hegel'schen Rechts-Philosophie.*
17. For example, Edgell Rickword objected to what he saw in the ode as the implications of a Nazi 'degradation of women and regimentation of the Strength through Joy variety', *New Verse*, Nov. 1937. Quoted in Fuller, p. 71.
18. Stan Smith makes much the same point: *The Orators* is 'making us ask that question of the wayward text which is asked in the "Epilogue"' (Smith, p. 56).

5. Spender (2) 'To will this Time's change'

1. Quoted from C. Day Lewis, *Collected Poems 1954* (1954; rpt London, 1970).
2. Quoted from review of *The Still Centre* in W. H. Mellers, 'Modern Poets in Love and War', *Scrutiny*, vol. 8, no. 1, June 1939, p. 119.
3. Quoted from *The Collected Poems of W. B. Yeats*, 2nd edn (1950; rpt London and Basingstoke, 1971).
4. *Stephen Spender and the Thirties*, p. 97.
5. *An Essay on Man*, Epistle 2, line 2, in *The Poems of Alexander Pope*, ed. John Butt (London, 1963).
6. See last sentence of poem, translated as 'You must change your life' in *The Selected Poetry of Rainer Maria Rilke*, ed. and trans. by Stephen Mitchell, with intro. by Robert Hass (London, 1987).
7. Quoted from *Friedrich Hölderlin, Eduard Mörike: Selected Poems*, trans. with intro. by Christopher Middleton (Chicago and London, 1972).
8. *Friedrich Hölderlin, Eduard Mörike: Selected Poems*, p. 238.
9. *Stephen Spender and the Thirties*, p. 212.

6. Auden (3) 'A change of heart'

1. Stephen Spender, 'W. H. Auden and His Poetry', in *W. H. Auden: A Collection of Essays*, Twentieth Century Views, p. 28.
2. *The Government of the Tongue*, p. 121.
3. *The Government of the Tongue*, p. 121.
4. Gavin Ewart can be heard adjusting himself to Auden's new voice in his review of *Look, Stranger!* (the volume in which 'Out on the lawn I lie in bed' first appeared): 'Since his first book, Mr. Auden's verse has undergone a considerable simplification and a more severe formal discipline'. *W. H. Auden: The Critical Heritage*, ed. John Haffenden (London, Boston, Melbourne and Henley, 1983), p. 220.
5. For a useful summary of the poem's historical context see Smith, pp. 81–2.

6. See discussion of Auden's debt to Yeats in Mendelson, pp. 179–80.

7. Compare the 'rook-delighting heaven' in Yeats's 'The Cold Heaven'.

8. *Paradise Lost*, Book 12, line 646. Quoted from *Milton: Poetical Works*, ed. Douglas Bush (1966; rpt London and Oxford, 1969).

9. The point is made by Smith, p. 24.

10. See 'On "September 1, 1939" by W. H. Auden' in Joseph Brodsky, *Less Than One* (1986; rpt Harmondsworth, 1987), pp. 304–56.

11. 'On "September 1, 1939" by W. H. Auden', p. 338.

12. Seamus Heaney, *The Haw Lantern* (London and Boston, 1987).

13. See Smith, pp. 73–5, esp. p. 75.

14. 'Dover Beach', lines 21, 28.

15. John Fuller's word and point, Fuller, p. 107.

16. The numbers refer to the sonnets as arranged in *In Time of War*, not as re-arranged in the 1965 revision of the sequence, *Sonnets from China*.

7. MacNeice (2) *Autumn Journal:* 'A monologue is the death of language'

1. Quoted in *The Cave of Making*, p. 43.

2. Quoted from *John Donne: The Elegies and The Songs and Sonnets*, ed. Helen Gardner (Oxford, 1965). Subsequent quotations of Donne's poetry are from this edition.

8. Poetry of the Spanish Civil War 'See Spain and see the world'

1. *Poetry of the Thirties*, ed. Robin Skelton (Harmondsworth, 1964), p. 19.

2. Quoted from W. H. Auden and Louis MacNeice, *Letters from Iceland* (1937; rpt London, 1967).

3. Quoted in *Contemporary Poets*, ed. James Vinson, 2nd edn (London and New York, 1975), p. 49.

4. Quoted in Monroe K. Spears, *The Poetry of W. H. Auden: The Disenchanted Island* (New York, 1963), p. 157.

5. Quoted in *The Poetry of W. H. Auden: The Disenchanted Island*, p. 157.

6. Christopher Caudwell, *Illusion and Reality: A Study of the Sources of Poetry* (1937; rpt London, 1946), pp. 282, 283. Caudwell, a poet and Marxist critic, served in the pro-Republican International Brigade in Spain and was killed in 1937.

7. See discussion in Smith, pp. 170–3, esp. 172, where Smith argues: 'At issue in both poems is the sense of history made up of changing and unrepeatable human subjects.... And the deepest distress they share ... issues from a sense of the essential frivolity of art'.

8. Quoted from *Letters from Iceland*.

9. From *Authors Take Sides on the Spanish War* (1937), quoted in *Spanish Front: Writers on the Civil War*, ed. Valentine Cunningham (Oxford and New York, 1986), p. 55.

10. Louis MacNeice, *The Poetry of W. B. Yeats*, p. 126.

11. Hugh Thomas, *The Spanish Civil War* 3rd edn (1977; rpt Harmondsworth, 1984), p. 272.

12. See discussion in *The Spanish Civil War*, p. 864.

13. Franz Borkenau, *The Spanish Cockpit* (1937; rpt London and Sydney, 1986), p. x.

14. *The Spanish Civil War*, p. 155.

15. See MacNeice's unfriendly words about Marxists in his account of this trip to Spain, *SAF*, p. 161.

16. 'To-day the Struggle', first printed in *New Statesman & Nation*, 5 June 1937, rpt in *Spanish Front: Writers on the Civil War*, p. 325.

17. First line's 'ironic echo' of 'Ode to a Nightingale' pointed out in *The Poems of Wilfred Owen*, p. 163.

18. This and the subsequent quotation from Wordsworth taken from *Wordsworth: Poetical Works*, ed. Thomas Hutchinson, new ed. Ernest de Selincourt (1936; rpt London, 1967).

19. *The Prelude*, 1850, Book XI, lines 142–4.

Index

249